od A., 1948-

GOOD SEX

GOOD SEX
Perspectives on
Sexual Ethics

Raymond A. Belliotti

 UNIVERSITY PRESS OF KANSAS

© 1993 by the University Press of Kansas
All rights reserved

Published by the University Press of Kansas (Lawrence, Kansas 66049), which was organized by the Kansas Board of Regents and is operated and funded by Emporia State University, Fort Hays State University, Kansas State University, Pittsburg State University, the University of Kansas, and Wichita State University

Library of Congress Cataloging-in-Publication Data

Belliotti, Raymond A., 1948–
    Good sex : perspectives on sexual ethics / Raymond A. Belliotti.
      p. cm.
    Includes index.
    ISBN 0-7006-0604-1 (alk. paper). — ISBN 0-7006-0605-X (pbk. :
alk. paper)
     1. Sexual ethics. I. Title.
HQ32.B45 1993
176—dc20   93-9851

Printed in the United States of America
10 9 8 7 6 5 4 3 2 1

The paper used in this publication meets the minimum requirements of the American National Standard for Permanence of Paper for Printed Library Materials Z39.48-1984.

In Memoriam

Rosario (1893–1959) and Agnes Rizzo Belliotti (1891–1956)
Giuseppe (1885–1963) and Graceia Giordano Leonardo (1886–1968)
Angelo (1913–1990) and Louise Leonardo Belliotti (1918–1980)

Nun aviri famigghia e comu essiri un nuddo miscatu cu nenti

CONTENTS

PREFACE

In 1977 I was asked to make a presentation on the topic of sexual ethics for a colloquium sponsored by the University of Miami School of Medicine. At the time, filled with the typical smugness of a graduate student immersed in the inflated self-image of analytic philosophy, I thought that sexual ethics constituted lightweight issues pondered only by people with enfeebled intellectual capacities, excessive prurient interests, deep sexual insecurities, or (thinly veiled) ulterior motives of sexual conquest. After only two minutes of deliberation, however, I accepted the invitation to speak and thus abrogated my philosophical smugness and joined the aforementioned brigade of intellectual lightweights. I was still, though, unsure of which of the four units of that brigade could most plausibly claim my membership.

On the afternoon prior to the scheduled colloquium, I sat down and sketched the paper, "A Philosophical Analysis of Sexual Ethics," that would serve as the basis of my presentation. The next day I arrived at the medical school in my typical graduate school garb: sandals, jeans, and a tank top with the guileless slogan, For Luck Today, Kiss An Italian (which perhaps suggested membership in the second or fourth unit of the lightweight brigade). Much to my surprise, the colloquium had been advertised as a debate between secular philosophy, as represented by me, and theology, as represented by "a minister of God." I was joined on stage by a six-foot three-inch beatific vision with carefully coiffured blond hair and a fresh manicure dressed in a cream, three-piece suit and stylish shoes. This vision was introduced as the minister Milton Chatsworth, doctor of theology.[1]

We each gave a 20-minute presentation, responded to specific points the other had made, then confronted questions posed by the large audience. While I was intense, rhetorical, and incantatory, Dr. Chatsworth was poised, charming, and soothing. While I invoked the inexorable conclusions of logic infused with passion, Dr. Chatsworth appealed to eternal verities, human soul making, and heavenly perfection. The audience judged our unrehearsed dog and pony show a success, although I am quite certain that at times the people attending were convinced they were witnessing a philosophical/theological version of Danny DeVito meets Robert Redford!

This colloquium was my introduction to the philosophical issues of sexual ethics. Shortly thereafter, my paper was accepted for publication,[2] and although I considered the work valuable mainly for personal amusement and as a warm reminder of my intellectual scuffle with Dr. Milton Chatsworth, "A Philosophical Analysis of Sexual Ethics" was eventually reprinted in several leading anthologies on current moral issues.[3] The article, invariably labeled, somewhat inaccurately, as representative of a "liberal" or "contractualist" model of sexual ethics, proved to be both a source of pride—writers are always pleased when their work reaches a larger readership than expected—and a wellspring of distress—it was woefully incomplete and advanced several arguments that I later recognized as unsound. But other projects demanded my attention, and although I vaguely aspired to write a refined version of the article, I failed to follow through. Perhaps there still lingered the prejudice that the issues of sexual ethics were lightweight fodder for the mind.

Two events aroused me from my inertia. First, I began to notice how the best-selling anthologies on current moral issues invariably categorized sexual ethics under three rubrics: conservative-conventional, sex with love, and liberal. Little or no direct attention was paid to leftist or feminist perspectives on the nature of the family and sexual relations. Such perspectives were often included in the anthologies, but only within their own marginalized intellectual ghettos. Clearly the implicit message was that the three mainstream perspectives constituted the range of legitimate philosophical views and any ideology to the political right or left could be stigmatized as extremist and implausible. Again, I vowed that someday I would provide a more complete description and analysis of sexual ethics.

The second energizing event occurred in 1989 when Peter Singer invited me to contribute a piece on sexual morality for his encyclopedia, *A Companion to Ethics.*[4] Surely this was the prime time to revise the thesis of "A Philosophical Analysis of Sexual Ethics" and to underscore the richness of the leftist critique of mainstream sexual morality. I finished my contribution to Singer's encyclopedia, but dissatisfaction soon surfaced. Whether the result of severe space limitations, my preoccupation with other concurrent projects, or my failure to dissect certain issues sufficiently, I soon became disappointed with my contribution.[5] Finally, I concluded the obvious: only by writing a book could I clarify my thinking on sexual ethics and redeem my previous failings. Such is the genesis of this book.

I have numerous people to thank. Without the support of my wife, Marcia Dalby Belliotti, this book would not have been completed, and her love and understanding are more than I deserve. My children, Angelo and Vittoria, also earn mention. Their steady stream of noise—laughing, crying, hollering, disputing—while I was working on the manuscript forced me to develop extraordinary abilities to focus. Their noise also reminded me of the passions that must accompany a life worth living. Deep gratitude also goes to Mary Ann Belliotti Conroy, the sister who taught me more than even she realizes.

Thanks go to Peter Singer for inviting me to make a contribution to his *A Companion to Ethics* and thus to rethink much of my position on sexual morality. Cynthia Miller, my editor, provided wise counsel and an unending supply of patience for an impatient author. Megan Schoeck, production editor, and Barbara Dinneen, copy editor, improved the manuscript significantly by correcting my numerous errors. The two readers, Mike W. Martin and Anita L. Allen, who evaluated this book for the University Press of Kansas, provided uncommonly helpful suggestions and generous encouragement. Also, special appreciation goes to Guilio Mannino, who helped me put a necessary finishing touch on the book. I suspect that he counts his contribution as minor; if so, he is incorrect.

Finally, I would like to thank the editors and/or publishers of the following journals and books for permission to adapt material from my articles: "Sex" in *A Companion to Ethics*, ed. Peter Singer (Oxford: Basil Blackwell, 1991), 315–326; "Marxism, Feminism, and Surrogate Motherhood," *Social Theory and Practice* 14 (1988): 389–417; "A Philosophical Analysis of Sexual Ethics," *Journal of Social Philosophy* 10 (1979): 8–11; and "Do Dead Humans Have Rights?" *Personalist* 60 (1979): 201–210.

INTRODUCTION
Sex and Moral Theory—
The Terms of the Debate

This book addresses some of the major sexual issues about which philosophers puzzle. The first set of issues is basic: Are gender and reproductive roles natural or are they socially constructed? Must morally permissible sex have only one function? Must it be heterosexual? Must it occur within the confines of the institution of marriage? Must it be accompanied by requisite emotions such as love and intimacy?

The second set of issues is more complex: How important is the notion of mutual consent when evaluating the moral character of sexual interactions? Is mutual consent a persuasive concept in a society permeated with gender oppression and domination? Which kinds of sexual activity, if any, are morally impermissible under what sort of circumstances?

Sex provides perhaps the most compelling context in which to assess the respective claims of our classical religious and philosophical moral theories. In addition to presenting my own views, this book includes a critical survey of a number of philosophical approaches to sex and moral decision making. In the context of classical and contemporary theories, it addresses the rationality and irrationality of sexual activity; the role, if any, of third party reactions in assessing the moral validity of sex between two parties; the limits of mutual consent as a sufficient condition of morally right sex; the force, if any, of appeals linking approved forms of sexuality with human nature, the need for nuclear families, and stable societies; and the power of leftist and feminist critiques of traditional Western sexual morality.

Such issues do not *define* sexual ethics. Clearly, there are numerous important questions not confronted here and several applications of ethical theory that are addressed obliquely or not at all: How may sexual pleasure be enhanced? Should sex education be part of public school curricula? What are appropriate policies of HIV testing and disclosure? How does one's sexual orientation help form personal identity? In this book, I address only certain fundamental questions embodied within the genre of sexual ethics; I do not pretend that it is a definitive work which could set the boundaries of sexual ethics.

In Part I, I explain and analyze the core Western tradition of sexual ethics: the detached asceticism of classical Greece, the doctrine of natural law as it evolved in Judeo-Christian thought, contemporary perspectives that link love and sexual intimacy, and libertarian and Kantian contractualist principles. I begin by giving a historical sketch of the origins of mind/body dualism and discussing its repercussions for sexual ethics in ancient Greece and the development of this dualism in the Judeo-Christian tradition. I contend that neither the Old nor the New Testament stigmatizes erotic impulses as inherently evil. In fact, the Old Testament wholeheartedly accepts the material world and conceives of humans as a psychosomatic unity. Greek dualism and asceticism made its way into the Judeo-Christian tradition through such thinkers as St. Augustine and St. Thomas Aquinas. I give arguments for the historical acceptance of views such as Stoicism and Epicureanism that advised the subordination of sexual desire to reason, and I make the case for the arbitrary introduction of Augustine's and Aquinas's views on sexuality into the divine imperative of the Council of Trent and into the code of sexual ethics promulgated by the contemporary Roman Catholic church.

The opening chapters lay the groundwork for my own theory by undermining the traditional claim that sex should be confined to procreation within the institution of marriage. If the institution of the church, rather than divine scripture written in keeping with natural law, introduced this notion for specific historical reasons that we can articulate, then we are free to look elsewhere to ground sexual ethics. To put a finer point on the matter: the most conservative views on sex cannot be defended successfully without appeals to notoriously contestable religious claims. Moreover, it is not clear that the specific doctrines on sex embraced by Christianity are in fact required by divine scripture.

I then confront a secular counterpart to the religious argument: the notion that sex should only occur within a context of a loving and committed relationship. I argue that the sex-only-with-love literature demonstrates a limited appreciation for the numerous permissible functions of sex and is preoccupied by a false dichotomy between a "unity of selves" image associated with committed love and a war of "each against every" in which independent sexual marauders seek to satisfy their ravenous urges without regard for the humanity of their partners.

I conclude Part 1 by turning to my preferred sociopolitical ground for sexual ethics: a libertarian position that emphasizes autonomy and mutual consent, modified by the Kantian qualification that one should never "use another as a mere means." There are, however, a host of conceptual difficulties with this qualification that militate against unbridled acceptance of the libertarian-Kantian credo.

Such difficulties, including the need for a clearer interpretation of "using another as a mere means," lead me to turn to leftist and feminist critiques of society to give fuller normative content to notions of "exploitation" and "mere use." Thus, in Part 2, I highlight the leftist critique of the core Western tradition by addressing the concerns of Marxism and a variety of feminist perspectives.

In Part 3, I identify mistakes made by other theories and advance a framework for sexual ethics which I call "sexual morality in five tiers." If successful, this five-tiered analysis will transcend the limitations of other traditional and contemporary theories, limitations that often result from six common errors. First, "reductionism" wrongly subdues complex sexual phenomena into only one of their constitutive parts. Reductionism is thus the wrongful aggrandizement of one contextual feature as dispositive of moral worth and the wrongful relegation of other contextual features to the scrap pile of irrelevancy. Second, "abstractness" is a failure to focus on the social particularities, gender, and bargaining power of sexual partners; its error lies in obscuring our vision of numerous social differences that bear moral implications. Third, "ahistoricism" wrongly ignores the historical and social context in which sex takes place. It misguidedly pretends that we can discover a universal, timeless sexual ethic that is impervious to change or unwisely suggests that if a universal sexual ethic escapes us we can still sanguinely apply our current dominant ethic without regard for its historical genesis.

Fourth, "isolationism" narrowly attends only to the effects of sexual actions on the participants. By ignoring relevant third party effects, isolationism unnecessarily limits the scope of our moral conclusions and mistakenly conceives of sex as distinct from its social implications. Fifth, "rigidity" is the unrealistic demand for clearcut rules for and mechanical methods of morally evaluating sexual activity. Rigidity errs in becoming obsessed with wrestling hard cases into distinct categories, instead of accepting the moral ambiguity indigenous to such cases. Sixth, "assimilation" unwisely assumes that sexual contracts are no different from commercial agreements to exchange goods and services. Assimilation thereby ignores extant social meanings and their relevance for normative assessment. Many of the arguments and criticisms I lodge against classical and contemporary views on sexual ethics will emerge from the accusation that these views commit one or more of these six mistakes.

My preferred framework, sexual morality in five tiers, requires libertarian agreement, a contextual attentiveness to morality, considerations derived from Marxist and feminist theory of economic and sexual exploitation, examination of third-party effects—the effects of a sexual act between the participating parties on other people directly affected—and, last, examination of the effects of the sexual act on the wider social context. Thus, I adopt a standard framework of the libertarian notion of noninterference between mutually consenting individuals, with significant consideration of challenges to the libertarian premise that we are all equally free to give or to withhold consent and with serious consideration of moral principles which independently evaluate actual agreements.

Finally, in Part 3, I apply sexual morality in five tiers to a variety of hypothetical situations and to several uncommon sexual practices such as bestiality, necrophilia, and incest. Here I go some distance in connecting sexual ethics to sociopolitical theory and certain core philosophical issues. This effort is animated by the conviction that frameworks for sexual ethics create various problems and bear numerous ramifications that go beyond the specific issues involved in determining whether or not particular sexual acts are morally impermissible.

Let us examine briefly the case of homosexuality to illustrate some of the moral reasoning that fuels disputes about sexual ethics. One common argument against homosexuality is that it is "unnatural" in some sense.[1] In Chapter 2, I argue, in the context of natural law theory generally, that there are a variety of possible interpretations of "natural": what is statistically usual, statistically frequent, statistically possible, accomplished without human interference, and what is in accord with an entity's essential characteristics. None of these interpretations, however, establishes that homosexuality is necessarily or usually immoral. Notions dependent upon statistical normalcy or statistical possibility, for example, lack necessary moral significance: the mere fact that humans routinely or often engage in X does not necessarily imply that X embodies moral merit, nor does it necessarily imply that -X is immoral. A fortiori, the fact that humans *can* engage in X does not establish X's moral credentials: not everything a "natural" entity can do is necessarily moral. In fact, notions of statistical possibility, if they did bear normative significance, could be used to establish the inherent *morality* of homosexual practices. Likewise, an interpretation such as "accomplished without human interference" is insufficient to establish the immorality of homosexuality: numerous morally appropriate actions do require human agency, and numerous actions that are not generated by human agency are either without moral significance or are morally inappropriate.

The most promising interpretation of "natural" for critics of homosexuality is "what is in accord with an entity's essential characteristics and what facilitates an entity's progress toward its rightful purpose." In this vein, sometimes the term "natural" is invoked tautologically to mean "what is right." But such use of the term disables critics of homosexuality in an important respect: conferring the honorific title "natural" on an action becomes trivial for purposes of determining the action's moral merit because "natural" becomes just another way of saying "morally sound."

More plausibly, the term "natural" is invoked functionally: because X is compatible with essential human characteristics and purposes, it is natural; and because it is natural, X is morally sound. Nevertheless, this interpretation is fraught with grave difficulties. It can be argued persuasively, for example, that natural laws, at best, merely describe events in the universe, but they bear no necessary moral significance: even if it could be established that X is "unnatural," it does not necessarily follow that X is immoral. Moreover, attempts to bridge the descriptive and the normative depend invariably on a specialized picture of human nature, on a full account of the proper human telos, and on a particular rendering of the genesis of objective morality. These notions themselves rest on suspicious metaphysical underpinnings and, often, on question-begging assumptions. Thus, the term "natural" is most often used in conclusory fashion to express an antecedently held condemnation of a practice, rather than as a conceptual tool for *arriving* at a normative judgment. Furthermore, claims of "naturalness" often commit the error of reductionism by wrongly postulating that sex, or a sexual organ itself, has only one permissible function or behavioral manifestation. Too often, such reductionism does not mirror the imperatives of an alleged objective morality but the narrow conditioning and historical taboos of a culture. Accordingly, accusations of "unnaturalness" expose themselves as feckless analytic instruments for establishing the inherent immorality of homosexuality.

Another argument advanced against homosexuality is that it always or almost always leads to personal unhappiness: as a countercultural phenomenon, homosexuality is ultimately unfulfilling and contributes to personal rage or personal dejection.[2] This argument cannot be taken seriously. First, even if completely persuasive, it would not establish the *immorality* of homosexuality. At best, the argument establishes the imprudence or foolishness of homosexuality. One's failure to select his or her most prudent biological posture does not necessarily imply one is immoral. Second, any alleged unhappiness homosexuals endure may be largely a function of the intolerance and discriminatory actions of heterosexuals which cause homosexuals to be clandestine, defensive, and often deceptive. But surely intolerance and wrongful discrimination cannot be conceded any moral currency: we cannot plausibly argue that homosexuality is morally wrong because it often leads to unhappiness generated by responses to the intolerance and wrongful discrimination of the nonhomosexual majority. The intolerance of the nonhomosexual majority cannot reasonably translate to the inherent immorality of the oppressed homosexual minority. Third, claims about the unhappiness of homosexuals may be false or overblown. Fourth, growing evidence of a biological component to sexual orientation suggests that arguments that assume homosexuality is freely chosen and may be freely rejected on grounds of prudence or morality may be flawed from the outset.

A third argument against homosexuality concerns its alleged instability, "an instability that arises from the lack of the full dimension of raising a family."[3] Here the claim is that a complete family structure "places the married couple in a context larger than themselves, shields them from one another, so to speak, and opens up new avenues of realism and honesty" that presumably nourish stability.[4] But this argument claims that couples with children form more stable units than couples without children. Is that empirically true? Even if so, it no more follows that homosexual couples are immoral than it does that childless heterosexual couples are immoral. The "family" has no "natural" structure, and even if the dominant nuclear family is taken to embody such a structure, homosexuality need not unsettle it or be unsettled by it. Clearly, if the heterosexual majority were more willing to tolerate adoptions by homosexual couples, then more such couples would be able to enjoy the alleged stability the wider context allegedly provides. Again, much of the alleged instability of homosexual relationships may be the result of the intolerant and often discriminatory actions of the heterosexual majority.

A fourth argument against homosexuality faults its inherent "preoccupation with one's own sex."[5] This preoccupation is presumably noxious because "half the human mystery is evaded."[6] By focusing on a person of the same gender, a homosexual presumably evolves a less risky, less mutually vulnerable, less fulfilling sexual encounter: "For the homosexual, who knows intimately in himself the generality that he finds in the other, there may be a diminished sense of risk. The move out of the self may be less adventurous, the help of the other less required. In an important sense it is open to the homosexual to make himself less vulnerable and to offer, because he needs, less support."[7]

That argument is unique but unconvincing. Nothing in the argument permits a legitimate inference that homosexuality is immoral. The notions of risk, mystery, adventure, and mutual vulnerability lack inherent and unambiguous moral significance. There is no clear reason why a relationship with someone more instead of less similar to oneself should translate into an inherently unfulfilling liaison. Moreover, the levels of risk, mutual vulnerability, and adventure in a relationship may be more a function of the relative sameness of the participants taken as wholes than of gender difference taken in isolation. Thus, two people of the same gender who are radically different in socioeconomic, racial, and religious backgrounds may be more of a mystery to one another than two people of different genders who are similar in the other respects.

Accordingly, this argument against homosexuality requires independent support for the claim that gender differences uniquely and necessarily add to the risk, mutual vulnerability, and adventure that allegedly enhance sexual relationships. The argument thus seems to presuppose precisely what it most prove. Moreover, the argument falsely assumes that the "homosexual experience" is a unitary concept that transcends societal and historical reconstruction.

Critics of homosexuality also advance other claims against that sexual orientation: that homosexuality reveals or results in psychological illness, that it undermines society's moral fabric, and that it spreads virulent venereal diseases and the HIV virus. This book will unmask the weakness of these claims: what is statistically unusual does not imply psychological sickness; society's moral fabric does not depend on invariable heterosexuality but on widespread adherence to general moral principles, none of which are necessarily violated by homosexuality; and while the spread of disease raises special concerns that point in the direction of employing better prophylactic measures, it does not show that homosexuality is inherently immoral.

I conclude that homosexuality has not been shown to be inherently wrong,[8] and thus acts of homosexuality can be morally evaluated by the same criteria which judge heterosexuality: sexual morality in five tiers. There are, of course, considerations of third party effects and wider societal context attending homosexuality which do not accompany heterosexuality, but the converse is true as well. Accordingly, no special analysis of homosexuality will be undertaken here.

But sometimes critics of homosexuality are less concerned with showing the alleged immorality of that sexual orientation than with displaying how it fails dismally to constitute an acceptable sexual *ideal*. There are at least two senses of "ideal" that are relevant here: morally ideal sex, and maximally fulfilling sex. Throughout this book, I am most concerned with morally permissible and impermissible, not morally ideal, sex. Morally ideal sex, whatever that may be, goes above and beyond the call of moral duty. It would engender some extraordinary moral benefits to others not attainable in (merely) morally permissible sex. Because *Good Sex* is pitched to the morally conscientious, not necessarily the saintly, reader, the issue of morally ideal sex is touched obliquely if at all.

There are numerous acceptable but sometimes mutually incompatible ideals of maximally fulfilling sex, ideals among which a person may legitimately select in pursuit of self-realization. Such ideals embody descriptive and prescriptive assumptions about the degrees of mutual intimacy, commitment, desire, and understanding necessary for worthy human associations.

Once a person internalizes an ideal, she often thereby commits herself to a host of special moral obligations which such ideals generate. Furthermore, sound prudential reasons often exist for a person to prefer one of these ideals to another: psychological makeup, nonsexual goals, preferred lifestyle, sexual desires, notions of self-fulfillment, and so on. However, a person may freely choose from among the numerous acceptable moral ideals of sexual behavior. Accordingly, there is no universal moral obligation for humans to adopt one particular vision of maximally fulfilling sex. For this reason, I concentrate here on the *requirements* of morality in the sexual realm, instead of proselytizing for my preferred vision of maximally fulfilling sex.

My decision to address the requirements of morality, instead of arguing for a particular rendition of ideal sex, affects the tone of the book. Arguments about the moral requirements of sexual behavior are less susceptible to a profusely emotional writing style than are efforts to persuade others to one's preferred vision of maximally fulfilling sex. Accordingly, the unsentimental, indelicate, often lighthearted tone of the book underscores the need for a measure of analytic rigor and an open-minded, tolerant perspective in answering the questions I address. As a result, I offer few flowery paeans to the transcendent powers of ideal sex and love.

My theory advances five tiers of scrutiny: libertarian agreement, general moral considerations, sexual exploitation, third party effects, and effects on the wider social context. Accordingly, sexual morality in five tiers must attend to a host of concomitant issues, including the extent to which and circumstances under which mutual consent can be taken as strongly probative of moral soundness; the presence and moral consequences of power differentials between the consenting parties; the presence of general moral defects such as promise breaking, deception, and infliction of harm; the relevance, if any, of third party reactions to the sexual activity of the consenting parties; and the social context in which the sexual activity takes place. The thesis advanced here takes leftist and feminist critiques seriously, yet refuses to dismiss libertarian-Kantianism as mere sham and thinly veiled oppression. The theory demands thorough scrutiny of the five tiers that implicate moral evaluation and suggests a moral continuum of sexual behavior based on that aggregate evaluation.

Thus, in *Good Sex* I develop a new theory of sexual ethics that aspires to mediate the tensions between mainstream Western morality and its leftist and feminist critics. But why should we want to work out these tensions? Why not adjudicate the tensions between traditional Western and non-Western approaches, or between psychoanalytic and Marxist approaches, or between Judeo-Christian and Islamic or Hindu approaches?

The short answer is that I undertake this exercise in order to synthesize a new and better approach to sexual morality from the strengths of the older and contemporary vantage points. Moreover, mediating the tensions between mainstream Western morality and its leftist and feminist critics reveals a genuine and sound alternative: a genuine alternative in the sense of an option that is a real and practical possibility given our historical position, and a sound alternative in the sense that is it an option supported by strong moral reasons. In my view, libertarian-Kantian social and political visions provide solid ground for normative theory and practice but nevertheless exhibit limitations that can be ameliorated by Marxist and feminist perspectives. The arguments for these claims constitute the subtext of this study.

One final caveat. This work cannot present itself as embodying the inexorable normative conclusions of analytic philosophy. The formal techniques of analytic philosophy are formidable tools for categorizing, classifying, criticizing, analyzing, and testing coherency and consistency. But merely formal techniques cannot by themselves evolve one full normative vision and claim plausibly that its acceptance is required by Reason itself. It is fatuous to assume that the techniques of analytic philosophy could be used to re-think sexual ethics from the ground up and to reveal the necessary normative demands of unadorned, unsituated, neutral logic. Accord-ingly, any work such as *Good Sex* will necessarily embrace a host of contestable descriptive and prescriptive claims. Although the sub-text here argues that sexual morality in five tiers is a genuine and sound alternative to several popular perspectives on sexual ethics, that subtext cannot establish that readers who reject sexual morality in five tiers thereby transgress the demands of reason and are thus necessarily irrational.

In sum, this book embodies a story, a historical dialogue engaged in by Western theologians and philosophers on a theoretical level and reflected in the behavior and ideologies of the masses on a prac-tical level. Because sexual activity is unquestionably one of the most powerful animating human drives, its story reveals much about the people we are and the people we might become.

PART I
THE WESTERN TRADITION
Theology, Philosophy, and Passion

I

TRANSCENDING THE FLESH
Dualism and Asceticism

Sexual ethics do not emerge from a historical vacuum. What we take to be proper sexual behavior depends significantly on our attitudes toward our bodies and their role in facilitating human happiness and proper human ends. One of the earliest recorded brands of sexual advice in the West was the dualism of ancient Greece. Prescribing an asceticism inclined toward sexual self-denial and recommending preoccupation with intellectual activity, the dualists' call to transcend the flesh was a powerful philosophy of life that was often accompanied by a rich worldview.

The dualism of ancient Greece unnecessarily and unwisely arranged a war between mind and body. Forcing themselves to choose between the pleasures associated with mind and those linked with body, the Greek dualists, mirroring their own preference for intellectual pursuits and often chastised by the stifling material impoverishment of their societies, were led inexorably to devaluing their bodies and to venerating philosophies of self-denial. Accordingly, dualist prescriptions for proper sexual behavior are often contaminated by spurious assumptions about the relationships between "mental" and "bodily" activities, distorting preoccupations with the image of sexual profligates, contorted speculations about the nature of personal salvation and immortality, and artificial distinctions between "higher" and "lower" pleasures.

If the authority of such philosophies were confined to a discrete historical period, we might dismiss them as quaint anachronisms. But, on the contrary, the influence of Greek dualism resonates throughout history, particularly within Christian religion, and its imperatives of sexual denial retain currency today in a variety of social movements.

THE PYTHAGOREANS

Pythagoras (ca. 570–ca. 500 BC) was an Ionian Greek born on the island of Samos. When he was about 38 he left Samos and settled in Crotona, a city in southern Italy, where he lived for over twenty years. During this period he founded a society which embodied his religious, philosophical, and political aspirations.

Centuries before the birth of Christ, the Pythagoreans taught a sharp dualism between mortal human bodies and immortal human souls.[1] Animated by a belief in the unity of all life, they taught that individual souls were fragments of the eternal, divine, universal soul. As such, individual human souls, the essential part of humans, were considered immortal. Until individual souls return to the universal soul, Pythagoreans claimed that souls are imprisoned in bodies and endure transmigration: death dissolves the union of an individual soul with a particular body, and that soul transmigrates into a new body of a human or animal. Body was thus viewed either as an impurity itself or as evidence that the soul within it was still contaminated and presently unworthy of eternal return to its ultimate destiny. Pythagoreans contended that the proper goal of persons on earth should be a spiritual purity that prepared human souls for their proper return to the universal soul. For Pythagoreans "the ultimate aim was the annihilation of self in reunion with the divine."[2]

Accordingly, the Pythagoreans cultivated a strain of Western philosophy of enormous significance and influence. Here we see a stark dualism between the spiritual, eternal soul and the mundane, temporary body; primacy placed on the need for the essential part of a human being to become once again pure and liberated from the material; and the subordination of the physical and sexual to the intellectual. This view relegates sexual activity to an abjectly inferior role in human flourishing. Because sex is necessarily linked with the body it was viewed as of minor importance and, worse, often a hindrance to spiritual salvation.

PLATO

Although eventually disappearing as a society and subculture, Pythagoreanism enjoyed continuing vitality. Certainly, the Pythagoreans had significant influence on Plato's (ca. 428–ca. 348 BC) doctrines of the immortality of the soul, the existence of Universals in a world of higher Truth and Reason, and philosophy as preparation for human assimilation with the divine.[3]

For our purposes we need only absorb the thrust of Plato's position: humans can discover, but do not create, Universals; this discovery is one of intellectual ascension; Universals are independent of the transient world of sense-particulars; and as eternal, objective entities, Universals have superior ontological status.[4]

Plato underscored a recurrent theme: reason is the greatest gift bestowed on humans, and its proper functioning is the highest human activity. Without the proper functioning of reason, there can be no internal harmony and health, and thus no justice. Both spirit and, especially, appetite—the other alleged parts of the soul—must submit to the rightful authority of reason.

> When the gentler part of the soul slumbers and the control of reason is withdrawn, then the wild beast in us, full-fed with meat or drink, becomes rampant and shakes off sleep to go in quest of what will gratify its own instincts. As you know, it will cast away all shame and prudence at such moments and stick at nothing. In fantasy it will not shrink from intercourse with a mother or anyone else, man, god, or brute, or from forbidden food or any deed of blood.[5]

Plato believed in personal immortality: for the duration of a life the soul, incorporeal yet substantial, is imprisoned in its body. Upon the death of its body, the soul persists and transmigrates into another body in accordance with the type of life it manifested prior to its body's death.[6] Continual reincarnations and philosophical explorations may refine the soul and prepare it for its highest reward: coalescence with the Forms themselves.[7] It is, however, unclear how seriously Plato intended his doctrine of successive reincarnations.[8]

Plato punctuates his theory of soul with renewed attacks on sensuality and continued exhortation to the contemplative life: "None

but the philosopher or the lover of knowledge, who is wholly pure
when he goes hence, is permitted to go to the race of the gods . . .
the true philosopher is temperate and refrains from all the pleasures
of the body, and does not give himself up to them."[9] Sexual activity,
although not inherently evil under Plato's scheme, is ersatz behavior: tolerated as sometimes necessary, stigmatized as dangerous, recognized as distracting, and feared as potentially enslaving.

Perhaps Plato's most specific passages on sexual ethics are contained in *The Laws*. There, the Athenian, the work's main protago-
nist, argues that the state would benefit greatly if erotic pleasures
were restrained effectively. The Athenian identifies reproduction as
the natural function of intercourse and argues that prohibiting all
other unnatural sexual activity is greatly desirable, if impractical.
However, certain rules are enforceable: "[that] no freeborn citizen
should dare to touch any but his own wedded wife, and that there
should be no sowing of unhallowed and bastard seed with concubines . . . if a man should have to do with any [such prohibited acts]
. . . and his act become known . . . he [should] be deprived of the
honors of a citizen."[10] In practice, then, those who stray from marital sex should place a premium on secrecy and discretion. The price
of disclosure of sexual promiscuity should be severe: treatment as an
alien was a grave retribution in the ancient Greek world.

Thus, Plato exhibits a clear intention to control sexuality within
the bounds of rationality. The path of rampant sexuality is anathema
to the path of philosophical and spiritual salvation. The sexual libertine, preoccupied with the material and a slave to the sensual, is a
prime example of one whose appetites are untempered and uncontrolled by the rightful authority of reason. Accepting a stark dualism
between body, transitory and condemned to the world of the senses,
and soul, ineffable and with potential for the fullest knowledge and
highest existence, Plato must regard robust sexuality as an insurrection against reason. Plato confers the greatest ontological status on
the Forms, which subsist transcendent, uncontaminated by the material, and sexless. Knowledge, goodness, and reason are glorified.
Sexual desire, a potentially dangerous appetite and a potential obstacle to the good life, must be tempered and viewed with extreme suspicion.

The views of the Pythagoreans and Plato rest clearly on a notoriously suspect dualism between mind and body. Plato's dualism lo-

cates a person's identity totally in "mind" while it disparages "body" as a temporary tomb which hinders ascent to the Forms. Personal liberation requires exoneration from body. Sexual desire is a cruel reminder of how far humans reside from true realization.

Several dubious philosophical connections emerge here. First, dualists have the impossible task of explaining the alleged interaction of two wholly disparate entities, mind and body,[11] which often seduces them into a conception of mind that is mysterious and implausible.[12] Second, any explanatory power enjoyed by dualism is equaled or exceeded by a robust materialism that conceives of humans as psychosomatic unities.[13] Third, appeals to mind or soul as separate substances reduce to either question-begging claims or reiterations, rather than solutions to the problem of distinguishing humans from other sentient creatures.[14]

Moreover, dualism includes unnecessary and ill-advised devaluing of bodily pleasures and associates them with enslaving desire. The bifurcation of sensual and intellectual pleasure is artificial because it fails to honor the phenomenology of pleasure taken as a unified experience. Sex can be seen as a facilitator of, not necessarily an obstacle to, the realization of the highest values: human flourishing and well-being. The ancient Greek dualists manifested little awareness of the salutary effects of sex on human health, its role in enhancing the pleasures of the "mind," and the possibility of prolific but not degenerative sexual activity. The stark contrast between mind and body, then, is not simply an unfortunate philosophical mistake. Instead, it issues in an error of social practice which wrongly subordinates and indicts sexual activity and deteriorates into an unwholesome self-denial that pits immortal salvation against bodily pleasure.

Dualists are too often hostage to the image of profligates whose sole raison d'etre is exercising their sexual organs to the exclusion of other human needs and activities. Such libertines, however, like trolls, hobgoblins, and witches, are more easily imagined than found.

STOICS

For a period of over five hundred years, beginning at about the end of the fourth century BC, Stoicism was the dominant philosophy of the

Greco-Roman world. Founded by a Phoenician merchant from Cyprus, Zeno of Citium (ca. 336–ca. 264 BC), Stoicism is best exemplified by Chrysippus (ca. 280–ca. 207 BC), Seneca (ca. 4 BC–AD 65), Epictetus (ca. 50–138), and Marcus Aurelius (121–180). Stoics embodied a worldview as well as practical advice for living well: the ideal of inner tranquility based on self-discipline and freedom from passion, an ideal accomplished in part by withdrawing from the material world and its physical preoccupations in deference to ascetic, spiritual concerns. Preaching indifference to both grief and joy, Stoics advocated living in accordance with nature. The most important existential choice for humans is whether to submit or rebel when confronted by Fate. Although they recognized a range of human freedom, the Stoics believed practical wisdom consisted of correlating personal attitudes with natural law and submitting to the divinely anointed order of the universe. Stoics viewed such attitudes as constitutive of the proper use of reason. Conforming one's interior attitude to and consciously affirming the laws of nature were paramount.

Stoics stigmatized standard emotions such as pleasure, sorrow, desire, and fear as evil obstacles to inner health: "It is not so much a question of moderating and regulating them as of getting rid of them and inducing a state of Apathy. At least when the passions or affections become habits they have to be eliminated."[15]

At the heart of Stoicism's recommendations is the counsel to distinguish carefully between those events within human control and those events beyond individual agency. This distinction was explained most clearly by a former slave turned philosophy instructor, Epictetus:

> Of things some are in our power, and others are not. In our power are opinion, movement toward a thing, desire, aversion, and in a word, whatever are our own acts; not in our power are the body, property, reputation, offices, and in a word, whatever are not our own acts. And the things in our power are by nature free, not subject to restraint . . . but the things not in our power are weak, slavish, subject to restraint, in the power of others . . . if you think only that which is your own to be your own, and if you think that what is another's, as it really is, belongs to another, no man will ever compel you, no man will hinder you . . . no man will harm you, you will have no enemy for you will not suffer any harm.[16]

The virtuous life consists of many of the familiar moral bromides still handed down in Western culture from parents to children: veracity, loyalty, piety, modesty, temperance, avoidance of bad companions, and a cosmopolitanism that transcends narrow parochialism and nationalism. Unsurprisingly, chastity is a part of this moral prescription, as Epictetus, while recognizing that marriage and family are in accord with right reason, specifically scorns adulterers. Interestingly, Stoics seem to have accepted a duty to facilitate an orderly world social structure that would reflect the rationally ordered physical universe. It should be clear that Stoic happiness does not consist of the satisfaction of hedonistic indulgences or worldly success, but of a peaceful state of mind. Tranquility, contentment, and serenity triumph in a Stoic cosmos while raging desire and wild-eyed passion are denigrated as inimical to the good life.[17]

Stoicism may be fairly charged with a number of flaws. First, the doctrine wrongly takes a rule of conduct that is salutary under the most trying circumstances and mistakenly inflates it into a maxim of life that purports to be generally applicable. Second, Stoicism demands a nearly neurotic indifference to one's environment and may well be beyond the capacity of sane humans. Third, it is too cautious and conservative, thus stifling to the full range of human response. Fourth, it draws inaccurately the distinction between events within our control and events beyond our control. Fifth, its universal adoption would probably result in less, and not more, aggregate human happiness. Sixth, it aims, perhaps inadvertently, at severing us from what is partly constitutive of our being. Accordingly, Stoicism seems fundamentally suspicious of humans themselves.

Stoicism represents another strain of Greek dualism, a philosophy which not only has theoretical pretensions, but practical goals. Cautioning against frenzied desire and advising the subordination of the sensual to the contemplative, Stoicism is another link in an influential tradition which designed the domestication of sexual desire.

EPICUREANS

The main philosophical rival of Stoicism during this period was Epicureanism. Founded outside of Athens by Epicurus (ca. 342–ca. 270 BC), and popularized in the Roman world by Lucretius (ca. 91–ca. 51

BC), this movement differed from Stoicism in a number of ways. First, Epicurus rejected the natural order of the cosmos emphasized by Stoicism. Abrogating appeals to functional and teleological explanations, Epicureans had little appreciation for mathematical and scientific pursuits. Second, Epicureans rejected the possibility of personal immortality and belief in divine providence. Viewing the gods as role models who did not interfere in human affairs, Epicurus concluded that death should not be feared because it is merely the absence of all consciousness and feeling.[18] Third, rather than striving for indifference to sensations, Epicureans embraced sensations as the sole normative criterion and posited pleasure as the greatest good.

Given this endorsement of pleasure and the contemporary notion of an "Epicurean" as a sort of fun-loving gourmet, one might be tempted to conclude that in his day Epicurus must have provided a clear antidote to the asceticism of Greek dualism. Such a conclusion would be wildly off the mark. Pleasure was conceived by Epicureans as mental serenity, internal peace, and freedom from anxiety.

> By pleasure we mean the absence of pain in the body and of trouble in the soul. It is not an unbroken succession of drinking bouts and of revelry, not sexual love, not the enjoyment of fish and other delicacies of a luxurious table, which produce a pleasant life; rather it is sober reasoning, searching out the grounds of every choice and avoidance, and banishing those beliefs through which the greatest tumults take possession of the soul. Of all this the beginning and the greatest good is prudence.[19]

Like their Stoic brethren, Epicureans aspired to a contentment of mind forged in part by suppressing raging physical desires. Accordingly, the Epicureans aspired to an absence of passion and frustration achieved by minimizing one's desires; avoiding momentary sensual stimulations; cultivating long-term satisfactions such as intellect, beauty, and friendship; and de-emphasizing social involvements such as politics and marriage. Regarding erotic impulses specifically, Epicurus's evaluation could not have been harsher: "Sexual intercourse has never done a man good, and he is lucky if it has not harmed him."[20]

Clearly venerating the enduring, the cerebral, and the simple, Epicurus strove to minimize human fears and maximize self-sufficiency. One source of alleged anxiety is unnecessary social involvement. Friendships are needed for security and mutual tranquility, but political activism engenders emotional turbulence and attracts undue attention to oneself. Family, marriage, and sexual activity are sure sources of annoyance. It goes without elaboration that Epicureans opposed overindulgence in food and drink.[21]

Despite significant disagreements with Stoicism, Epicureanism has much the same flavor: moderation, asceticism, self-control, independence, philosophical insight. Epicureanism, too, is a philosophy born of social context and circumstance. Where antecedent prospects for world success are transparently thin, where real possibilities for influencing political institutions are virtually nil, where human misery is widespread and personal dissatisfaction rampant and predictable, such doctrines as Stoicism and Epicureanism that dispense practical advice on how to minimize suffering and maximize endurance may prove hygienic. Thus, reaction to these doctrines may be inversely related to one's perceived chances of achieving conventional notions of personal and political success.

There remain, of course, numerous nagging doubts about Epicureanism. Epicureans seem more concerned with avoiding possibly painful experiences than in seeking possibly pleasurable ones, thereby appearing too cautious. Moreover, they misunderstand the relationship between the "lower" sensual pleasures and the "higher" intellectual pleasures by failing to acknowledge that gratifying the former type is often a prerequisite for satisfying the latter. Epicureans are generally too abstemious in their outlook; they eschew moderation for self-denial. Like their Stoic brethren, Epicureans take prescriptions relevant to certain exceptionally brutal times and erroneously elevate them to universal imperatives.

This brief survey of Pythagoreanism, Plato, Stoicism, and Epicureanism is intended to illustrate that the seeds of dualism were firmly in place well before the birth of Christ and flourishing thereafter. This observation is not an apology for Christianity, but a clear historical fact. A major strain of Western sexuality emerged here: an asceticism that counsels detachment and freedom from sexual passion, or at least advises the subordination of sexual desire to reason; that tends to regard the body as a prison of the immortal human soul; and that is often accompanied by the view that our world is an ersatz version of truth and reality.

I am not necessarily suggesting that the doctrine of dualism caused or logically implied conclusions about asceticism; the relationship between the theory of dualism and the practice of asceticism is more subtle than that of simple causality. In addition, it would be an error to assume this variety of dualism defined Greek culture or that it stood haughtily unopposed by alternate visions. From the earliest writings of Homer in the eight century BC through the masterpieces of Aristotle (384–322 BC), the well-known Greek message of "moderation" persisted. Here those who were promiscuous or celibate suffered similar ridicule. The proper measure, the correct note, could be struck only by those who recognized that sordid sexual yearnings and prissy denial were equally harmful. The lascivious overindulgence of the profligate sanctifies physical passion at the expense of cerebral and spiritual objectives, while the abstemious withdrawal of the sexual recluse cringes at sensuality and thereby denigrates part of our constitutive nature. Under this view, sexual activity should be acknowledged as necessary and beneficial, a salutary human pursuit to be enjoyed temperately, without obsession or preoccupation. The Greek prescription of moderate indulgence, like the competing dualist call to transcend the flesh, would have considerable historical influence and never fade completely from ideological disputes concerning sexual ethics.

2

THE NATURAL LAW
Judeo-Christianity

It should now be clear that Christianity cannot accurately be identified as the intellectual source of the philosophical dualism that embodied a negative attitude toward the value of sexual activity. In this chapter, I provide brief sketches of the views on sex contained in the Old Testament, the words of Jesus, and the writings of St. Paul. Next, I examine more thoroughly the influence of St. Augustine, St. Thomas Aquinas, Martin Luther, and John Calvin as a prelude to unraveling the mature Christian, and specifically Roman Catholic, outlook on sexual ethics.

I conclude that the most conservative views on sex cannot be defended successfully without appeals to notoriously contestable religious claims. Moreover, it is not clear that the specific doctrines on sex embraced by Christianity are in fact required by divine scripture. The church introduced many of these doctrines at the Council of Trent for specific historical reasons that we can articulate, rather than from the unambiguous imperatives of divine scripture in keeping with natural law. Finally, I argue that the church's position is afflicted by confusing appeals to the "naturalness" of various acts, an ungrounded "indivisibility principle" that wrongly anchors the expression of sexual love to procreative intent, an unreasonable instrumentalist view of sex, and significant gender inequalities.

THE OLD TESTAMENT

The predominant view of the Old Testament emphasized the joy of sex, counseled fecundity, and assumed that marriage and parenthood were natural.[1] Motivated in part by a concern for reproduction

25

of family lines, Hebrew law accepted levirate marriages, in which the childless widow of a man could be impregnated by his brother and the resulting child regarded as the offspring of the deceased. W. G. Cole stresses that even the admonition against adultery "springs from the concern for the seed, the family line. That this is not anti-sexual is demonstrated by the glaring absence of any ban on fornication, an omission which embarrassed later Christians of puritanical hue."[2]

More generally, the Old Testament lacked the bifurcating urges manifested in Greek dualism. Accepting wholeheartedly the material world and conceiving of humans as a psychosomatic unity, the Hebrews displayed little inclination to denigrate the physical. Here we see no contrast between that which has supreme value, the spiritual and eternal, and that which is contaminating the transitory, the material and physical.[3]

Perhaps most significantly, the Old Testament portrays the unity of body and soul.

> The Genesis narrative does not assert that man was supplied with a soul but rather that he *became* a living soul. And the Hebrew word for soul is *nephesh*, which refers to the whole human being, not simply to some vague, spiritual entity. The Israelite use of *nephesh* is very close to what modern psychology means by the term 'personality.' It is the totality of the individual, that which marks him with his unique stamp, making him what he is.[4]

Finally, there are references to personal immortality which also consistently maintain the recurrent themes of appreciation for the material and physical and for a unitary concept of personhood. Accordingly, when contrasted to Greek dualism and asceticism, the attitudes of the Old Testament toward sex and the material world seem overwhelmingly positive: "In Jewish history coitus has been consistently and unambiguously valued for the sheer joy and pleasure of it, even where procreation was obviously impossible."[5]

JESUS

In the few recorded Gospel verses in which Jesus addressed sex, he condemned adultery and divorce. But he nowhere stigmatizes erotic impulses as inherently evil. Preaching a law of love and assessing people on the basis of their inner motives and intentions, Jesus castigates sex and the material world as obstacles to eternal salvation only when they become idols.[6]

Against the rigid legalism of the Pharisees, Jesus preached a philosophy of love which appealed to inner attitudes and motives as the criteria of moral virtue. Further, Jesus advanced the novel doctrine that God's love extends to all humans, regardless of their earthly deeds. Rather than underscoring reward for the virtuous and retribution for the evil, Jesus stressed that sinners may require greater divine concern based on their greater need. Humans themselves should love and pray for friends and enemies alike, and their concern and love should emulate divine benevolence.[7] Again unlike the legalistic Pharisees, Jesus at times abrogated conformity with general, abstract principles in deference to specific compelling circumstances.

Interpreted in light of these general inclinations—emphasis on inner motives, universal love, and antilegalism—what can be said about Jesus' teachings on sex? First, we must consider Jesus' Sermon on the Mount and his admonition against adultery, which words are recorded in the Gospel of Matthew: ''You have heard that it was said, 'You shall not commit adultery.' But I say to you that every one who looks at a women lustfully has already committed adultery with her in his heart.'' While these verses might be construed as manifesting a commitment to Greek asceticism, they may be better placed in the framework of Jesus' concern for inner motives as the criteria of moral virtue.[8]

In the Sermon on the Mount, Jesus also spoke harshly against divorce. His sentiments against divorce are chronicled in Matthew (5:27–30, 19:1–12), Mark (10:2–12), and Luke (16:18). Matthew records: ''It was also said 'Whoever divorces his wife, let him give her a certificate of divorce.' But I say to you that everyone who divorces his wife, except on the ground of unchastity, makes her an adulteress; and whoever marries a divorced women commits adultery.'' Here some have interpreted Jesus as an absolutist.[9] But if we take seriously Jesus' sanctification of inner motives, it is not entirely clear to which version of sexual ethics we should subscribe. The problem here, of course, is that another's inner attitudes and motives are rarely transparent and thus it is difficult for society, saddled inherently with fallibilism and partial information, to base its ethic on criteria which is fully accessible only to God.

It is clear that human action is not necessarily dispositive of human inner attitudes. Is the married couple who stay together and who violate no obvious societal sexual prohibitions, while inwardly despising one another, morally virtuous? Is the unmarried couple who do not live together, but who share an abiding consummated love, thereby sexually immoral? How would Jesus evaluate such questions? On the basis of whether a sincere, mature love was present? On the criterion of whether the couple was officially (or unofficially) married? On the principle of whether sex is consummated with one and only one sexual partner? On the basis of the reasons why sex was consummated? On the criterion of whether the parties kept their word to the other: they married, remained so, were faithful, and shared a measure of love? The answers to such questions are not contained unambiguously in the recorded words of Jesus.

Those who antecedently long to interpret Jesus' words in nonconventional fashions may seize upon his antilegalism and appeal to the contextualism of inner motives. Accordingly, they may argue that contemporary Christian sexual morality is at best a concession to society's epistemological inability to discern accurately the inner attitudes of sexual partners, while at worst it is a distortion of the spirit of Jesus' teachings and a reversion to the discredited legalism of the Pharisees. Those who antecedently yearn to interpret Jesus' words as the seeds from which contemporary Christian sexual morality blossomed may appeal to the absolutism of Jesus' specific teachings on divorce and adultery. Thus, they may argue that divorce and adultery are strictly prohibited and that even lusting after another is morally tantamount to consummating the forbidden act.

We may say with confidence, however, that Jesus nowhere stigmatizes erotic impulses as inherently evil. Never accepting the most extreme forms of asceticism extant in the Greek world, Jesus castigates sex and the material world as obstacles to eternal salvation only when they become idols.[10]

ST. PAUL

Unlike Jesus, who had virtually no contact with the world outside of the immediate Palestinian area, Paul was born in the seaport city of Tarsus, which was the center of a respected university. Literate in Greek and a frequent traveler, Paul moved relatively easily in the Roman world.

Perhaps as a result of his dual major influences, his Hebrew origin and Greek learning, Paul's writings on sex and marriage manifest sharp ambivalence. The incongruity manifests itself even in his attitudes toward women. On one hand, he accepted the irrelevancy of all social distinctions; once we are seen as children of God and accept the faith, "there is neither Jew nor Greek, there is neither slave nor free, there is neither male nor female; for you are all one in Christ Jesus" (Gal. 3:28). Moreover, he suggests specifically that gender inequalities are artificial: "In the Lord woman is not made independent of man, nor man of woman, for as woman is made from man, so man is now born of woman. And all things are from God" (1 Cor. 11:11–12). Paul also seemingly accepted that it is appropriate for women to pray and prophesy publicly (1 Cor. 11:5). Finally, the duties of marriage were generally presented as reciprocal: where the women was required to be obedient to her husband, the husband was commanded to venerate and protect his wife.[11]

On the other hand, in numerous passages Paul clearly affirms the subjugation of women to men. He talks of a wife being responsible to her husband, as her husband is responsible to Christ (1 Cor. 11:3); of the requirement that a woman who publicly prays wear a covering on her head as a sign of her husband's dominion over her (1 Cor. 11:5); and of the need for women to remain silent during church meetings because of their subordination to men (1 Cor. 14:33–35). The Epistles to Timothy, although no longer commonly taken as authored by Paul, underscore such attitudes by counseling women to be quiet, sensible, humble, never presuming to teach men, and always cognizant that the suffering they bear in childbirth is a direct result of the fact that the first sinner was a woman, Eve (1 Tim. 2:9–15).

After reading these paragraphs one may well conclude with Cole that "there is no consistent interpretation of sex to be found in Paul's epistles and one can be purchased only at the price of distortion."[12] Although it is undeniable that St. Paul wrote ambivalently on gender roles, the bulk of his words imply that God intended that men rule over women because of natural male superiority.

Unsurprisingly, Paul also manifests paradox when discussing the institution of marriage. It was he who first presented the Christian ideal of celibacy: "It is well for a man not to touch a woman . . . I wish that all men were as I myself am'' (I Cor. 7:7). But he also advised against long periods of sexual abstinence within marriage for those whose passions precluded chastity: "If they cannot restrain themselves, let them marry. Better marry than be aflame with passion!" (I Cor. 7:9). He cautions that sex, along with all other things merely of this world, must be subordinate to earning eternal salvation: "The unmarried man is anxious about the affairs of the Lord . . . but the married man is anxious about worldly affairs, how to please his wife, and his interests are divided" (I Cor. 7:32–34). Moreover, those who are married should not remain sexually continent for long periods, lest they be tempted to adultery: "Every man had better have a wife of his own and every woman a husband of her own. The husband must give the wife her conjugal dues, and the wife in the same way must give her husband his; a wife cannot do as she pleases with her body . . . and in the same way a husband cannot do as he pleases with his body" (I Cor. 7:2–4).

Here, however, the paradox can be unraveled. For St. Paul, celibacy is the highest calling, for it alleviates numerous mundane anxieties and ameliorates the dangerous effects of social institutions, thereby increasing the potential for achieving divine salvation. Accordingly, his initial advice to the unmarried or widowed is, "Remain unattached!" But this counsel is not obligatory, and most people will be driven by passionate urges to marry. In fact, Paul acknowledges that this is not only permissible but even advisable for those who are so inclined. Mirroring Jesus' teachings about inner attitudes as the criteria for morality, Paul understands that there is no virtue in remaining single while inflamed with lust. Furthermore, those who are married should not try to restrain artificially their sexual desires.

Accordingly, Paul honors celibacy as the highest estate because of its alleged instrumental value in increasing prospects for eternal happiness. But he does not denigrate sexual passion as unnatural, nor does he advise ascetic self-discipline as a way of overcoming passion. Although St. Paul posited an ideal which contrasts with the counsel of the Old Testament, and albeit he was affected by Greek dualist tendencies, he fell short of suggesting that sex is inherently evil.[13]

ST. AUGUSTINE

As the church sought converts among the Gentiles, its Jewish heritage tended to diminish while Greek influence increased. In the first centuries AD, with the rise of the Gnostics, virginity became an important virtue and marriage an allowance for the spiritually weak. Although most Gnostics were ostensibly Christians, their teachings were a strange and heretical blend of Greek, Jewish, Iranian, Babylonian, Egyptian, and Oriental traditions. Dualism, however, dominated the Gnostic way and led most followers to the conclusion that avoiding unnecessary contamination from the material world was obligatory and prudent. Generally, Gnostics identified the soul and things spiritual with good, and the body and things material with evil. Accordingly, most Gnostics accepted wholeheartedly an extreme asceticism which included abstention from sexual activity.

After renouncing his colorful past, St. Augustine (354–430), in his *Of Holy Virginity* and *On Marriage and Concupiscence*, became the chief systematizer and refiner of a tradition that exhorted humans to abrogate bodily pleasures for the higher ideal of contemplation. According to this line of thought, sex before the Fall of Adam and Eve was uncontaminated by raging passion and was controlled and restrained by the mind. With original sin came burning sexual desire and much loss of control over the body. Accordingly, all sexual desire was thought to be tainted with evil because of its source. Moreover, original sin itself was thought to be transmitted generationally through sexual intercourse. Thus the requirement of the virgin birth: Jesus could be free from original sin only if he were not begotten through the sexual act. Chastity was reaffirmed as the highest ideal, and sex within marriage was regarded as an evil necessary for the continuation of the species: morally permissible only if it was motivated by a desire for children, realized by an act which did not by its nature preclude procreation, and engaged in moderately and decorously.

To understand Augustine's teachings we must note the circumstances under which he converted to Christianity. After a youth characterized by sensual pursuits but accompanied by serious guilt, Augustine believed that he had received a message from God to convert to Christianity and to renounce his past, including the pursuit of sexual pleasure.

I will now call to mind my past foulness, and the carnal corrup-
tions of my soul: not because I love them, but that I may love
Thee, O my God. For love of Thy love I do it; reviewing my most
wicked ways in the very bitterness of my remembrance, that
Thou mayest grow sweet unto me. . . . For I even burnt in my
youth heretofore, to be satiated in things below; and I dared to
grow wild again, with these various and shadowy loves: my
beauty consumed away, and I stank in Thine eyes.[14]

Here we see the ideological battle lines drawn: either sex or religion, either the pleasures of this world or God. One might be
tempted to conclude that I have drawn the distinctions too crudely.
Surely, Augustine could have chosen a middle ground which would
condemn promiscuity as an obstacle to salvation, but retain appreciation for moderate enjoyment of sexuality. Although this conclusion
is reasonable and as a matter of logic was clearly possible, it is just as
clear that Augustine rejects it. Augustine rebelled so thoroughly
against his past and was so firmly convinced that sexuality had
proved his moral undoing that he came to view women as representative of all the worldly seductions that hinder full commitment to
Christianity and pursuit of divine salvation: "I perceive that nothing
more saps the citadel of manly strength, whether of mind or body,
than female blandishments and familiarities."[15] Thus, sexuality becomes a focus of religion.

Even Augustine, however, conceded the obvious: sex as reproduction is necessary for the survival of the species, and marriage is a divinely created, "natural" condition. Accordingly, Augustine acknowledges the (limited) moral appropriateness of sex: "For what
food is unto the conservation of the man, this sexual intercourse is
unto the conservation of the race."[16] But, unsurprisingly, Augustine's virulent misogyny resurfaces when he insists that a husband
must love the humanity of his wife but lament the fact that she is a
woman: "Love in her what is characteristic of a human being . . .
hate what belongs to her as a wife."[17] As a creation of God, women
are equal children seeking eternal salvation; but as women qua
women, they constitute one of the chief worldly temptations standing in the path of man's spiritual purity.

In this manner, Augustine fashions his position on sexual ethics.
One part of this sexual ethic is based simply on pure necessity:

"God . . . alone is to be loved; and all this world . . . all sensible things, are to be despised—while, however, they are to be used as this life requires."[18] Another part is founded on the perceived need to subordinate sensuality to the authority of rationality: "For necessary sexual intercourse for begetting is free from blame, and itself is alone worthy of marriage. But that which goes beyond this necessity, no longer follows reason, but lust."[19]

A third part is based on Augustine's understanding of the Fall of Adam and Eve. Augustine considers seriously two portrayals of sex in Paradise. One possibility was that sexual feelings were conjured by reason and under complete control of the will.[20] The second possibility was that erotic feelings did not accompany sex in Paradise.[21] Either of these portrayals of sex in Paradise is acceptable for Augustine because each provides a picture of sex congenial to a dualist's aspirations: the docile subordination of the passions to the rightful authority of reason.

Now Augustine applies the clincher: one of the punishments that befell Adam and Eve after the first sin was the loss of rational authority over their erotic impulses. Unable to assert full command over their bodies by acts of volition, Adam and Eve first experience shame over their nakedness: "Did not they—he in the open, she in the hidden impulse—perceive those [sexual organs] to be disobedient to the choice of their will, which certainly they ought to have ruled like the rest by their voluntary command?"[22] Thus, excessive sexual passion—those erotic impulses beyond the level required for moderate, decorous sex aimed at reproduction—stems from the first sin and bears no virtue.

But matters do not end there. St. Augustine also argued that original sin itself is transmitted generationally through sexual intercourse. There is only one escape from this original sin: one must be conceived without sexual intercourse. Thus, the requirement of the virgin birth: "Now, the devil found no carnal concupiscence in the Lord because the Lord did not come as a man to men by its means."[23]

Born of sin and bequeathing sin, sexual intercourse is permeated thoroughly with evil. Thus, Augustine sanctifies the condition of chastity. He recognizes, in clear lockstep with Christian tradition, that outward abstinence from sex is insufficient for true chastity; the proper inner attitude is also necessary if one is to achieve purity and virtue. Perhaps recalling his own internal struggles, he tells us that the highest end of Christian sexuality is to transform the erotic so that inner conflict between the rational and physical subsides.

The institution of the church and the sacrament of marriage can, however, morally legitimate sex of the requisite type and render non-procreative sex within marriage merely venial sin.

> For intercourse of marriage for the sake of begetting hath not fault; but for the satisfying of lust, but yet with husband or wife, by reason of the faith of the bed [the sacrament of marriage], it hath venial fault: but adultery or fornication hath deadly fault [mortal sin], and, through this, continence from all intercourse is indeed better even than the intercourse of marriage itself, which takes place for the sake of begetting.[24]

Even moderate, decorous sex, undertaken by married couples for purposes of procreation, brings limited Augustinian recommendation: "The better [spouses] are, the earlier they have begun by mutual consent to contain from sexual intercourse with each other."[25] Thus, even within marriage the highest aspiration is close companionship accompanied by sexual continence. Where lust is present, marriage domesticates eroticism and harnesses it toward procreation and faithful monogamy. As a sacrament, marriage constitutes a divinely instituted connection between husband and wife. Accordingly, divorce, birth control, abortion, infanticide, masturbation, fellatio, and cunnilingus, among others, are morally prohibited. Even the "rhythm method" of birth control, a practice sanctioned by later Christians, is excoriated by Augustine as remaking a wife into a kind of prostitute.[26]

Augustine's own disparagement of sexual pleasure seems to be founded on his speculation about the relationship between sex and volition before and after the Fall, his Manichaean heritage and dualist inclinations that venerate the spiritual and mental, his personal difficulties in dealing with his rather exciting life prior to Christian conversion, and his apparent fear or hatred of women.[27] Although he sought biblical documentation for most of his claims, surely his disparagement of sexual activity goes far beyond biblical injunctions. Not even the passages of St. Paul, many of which themselves are labeled Paul's "counsel" or "opinion" and not God's word, can reasonably be invoked to establish Augustine's more extreme conclusions about sex.

Having said this, I do not wish to blunder into a genetic fallacy: the suggestion that a writer's conclusions are *proved* false by stigmatizing the genesis and psychological conditions from which they arose. But we must acknowledge that St. Augustine's position on sex is in many respects not demanded by Scripture. This fact, combined with his question-begging speculations about sex before the Fall, at the very least provides significant inductive evidence against his conclusions.

ST. THOMAS AQUINAS

During the Renaissance in Europe, the thought of the greatest medieval theologian, St. Thomas Aquinas (1225–1274) emerged. The leading theoretician of the pro-Aristotelian Dominican order of priests, Aquinas echoes most of Augustine's account of sex in his *Summa Theologica*, but ameliorates to some degree Augustine's distrust of bodily pleasure and joy within marriage.

Aquinas's vision of natural law includes apprehending eternal human nature by human reason and drawing moral obligations from that human nature, which obligations demand that we bind our wills to those actions necessary for the flourishing of our natures and the attainment of our final ends. Thus conceived, the discovery of what morality and law are must be an a priori exercise, not an empirical investigation of particular societies.[28]

Like Augustine, Aquinas recognizes that as an agency created by God, sex is good once its proper functions are identified and fulfilled. In Paradise, erotic impulses were under the full control of reason, but after the Fall one part of divine retribution to humans was the loss of this control and the emergence of concomitant experiences of shame. Where Aquinas diverges from Augustine is on the role of pleasure in sex. In Paradise, sexual activity, if anything, would have been accompanied by *more* pleasure than experienced after the Fall, because in Paradise there was "greater purity of nature and greater sensibility of the body."[29] Aquinas strays from rigid asceticism as he acknowledges the positive possibilities of sensations of pleasure. He distinguishes between good pleasures and bad pleasures on the basis of their genesis: if in accord with reason, the pleasure is good. Thus, sexual pleasure in Paradise was entirely good because it was entirely subject to rationality.[30]

But there are clear distinctions between sexual pleasure in Paradise and after the Fall.

> Beasts are without reason. In this way man becomes, as it were, like them in coition, because he cannot moderate concupiscence. In the state of innocence nothing of this kind would have happened that was not regulated by reason, not because delight of sense was less, as some [such as Augustine] say (rather indeed would sensible delight have been greater in proportion to the greater purity of nature and the greater sensibility of the body), but because the force of concupiscence would not have so inordinately thrown itself into such pleasure being curbed by reason, whose place it is not to lessen sensual pleasure, but to prevent the force of concupiscence from cleaving to it immoderately.[31]

Thus, to the extent that reason is overwhelmed by concupiscence, bodily pleasures become evil. Again, we see that physical pleasures must be subordinate to the rightful authority of reason.

Moreover, Aquinas, relying on the example set by Christ, reiterates that virginity is an estate superior to marriage. But he also repeats the Christian view that inner motivations are the foundation of moral virtue and that marriage embodies important functions. Therefore, one who is, as a matter of fact, a virgin is not by that condition alone morally superior to those wedded.

Like Augustine, Aquinas displays an abundant measure of what would today be termed sexism.[32] This sexism extends to Aquinas's account of the sins of lust. For example, he regards the seduction of a virgin less seriously than adultery because the latter, unlike the former, involves a violation of a husband's proprietary interests.[33] Notice that Aquinas invokes the alleged harm done to the husband or father of the woman involved, not the degree of harm befalling the woman, as the criterion of the gravity of the sin. Unequivocally supporting the subordination of women to the authority of men, Aquinas's nonegalitarian picture of sexual ethics extends to his account of the sins of adultery. W. G. Cole explains:

Adultery makes the woman guilty of three sins: infidelity to the law of God, offense to her husband, leaving him uncertain whether his children are really his, and bearing the offspring of a man not her husband. The sins of the adulterous man are only two: his union with another woman is not good for his own children and he hinders the good of another's progeny.[34]

Another example of Aquinas's asymmetrical rendering of sexual ethics is his description of the marital debt: a wife, regardless of her antecedent inclinations, must submit to her husband's sexual desire to protect him from the temptations of adultery.[35] This suggests that should a wife refuse the marital debt and her husband seek sexual consolations from another woman, the wife is partially (entirely?) culpable for the sin of her husband. Thus, marriage becomes an antidote for sin. In all fairness, we must note that Aquinas also recognizes a marital debt on the part of the husband to his wife. Theoretically, he, too, was counseled to render the marriage debt upon demand or obvious need of his wife. But such advice was softened by the belief that a wife would be less likely to be consumed with the passion that triggers the demand and by an important corollary to the principle of marital debt: a husband is not obligated to render the debt if his wife is menstruating. It should come as no surprise that this corollary is not reciprocal: a wife who is menstruating is still obligated to render the debt upon the demand of her husband. Again, keeping the husband from the temptations of adultery is paramount.

Clear pictures of husbands and wives emerge. The man is often consumed with sexual passions so powerful that they must find expression. The woman is rarely beset by erotic impulses and is thus assigned the role of keeping her husband from the lure of extramarital sin. He has urges, she has duties. Should she fail to render the debt upon her husband's request, she at least shares culpability for any resulting adultery.

But notice another aspect to this issue. For Aquinas it is sinful to engage in sex from solely lustful motives. Thus, a man who desires sex with his wife because of his own consuming passions, and not for procreative reasons, seemingly is guilty of sin upon consummation of his lustful urges with his wife. The wife's rendering the marital debt, however, presumably confers merit and virtue on the sexual act. Accordingly, when a woman renders the debt to her husband she not only prevents his potential sin of adultery, but she also eradicates, or at least ameliorates, the moral taint of her husband's lustful motives.

One might be tempted to view this as empowering women, giving them a partial ability to absolve or prevent their husband's moral transgressions. But we must not neglect that the marital debt is a duty. Wives who fail to fulfill this duty are themselves subject to moral disapproval. Lacking true choice, women lack true power. Hence, the concept of rendering the marital debt is more reasonably depicted as yet another illustration of the explicit subjugation of women to the projects and purposes of men, particularly their husbands.

Thus, Aquinas echoes most of Augustine's account of sex, but ameliorates to some degree Augustine's distrust of bodily pleasure and joy within marriage. He refuses to label pleasure as in itself evil, but he also denies that pleasure should be sought for its own sake, instead reaffirming the primacy of reason and the allegedly natural functions of humans. His portrayal of eroticism before the Fall parts company with Augustine, but his innovative doctrine of the marital debt and his general account of male/female relations sustain and reinforce the gender inequalities that constituted much of the church's dogma on sexual ethics.

THE PROTESTANT REFORMERS

In 1517, Martin Luther (1483–1546), an Augustinian monk from Wittenberg, responding to widespread perceived abuses in the church, posted a document that listed ninety-five theses arguing against the church's policies on selling indulgences. Having no antecedent desire to break radically from most of the church's traditions, Luther was confident that significant internal reforms were likely. This conviction soon proved incorrect.

In general, Luther contended that sin and evil pervade history. The quest for human moral perfection is doomed to failure. The church itself was guilty of aspiring to transform itself, a mortal and fallible enterprise, into a Godlike final authority.[36]

While agreeing with most of the Augustinian-Thomist position on sex, Luther rejected celibacy as an ideal. Luther observed that few are liberated from erotic impulses. Thus, God initiated and demands marriage as a duty for all but a few: "Whoever is ashamed of marriage is also ashamed of being a man or being thought a man, or else thinks that he can make himself better than God made him."[37]

Affirming that *all* work was sacred, Luther refused to acknowledge the supremacy of the monastic calling. Moreover, his appreciation for marriage was enhanced by his contempt for vows of chastity. "There is never less chastity than in those who vow to be chaste. Almost everything about it is befouled, if not by unclean seminal emissions, then by the continual searing of lust which never dies out . . . if anything fictitious has to be vowed in the monastery, it should be fictitious chastity."[38]

Luther's preference for marriage was based on his belief that this estate was instituted and required by God and his observation that few, if any, are truly liberated from the powerful seductions of eroticism. He denied, however, that marriage is a sacrament and advised religious institutions to remove themselves from administrative authority over marital judgments.[39]

Despite his agreement with much of Augustinian-Thomist theory of sexuality, one major difference in Luther's approach is clear: when confronted with difficult practical problems in areas such as bigamy, adultery, and divorce, he boldly affirmed pragmatic solutions even where such solutions varied from his theoretical musings.[40]

The other towering figure of the Reformation, John Calvin (1509–1564), set out explicitly to imagine and create a theocracy in Geneva. No minion of the doctrine of separation of church and state, Calvin envisioned a virtuous and just social order under the auspices of clergy. He echoed Luther's theme that marriage was paramount but also tended toward the view that sexual activity within marriage must be restrained and decorous.[41]

Calvin's condemnation of unrestrained and intemperate sex within marriage would resonate pleasingly to the most doctrinaire Augustinian: he vilified those "adulterers of their own wives [who] have no regard to modesty or decorum."[42] He retreated from his exaltation of marriage by praising celibacy as "better than marriage because it has more liberty, so that persons can serve God with greater freedom."[43] Calvin tried to reconcile his paradoxical claims about celibacy and marriage by pointing out that his true objection to Roman Catholic celibacy was the fact that it was a *required* vow of the clergy. Apparently, he never wished to deny the inherent value of celibacy, only its imposition by church authorities.

Perhaps a better way to unravel Calvin's paradox is to view him as counseling against two radical positions: an extreme asceticism that denigrates all sex as inherently inferior, and an extreme hedonism that accepts uncritically any sexual act indulged in by married couples. This solution has the comforting feature of portraying Calvin as a moderate centrist on sex, one who prudently perceives the twin vices of excess and abstention, but it may create the illusion that Calvin was more consistent and more broad-minded on sexual matters than he truly was.

In any event, for Calvin, marriage has three functions: companionship, reproduction, and avoidance of fornication. He also recognizes measures of gender equality with respect to conjugal rights that elude Augustine and Aquinas. But always there lurks the specter of Calvin's three horseman of sex: inevitability, delicacy, and propriety. Rather than being inherently valuable, sex is inevitable because of the prevalence of concupiscence. Rather than being valuable in themselves and often expressive of love and sharing, sexual passion and pleasure must be moderated. Calvin venerates delicacy and propriety, but merely resigns himself to erotic impulses.

Accordingly, although the Protestant reformers add some nuances to the Augustinian-Thomist tradition of sexual ethics, and in spite of Luther's admirable pragmatism in solving concrete moral dilemmas, it is fair to conclude that procreation and avoidance of sin remained for the Protestant reformers the main positive functions of sex.[44]

THE COUNCIL OF TRENT

The Council of Trent met numerous times from 1545 to 1563. Here official Roman Catholic doctrine was formulated and promulgated. Besieged by burgeoning criticism and riddled with internal conflict on a host of theoretical concerns, the church sought orthodoxy both as a way to circle the wagons against external attack and as a way to solidify doctrinal conformity.[45]

In its twenty-fourth session in 1563, the council advanced its canons and decrees relevant to the sacrament of marriage. Among other things, the council concluded the following: clandestine marriages in which the parties consented to live together and in which they consummated their union sexually were forbidden. A marriage fully sanctioned by the church as sacrament must include an ecclesiastical ceremony presided over by a priest and conducted in the presence of at least two other witnesses. Marriage was thus defined as an eternal and indissoluble bond, instituted by God, and honored as a sacrament by Christ. Although "indissoluble," marriages could be annulled for certain carefully circumscribed reasons: for example, vow of celibacy by either party. The council declared officially the moral superiority of virginity and celibacy to marriage, and affirmed the requirement of clerical celibacy.

The catechism of the Council of Trent explained the three legitimate purposes of marriage: mutual support and companionship, reproduction, and remedy for potential sin. Concupiscence was described officially as a consequence of the Fall. As a sacrament, marriage must be fully under the domain of the church's administration, dissolution of a marriage by human legal processes does not imply dissolution in the eyes of God. Thus, one who divorces by dint of legal procedures and who subsequently engages in sex with another is culpable of the sin of adultery: Caesar cannot absolve what God disparages as sin.

Two other issues of prime importance for our purposes were clarified and solidified as dogma. First, the question of the role of pleasure in marriage. Here the council "exhorted the faithful to avoid sex that is motivated by sensuality or pleasure and urged them to abstain, at times (at least three days before receiving Holy Communion and often during Lent), from the marriage debt in order to devote themselves to prayers and meditations."[46] The catechism emphatically demanded the complete domestication of sexual pleasure within marriage.[47] Second, procreation and rendering the marriage debt are specified as the only morally legitimate motives for sex within marriage. The council and its catechism also proceed to refine moral culpability where the marriage debt is consummated: "The one who demands payment [translated, the man], who seeks sex for pleasure, or out of love . . . is guilty of sin, albeit a venial one [far less grave than mortal sin]. The partner who renders the debt [translated, the woman] is not in sin, for she . . . merely submits; she does not seek pleasure."[48]

No longer would theological writings on sex be mere opinions, philosophical speculations, or efforts of theoretical suasion. With even sex as an expression of love stigmatized as a motive insufficient for the church's moral imprimatur, the seeds of Greek dualism had blossomed and now were reaped. People challenging or violating what were then and henceforth articles of Roman Catholic faith jeopardized their own eternal salvation. The superiority of the spiritual and ascetic, once a response to a cruel scarcity of material resources and a brutal hierarchy of social power, was now divine imperative. The die had been cast.

CONTEMPORARY ROMAN CATHOLICISM

The Roman Catholic position on sex has been reaffirmed numerous times in papal encyclicals by Pope Leo XIII (1880), Pope Pius XI (1930), Pope Pius XII (1944), Pope John XXIII (1961), Pope Paul VI (1968), and the Vatican's *Declaration on Certain Questions Concerning Sexual Ethics* (1975): sex is morally permissible only if it occurs within the institution of marriage and the act is not deliberately rendered incompatible with human reproduction. Under this view, all sexual activities that occur outside the institution of marriage (e.g., adultery, promiscuity) and all sexual expressions that are deliberately incompatible with human reproduction (e.g., masturbation, homosexuality, oral and anal sex, and even the use of a contraceptive device) are stigmatized as "unnatural" and thus immoral.

We must now attend to the specific arguments that purportedly sustain these conclusions. Pope Paul VI's encyclical, *Humanae Vitae* (1968), although most directly an argument against the practice of birth control by artificial means, contains the essential Roman Catholic position on sexual ethics. In this work, one is first struck by the characterization of reproduction as a "most serious *duty*" (emphasis added), and by the defining characteristics of conjugal love.[49] There are four essential attributes of love: First, conjugal love must be "fully human"—an act of free will in which spouses become "one heart and only one soul" leading to greater human perfection—and not simply "a transport of instinct and sentiment." Second, conjugal love must be "total"—a unique form of friendship in which spouses "generously share everything, without undue reservations or selfish calculations." Third, conjugal love must be "faithful and exclusive until death." Fourth, conjugal love must be fecund, "for it is not exhausted by the communion between husband and wife, but is destined to continue, raising up new lives."[50]

Underlying such suppositions is the fundamental Roman Catholic vision: Humans can discover, but do not invent, moral law. There is a natural order, created by divine will and instituted by divine authority, immanent in the universe. Once this natural law is discovered, humans cannot legitimately appeal to consequential considerations as a strategy to carve out exceptions to their moral duties. One cannot "do evil so that good may follow therefrom."[51] The purpose of such objective, deontological laws is to guide humans to their moral end: eternal salvation and residence in the city of God. Accordingly, the institution of marriage and the practice of sexual intercourse are not subject to reimagination or reinvention by human agency.[52]

In *Humanae Vitae*, Pope Paul VI reaffirms the longstanding Roman Catholic position on sexual ethics: "Each and every marriage act [of sexual intercourse] must remain open to the transmission of life."[53] Thus, "direct interruption of the generative process already begun . . . directly willed and procured abortion . . . direct sterilization . . . and every action [of or accompanying sex] which as an end or means renders procreation impossible" are all morally illicit.[54]

However, the church recognizes the moral permissibility of "therapeutic means truly necessary to cure diseases . . . even if an impediment to procreation,"[55] provided such impediment, although foreseen, is not the direct motive of the therapy; and the church sanctions the "rhythm method" of birth control: "[It is licit] to take into account the natural rhythms immanent in the generative functions, for the use of marriage in the infecund periods only, and in this way to regulate birth without offending moral principles."[56] Here the church distinguishes between (a) illicitly impending natural processes, which presumably occurs in the prohibited acts described above, and (b) licit use of a natural disposition, such as the rhythm method.

But the church judges irrelevant all appeals to the consequential benefits of disregarding the church's position on sexual ethics. The Pope, in fact, shows clear awareness of the common litany of alleged social problems that might be ameliorated by alteration of the church's teachings on sexual ethics: overpopulation, economic difficulty in educating large numbers of children, diminished resources in relation to extant humans, changing perceptions of woman's role in society, increased technological ability to effect and control reproduction, changing perceptions of the variety of roles sex may assume in one's life, and general changes in working and housing conditions.[57] All such appeals are irrelevant to the Pope's analysis because they embody two false claims: they tacitly assume that it is morally permissible to "do evil so that good may follow therefrom"[58] and that appeals to consequences have merit for a deontological ethic.

Thus far I have described Pope Paul's conclusions, which are in no way novel when compared with past teachings of the church. Still, we need to examine the argument from which these conclusions allegedly follow. *Why* are certain methods illicit impediments of natural processes? *Why* are sexual actions which are incompatible with reproduction thereby morally impermissible? *Why* are most birth control methods and hedonistic motives inherently evil and thus not morally redeemable by consequentialist appeals?

The answers are provided by one fundamental principle. The church decrees that there are two indivisible aspects of sex within marriage: the unitive and the procreative. The unitive function permits the intimate joining of spouses as "husband and wife become only one heart and only one soul."[59] The procreative function facilitates the fecundity of marriage: "Marriage and conjugal love are by their nature ordained toward the begetting and education of children."[60] God decrees, and the church relays the message, that these dual, indivisible meanings define the conjugal act.[61]

From this "indivisibility principle" flow numerous conclusions on sexual ethics. All acts, such as artificial birth control and abortion, that deliberately aim at preventing procreation during sexual intercourse or that aim at preventing a human embryo from coming to term are immoral because they repudiate procreative meaning. All sexual acts—such as oral sex, anal sex, homosexual sex, and masturbation—that are by their nature incompatible with human reproduction are immoral because they contradict procreative meaning. All sexual acts, such as adultery and promiscuity, that occur outside the institution of marriage are immoral because they deny both unitive and procreative meaning: they take place outside the sacrament ordained by God for licit satisfaction of erotic urges and human reproduction. All acts of sexual intercourse that are "imposed upon one's partner without regard for his or her condition and lawful desires"[62] are immoral because they are not "true acts of love"[63] and thus disdain unitive meaning.

It must be emphasized that such acts are *inherently* immoral, by their very character they denigrate God's design and transgress natural law, and thus their moral stigma cannot be absolved by appeals to any allegedly good consequences they produce. Moreover, the indivisibility principle applies to *each* conjugal act. A married couple cannot argue successfully that a *particular* act, for example, of sex with use of a contraceptive device or of oral sex, is morally permissible because their sexual activity taken as a whole produced numerous children.[64]

The church recognizes that, although prohibited acts are without exception grave transgressions of moral law, the subjective culpability of the transgressors may vary somewhat in relation to circumstances. We must also underscore the church's contention that it is merely passing along divine imperatives, not inventing ethical principles: "Of such laws the Church was not the author, nor consequently can she be their arbiter; she is only their depository and their interpreter, without ever being able to declare licit that which is not so by reason of its intimate and unchangeable opposition to the true good of man."[65]

Still, the church's position may seem disappointing. Why should we embrace warmly the indivisibility principle? Is it not merely a question-begging declaration that lacks deeper insight: sex within marriage must be compatible with reproduction because the indivisibility principle says that reproduction is one of the inseparable meanings of the conjugal act? Don't we need a further argument or deeper reasons to accept the indivisibility principle in the first place?

In *Humanae Vitae* we find virtually no argument in favor of the indivisibility principle except an appeal to the church's long-standing teachings on this subject;[66] continued assertions that the principle is required by natural law;[67] and descriptions of the church's authority to speak on and interpret such matters.[68] All of these appeals are questionable.

First, the appeal to tradition has most direct application in the area of secular law where, because of the fear of state oppression of individuals or of defeating citizens' reasonable expectations, it is paramount that citizens have prior notice of the law's requirements. In order to avoid, to the greatest extent possible, the application of retroactive (ex post facto) law, judges appeal to precedent as a powerful factor when deciding hard questions of law. The assumption here is that easy cases and many hard cases should be decided by precedent and that judicial overturning of settled law should occur, if at all, only for overwhelmingly exigent reasons. Part of this judicial philosophy is based on separation of governmental powers: the legislature, as an elected branch of representatives, is the more appropriate local for lawmaking; the judiciary, whose most powerful units are unelected, is the appropriate place for interpreting and applying law.[69]

These elements are lacking in the church's invocation of tradition. With no clear, authoritative, unequivocal divine revelation, the tradition of the church's teachings on sexual ethics has its source mainly in the extensive writings of Augustine and Aquinas. Although both were powerful philosophical thinkers, neither, on the church's own policies of papal infallibility, were protected from error by divine confirmation at the time they wrote. At the Council of Trent what had hitherto been merely the opinions and speculations of clerics became codified into official church dogma. Recall the circumstances under which that council was convened: extensive internal abuses, political pressure from reformists, and considerable doctrinal conflict.

The other primary source of the church's teachings on sexual ethics is St. Paul. But interpretation of Scripture is itself problematic. Scholars now admit that biblical passages pertain to specific contexts and social circumstances and concede that we must be cautious when applying the apparent prescriptions of such passages more generally.[70] Scripture may well be invoked in support of heterosexual relations and of the inviolability of the marriage agreement, but there is much indeterminacy in its counsel on a host of concrete problems of sexual ethics.[71]

Appeals to the authority of Scripture engender problems analogous to those accompanying pleas for "originalism" in the judicial interpretation of law.[72] The interpretation of Scripture, as a reading of texts written centuries ago in a cultural context far different from our own, is plagued with problems of reconciling various levels of intentions, different social renderings of cultural practices, and projected literal meanings of words. The church would rejoin, of course, that there are at least two differences between mundane legal interpretation and biblical analyses: Scriptures are divinely inspired texts, and changing social contexts are therefore irrelevant; and papal declarations of Scriptural content embody a divine imprimatur and are thereby infallible. The pervasiveness of human agency in the interpretation of Scripture and the seeming conflict among many of the various parts of Scripture, however, leave many thinkers skeptical of the church's claims.

Second, the church appeals to natural law in support of its rendering of sexual ethics. But this appeal may run counter to Aquinas's own position. Aquinas held that in natural law there is a distinction between primary and changeless general principles (e.g., "do good," "avoid evil"), and secondary and changeable principles (specific conclusions to concrete cases drawn from primary principles).[73] The application of primary principles could vary, among other reasons, because of changes in social reality. Thus, unless it is shown that the indivisibility principle is a general, primary one of the requisite sort, it is possible to argue that truculent appeals to tradition as morally dispositive undercut the accompanying appeal to the authority of natural law. It may well be that in discussions of sexual ethics based on natural law, consequentialist considerations, many of which are based on perceptions of a changing social and economic environment, are relevant after all.

Third, the church reaffirms its own authority to speak conclusively on the topic of sexual ethics. This authority is undoubtedly recognized by most Roman Catholics. But recall that the church's pretension to "infallibility" when addressing matters of faith was one of the focuses of the Protestant reformers' attack.

Beyond these remarks, some internal tensions also exist within the explicit aspirations of *Humanae Vitae*. The presumed inexorable link between the procreative and the unitive meanings of the conjugal act may be unstable. To the extent that sexual activity within marriage must be limited to intercourse with procreative intent, spouses will often be confronted with a dilemma under those economic and social circumstances where pregnancy is unwelcome: either refrain from sex or have sex with risk of unwanted pregnancy. Such pressures, exerted by the procreative meaning of sex, are unlikely to enhance the unitive possibilities of conjugal acts.[74]

Ironically, given the church's tradition of recognizing the presence of strong erotic impulses in some people (read: men), the choice of refraining from sex or limiting it in accordance with the rhythm method to avoid unwanted pregnancy resurrects another of the church's traditional fears: lack of sufficient sex within marriage luring concupiscence-driven men to extramarital relations. Perhaps, though, this fear has subsided. For example, the embarrassing doctrine of the marital debt, formulated as a remedy for extramarital sin, is not invoked by Pope Paul in *Humanae Vitae*.

In late December 1975, the Sacred Congregation for the Doctrine of the Faith issued, with approval of Pope Paul VI, its "Declaration on Certain Questions Concerning Sexual Ethics" ("Questions Concerning Sexual Ethics"). Here, traditional Roman Catholic doctrine on this topic was repeated and further clarified. The document begins by underscoring the importance of sexual questions: "The human person . . . is so deeply influenced by his sexuality that this latter must be regarded as one of the basic factors shaping human life."[75] After reaffirming its longstanding commitment to an objective moral order embodied in natural law, the authors soften the church's earlier allegiance to moral evaluation on the basis of inner motives: "The moral goodness of actions . . . does not depend only on a sincere intention and the evaluating of motives, but must be judged by objective standards."[76]

The document applies the church's doctrine to three concrete issues: premarital relations, homosexuality, and masturbation. Premarital sexual relations are ruled illicit because "these unions cannot guarantee the sincerity and fidelity of the relationship between man and woman, and, above all, cannot protect the relationship against the changeableness of desire and determination."[77]

Tacitly relying on the indivisibility principle, the authors also quote Scripture approvingly: "The Creator made . . . male and female and declared, 'For this reason a man shall leave his father and mother and cling to his wife and the two shall become as one.' Thus they are no longer two but one flesh."[78] The authors also rely heavily on St. Paul's epistles and cite in a footnote a variety of verses which purportedly condemn extramarital intercourse.[79] Finally, the authors advance what at first blush looks like a consequentialist argument but which can be recast easily as continued subsidy of the indivisibility principle: "Premarital relations . . . most often exclude any prospect of children. Such love claims in vain to be conjugal since it cannot . . . grow into a maternal and paternal love; or, if the pair do become parents, it will be to the detriment of the children, who are deprived of a stable environment."[80]

The authors' invocation of Scripture here is troubling. Many of the verses advanced as documentation in support of a general condemnation of all premarital sexual relations seem more obviously directed at adultery or homosexuality, or seem too vague to sustain outright censure of all premarital relations.[81] More generally, the authors' entire methodology of appealing to Scripture is questionable. As Philip Keane points out:

> At times the method seems to border on proof texting, i.e., taking single scriptural passages as completely decisive for all moral cases that might relate to the passage. Today we are aware of the great difficulties involved in using any single scriptural passage as decisive for all cases. There is the question of the original context in which the passage was used, the question of how the passage's context may have been shifted by later biblical authors, and the question of how a particular scriptural passage relates to other passages on the same topic. . . . ["Questions Concerning Sexual Ethics"] does not seem to give sufficient attention to hermeneutic issues pertinent to the biblical passages it cites. . . . The document . . . can leave uninformed Catholics with the [mistaken] impression that Scripture offers complete concrete answers to sexual dilemmas.[82]

The authors of "Questions Concerning Sexual Ethics," while urging understanding and encouragement to those afflicted, unequivocally condemn homosexual behavior. Again, homosexual actions transgress against the indivisibility principle, and are presumed to be "serious deviations" from natural law. The authors stress Scripture here: "In consequence, God delivered them up in their lusts to unclean practices; they engaged in the mutual degradation of their bodies, these men who exchange the truth of God for a lie and worshipped and served the creature rather than the Creator. . . . Their women exchanged natural intercourse for unnatural, and the men gave up natural intercourse with women and burned with lust for one another. Men did shameful things with men."[83]

Unsurprisingly, the authors of "Questions Concerning Sexual Ethics" also reject masturbation, labeling it "an intrinsically and seriously disordered act."[84] Lacking the requisite marital relation, masturbation clearly violates the indivisibility principle: "The chief reason for [the moral impermissibility of masturbation] is that, whatever the motive, the deliberate use of the sexual faculty outside of normal conjugal relations essentially contradicts its finality."[85]

The tone of "Questions Concerning Sexual Ethics" is uncompromising in refusing to entertain the circumstances and full context in which sexual actions take place, and, instead, in solidifying adherence to the indivisibility principle and the absolutism of natural law. As such, the authors of the document, with papal blessing, ratify an instrumental view of sex: sex is valuable only to the extent that it honors the unitive and procreative functions of the indivisibility principle. Accordingly, in the vision of the church, sexual activity has no inherent value.

Perhaps an instrumental view of sex is a direct consequence of Augustine's theory of the genesis of concupiscence. If concupiscence is born from sin, then such desire cannot have inherent value. Any benefits to be derived from sexual desire can only be justified as facilitating the natural ends and functions of humans. Thus, any sexual activity that violates the instrumental values captured by the indivisibility principle must be morally impermissible.

In any event, there are actually four parts to the church's contemporary position on sexual ethics: (1) sex must take place within marriage; (2) sex must be limited to male-female intercourse; (3) intercourse must not be accompanied by artificial birth control measures; and (4) the totality of a married couple's compliance with the above cannot cleanse the moral taint of any particular sexual acts of noncompliance. Again, the church takes herself to be the repository of a divinely ordained doctrine which defines what is natural for humans: that which is unnatural is morally wrong. But what does it mean to call an act "natural"? And of what normative significance is the term?

There are a variety of possible interpretations of "natural": what is statistically usual, statistically frequent, statistically possible, accomplished without human interference, and in accord with an entity's essential characteristics.

The notions of "statistically usual" and "statistically frequent" are unhelpful in discerning the church's meaning. Numerous actions, both external to and within the area of sexual ethics, that occur usually or frequently would still be stigmatized as "unnatural" by the church. Notions dependent upon statistical normalcy lack the necessary moral significance upon which the church's position depends. The mere fact that humans routinely or often engage in X does not necessarily imply that X embodies moral merit, nor does it necessarily imply that X is natural to humans. Thus, one cannot successfully argue that because procreation sometimes follows sex it is the natural function of sex. Numerous other events and experiences accompany or follow sex at least as frequently as procreation. Moreover, of the many possible sexual acts, only intercourse can result in procreation. Does that prove that only intercourse within marriage is natural sexual activity? Or does it suggest that there are numerous possible natural functions of sex?

A fortiori, the notion of "statistically possible" is insufficient for the church's aspirations. The church does not subscribe to the view that whatever humans *can* do is natural for them *to* do, or to the general principle that everything a natural entity does is natural to that entity. Rather, the church would endorse the proposition that the mere fact that an entity can physically perform X does not necessarily imply that X embodies moral merit, nor does it necessarily imply that X is natural to that entity.

The notion of "accomplished without human interference" comes much closer, but still does not capture the church's usage. It comes closer than the statistical notions because it seems to encompass, for example, the distinction between illicit artificial birth control methods, which require some sort of human intervention or some sort of technical device, and the licit rhythm method, which requires no technical aids and which does not owe its reality to human agency. But "accomplished without interference" still falls short of defining the church's meaning because numerous actions that the church venerates as "natural," in the sense of "morally appropriate," do require human agency; and some actions that are not generated by human agency are either without moral significance or are morally inappropriate.

The church's understanding of "natural" can be expressed in terms of "what is in accord with an entity's essential characteristics and which facilitates an entity's progress toward its rightful purpose." The charge that the church misunderstands what is natural because it fails to consider human behavior from a statistical standpoint misses the mark. The church's conception of natural behavior is self-consciously specialized: it depends on a certain portrayal of human nature, on a full account of the proper human telos, and on a particular rendering of the genesis of objective morality. Only such an understanding of "natural" is accompanied by the necessary normative significance which the church contemplates: what is natural must be morally sound.

Here we encounter different problems. If "natural" simply means "morally right," then to label X natural is by definition to approve of it as morally sound. But then conferring the honorific title "natural" on an action is trivial for purposes of *determining* its moral merit, because "natural" is just another way of saying "morally sound." Yet natural law theorists do not take themselves to be uttering moral tautologies when they speak; rather, they purport to be identifying some objective characteristic by virtue of which an act is morally wrong. Such objective characteristics must explicate the proper functions of various human organs. In other words, natural law theorists argue that *because* X is natural, X is morally sound, and *because* Y is unnatural, Y is morally unsound.

This discussion calls into question whether appeals to naturalness are important. The church seems to oscillate between a tautological and functional conception of the relationship between the natural and the right. The tautological conception is useless, while the functional conception is difficult to explicate without either begging the question or appealing to discredited statistical norms. Moreover, virtually every substantive remark the church wants to make in sexual ethics can be made without use of the term "natural." Accordingly, it may well be that appeals to the naturalness of various practices do nothing more than confuse debates on sexual ethics.

In any event, in order to accept the church's argument for sexual ethics, one must embrace a host of other fundamental principles and beliefs. Among these are the following: there is a God; God ordains an objective moral code and an immanent order; humans can know the natural law in unambiguous fashion; the recorded words of Jesus are accurate reflections of divine positive law which helps make eternal law, the law residing in God's mind, clearer to humans; God conferred upon the men whose words are recorded in the Bible authority to reveal eternal law; popes, as God's representatives on earth, are infallible interpreters of truth in matters of faith; the apparent misogyny and sexism that permeate the church's early teachings and that resonate throughout the church's traditions on sexual ethics are in fact part of the divine plan; much of the work of Paul, Augustine, and Aquinas, which was self-consciously written as opinion, speculation, and reasoned judgment, in fact embodies the core of the natural law on sexual ethics; the Council of Trent's interpretations and resolutions of prior doctrinal conflicts were correct renderings of truth; and all of the above is in accord with facilitating the eternal salvation of humans who are endowed with an unchanging essence or nature.

Reliance upon the existence and ultimate dominion of a supreme being, an unchanging human essence or nature, and objective standards of morality that are allegedly part of the "furniture of the universe"[86] seems mysterious and dubious to critics. They object that either such entities have been proved not to exist, or they are in principle and practice impossible to prove or disprove.[87] Natural law has traditionally aspired to translate physical and biological generalities into normative propositions. Betraying its rapture with the methods and the achievements of science, natural law theorists hope to discover similar laws of a moral nature embedded in nature. Unfortunately, most modern versions of this theory are wedded too closely with specific theologies, which even if correct may alienate those of different religious persuasions and thus fail to provide much common ground for normative reasoning. Moreover, even if an eternal human essence exists, how should we select which of its features reflect "natural law"? Neither the nature of the universe nor human nature sends us an unambiguous message about the world and our place within it. We must translate whatever universal descriptive elements we perceive into prescriptions for human conduct; but if nature transmits contradictory messages, then the advice "Follow Nature" is itself logically incoherent. The journey out of this quagmire has included, in Aquinas, for example, reliance upon a unique human telos. But it is precisely this maneuver that forces natural law theorists to embrace specific theologies and additional metaphysical suppositions which expose them to further criticism.

Further, the anthropological evidence is quite ambiguous as to the existence of a timeless human nature: variations in norms and customs are pervasive.[88] Also, it is difficult to separate the innate inclinations of humans (our nature) from environmental influences (our nurture). Only by heightening the level of abstraction and generality to triviality and definitional truths can natural law theorists persuasively demonstrate the human commonality they allege.

Although its application must adapt to variable, concrete social contexts, natural law has as its end that humans fulfill their function and achieve their essential purposes. But such functions and purposes are inherently contestable, at least to nonbelievers.[89]

There are, however, at least two important criticisms that cannot be raised legitimately against the church's position on sexual ethics: that it ignores the social and political dimensions of sex and that it ignores women by appealing to an abstract notion of a contracting, genderless, couple. The church recognizes explicitly that the sexual actions of two people, even if married, have wider effects than those borne by the couple and must answer to an authority higher than the presence of their mutual consent. Moreover, rather than rendering women invisible, church doctrine has always specified a particular role for women and has explicitly addressed gender differences.

Of course, to many people such words will yield faint consolation. Those critics who object to the substantive fashion in which the church addresses such issues excoriate the church's specification of natural moral law, mock its truculent refusal to consider the practical consequences of its policies in this world, and vilify what they take to be the sexism of the church's doctrine on women's role and on gender differences.

In sum, the Roman Catholic depiction of sexual ethics is often criticized for its underlying descriptive and prescriptive world vision: an ahistorical conception of human nature, an unchanging and limited perception of the proper place of sex within that nature, a specialized view of the one acceptable form of family, and a narrow perception of the function of human sexual activity. Rather than deriving moral theory from an objective analysis of human nature, those who make claims about what is "natural" for humans often seem to choose those elements of our nature that correspond to their own preconceptions about how we ought to behave. Serious questions linger: Why is sex within marriage for the purpose of procreation more in accordance with human nature than sex for the purpose of pleasure or for expression of love alone? Why does sex have only two proper functions, the unitive and procreative?

We must understand that the litany of questions and criticisms I have lodged here does not prove with deductive confidence the inadequacy of the church's policies on sexual ethics. Rather, if persuasive, the critique casts serious doubt on those policies and provides substantial evidence against the truth of the church's conclusions. And so it is with philosophical analysis of complex moral issues: few nontrivial normative disputes can be resolved with cognitive certainty. This is both philosophy's disappointment and its glory.

Despite my critique, religious faith will always play an important role for many people in their perception of sexual ethics. Accordingly, my aspirations here are limited: to undermine the false imperialism of the most conservative views on sex by showing that they cannot be defended without appeals to religious claims that are themselves notoriously contestable.

Some thinkers, unconvinced by the church's arguments and suspicious of the genesis of her view of sexual ethics, are nevertheless drawn to the church's sanctification of marriage and reverence of heterosexual love. Such philosophers often abrogate reliance on much of the church's metaphysical assumptions, yet strive to uphold the integrity of marriage and the value of love. Accordingly, they modify much of the Judeo-Christian traditions on sexual ethics, while simultaneously acknowledging their intellectual debt to those standing customs.

For example, one might hold that sex is morally permissible if it occurs within the institution of marriage, even when of a kind incompatible with reproduction. Thus oral and anal sex may be accepted because pleasure within marriage may be acknowledged as a legitimate goal of sex, while use of birth control devices may be permitted once the indivisibility principle is disassembled. It is to such images of sexual ethics that we now turn.

3

THE PRIMACY OF EMOTION
Love and Intimacy

One way of developing some of the basic classical positions is to contend that sex is morally permissible only if it occurs within the experience of love and intimacy. Such a position is supported by two main allegations: a view of human nature that interprets sex as a paramount human activity reflective of those aspects of personality closest to our being, and a claim that sex without love debases and ultimately fragments human personality. This approach is animated by the impulse to evade the allegedly dehumanizing effects of mechanical, merely promiscuous sex and, instead, to exalt sex as the most intimate physical expression of the human self—an act worthy of special concern because of its unique effects on our existential integrity.

Various modifications occur within this approach. Some proponents would contend that the requisite love and intimacy must be exclusive. Thus, morally permissible sex may occur with only one other person, but even here successive sexual interactions which implicate love would be morally permissible. Other proponents argue that sex may be nonexclusive because a person is capable of simultaneously loving more than one other person. Hence, simultaneous love liaisons could be morally permissible.

I will argue that the sex-only-with-love literature portrays vividly a powerful moral ideal. But this ideal is only one of many possible acceptable moral aspirations for worthwhile sex; it cannot issue in universal moral prescriptions. Moreover, this genre is too often mystified by the truncated choices embodied in two extreme images: the profligate who values sex only for his own pleasure and who consistently evades all commitment to others, or the chaste practitioner of sex only when full marital commitment or mutual love is antecedently in place. Thus, the sex-only-with-love literature ignores the possibility of deeply caring sex between parties who lack marital commitment or mutual love and assumes wrongly that sex between such parties necessarily involves pernicious objectification, commodification, or violence to existential integrity.

VINCENT PUNZO

An illustration of this genre is contained in Vincent Punzo's *Reflective Naturalism*.[1] Punzo denies that sexual activity must be evaluated by the same moral criteria as other human enterprises. He contends that those who oppose him on this issue are under the pervasive spell of the commodification of Western life: "Sexuality has come to play so large a role in our commercial lives that it is not surprising that our sexuality should itself come to be treated as a commodity governed by the same moral rules that govern any other economic transaction."[2]

Sexual activity is unique and thus cannot be justifiably assimilated to mundane matters of personal choice: "Sexual encounter is a definitive experience, one in which the physical intimacy and merging involves also a merging of the nonphysical dimensions of the partners . . . man moves beyond the negative concern with avoiding his or another's physical and psychological harm to the question of what he is making of himself and what he is contributing to the existential formation of his partner as a human subject."[3]

Underscoring the intimacy and totality that he thinks necessarily characterizes sexual activity, Punzo appeals to the historical aspects of the human self.

> The man and woman who engage in sexual intercourse are giving their bodies, the most intimate physical expression of themselves, over to the other . . . the man who has sexual relations with [a woman] has literally entered her. A man and woman engaging in sexual intercourse have united themselves as intimately and as totally as is physically possible for two human beings. Their union is not simply a union of organs, but is as intimate and as total a physical union of two selves as is possible of achievement.[4]

Having established to his satisfaction the sui generis character of sex and having thereby distanced it from evaluation by prevailing moral standards, Punzo argues that only sex accompanied by a marital commitment fulfills the relevant moral prescription of honoring the human self. His argument centers on the special capacities of humans to perceive themselves as beings existing through time and to reimagine and remake themselves through their choices and existential projects. Accordingly, much is at stake in sexual activity: not merely pursuit of pleasure and satisfaction of erotic impulses, not simply the fulfillment of a duty to procreate, but the fashioning and nurturing of human selves.

Punzo seemingly views the value of sex as instrumental: "Within the lives of those who have so committed themselves to each other, sexual intercourse is a way of asserting and confirming the fullness and totality of their mutual commitment."[5] Existential integrity is comprised in part by man's acceptance of "his body as a dimension of his total personality."[6]

The error of sexual libertines is that they act as if they can sever "bodily existence and the most intimate physical expression of their selfhood from their existence as historical beings."[7] Notice that Punzo is not claiming that physical or psychological harm must result from premarital or extramarital unions, but rather that the moral failure of such liaisons is their lack of the requisite existential integrity.

To glimpse more clearly what Punzo means by "existential integrity," we need to attend to his denunciation of premarital sex that is unaccompanied by serious mutual commitment.

Such unions are morally deficient because they lack existential integrity in that there is a total merging and union on the physical level, on the one hand, and a conscious decision not to unite any other dimension of themselves, on the other hand. [Such a] sexual union thus involves a 'depersonalization' of [the parties] bodily existence, an attempt to cut off the most intimate physical expression of their respective selves from their very selfhood. The mutual agreement of premarital sex partners is an agreement to merge with the other not as a self, but as a body which takes unto oneself, which one possesses in a most intimate and total fashion for one's own pleasure or designs, allowing the other to treat oneself in the same way.[8]

Apparently, for Punzo, such activity is tantamount to treating persons as if their bodies were separable from their selves and thus to objectify wrongfully.[9] For Punzo, then, morally appropriate sex between two parties implicates a deep intimacy which includes a full, mutual commitment to share a future fraught with vicissitudes.[10]

Punzo does not require ceremonial marriage as a prerequisite for morally licit sex, but he avoids contradicting his previous statements on the evils of premarital sex by replacing the ceremonial marriage reqirement with a deeper view of the necessity of mutual trust, acceptance, and reciprocal sharing. Thus, although Punzo does not require de jure marriage for morally permissible sex, he does demand a type of de facto marriage.[11]

Strictly speaking, Punzo's is not paradigmatically a "sex with love" approach. He would presumably reject the view that the presence of mutual love is sufficient for morally permissible sex. For, after all, two parties could express accurately their love for one another, yet decline to "share the problems and prospects of their historical existence in the world" through time.[12] Moreover, two parties could accept sincerely the mutual commitment of de jure marriage, yet not share an antecedent love for one another. For example, in many cultures marriages often are arranged years in advance for children by their parents or relatives. Under such circumstances, the couple, upon reaching marital age, may accept sincerely their union but recognize that they do not love one another. That is, they may be eager to "share the problems and prospects of their historical existence in the world" through time and may in fact come to love each other deeply, even though at the time of the marriage ceremony love is lacking. Presumably, given the circumstances, Punzo would not stigmatize their postmarital, or even preceremonial, sexual intercourse as immoral. Therefore, Punzo must view mutual love as neither sufficient nor necessary for morally permissible sexual intercourse.

The flavor and spirit of his work, however, places him in the "love and intimacy" camp. Clearly, he assumes that in the vast majority of cases love will accompany the requisite commitment and that intimacy is paramount in sexual interaction. Rather than appealing to procreative intention, Punzo exalts mutual commitment to share each other's life in its totality.

Be that as it may, Punzo is mired in a pernicious dichotomy: either two parties have the requisite marital commitment (of at least a de facto sort) and their sexual intercourse is morally permissible, or they lack full commitment and their sex is morally impermissible. This dualism is both uncompromising and untrue to life. Often, two parties may have a deep and significant commitment to one another which is apparent to them and to others yet fall short of Punzo's imperative to "share the problems and prospects of their historical existence in the world" through time. Under such circumstances, is it clear that sexual intercourse "involves a 'depersonalization' of [the parties'] bodily existence, an attempt to cut off the most intimate physical expression of their respective selves from their very selfhood"? Hardly.

Punzo offers us truncated choices embodied in two extreme images: the libertine or the chaste spouse. In fact, there are numerous degrees of (morally praiseworthy) mutual commitment which are reflected in experience. Putting aside for the moment whether the sexual libertine need be as morally deficient as Punzo claims, surely we may legitimately dispute the limited, stark contrasts Punzo conjures. Experience invalidates Punzo's "all or nothing at all" refrain.

Russell Vannoy expresses well the experiences of those who insist that sex without love and intimacy is neither inherently depersonalized nor self-denigrating:

Is sex without love superficial, as compared with the unity of heart, mind, and body that is claimed to exist between sex and love? Suppose . . . I find myself overwhelmed by an attraction for someone in both a sensual and sensuous sense. Such a person's beauty need not, of course, be physical. There are many things about this person which may stir my emotions, even though I may have no desire to become emotionally involved with her in the sense [embodied by marital commitment]. The experience is enriched by the beautiful setting, by the hopes of sharing an evening with her, by memories of previous encounters with such charming individuals, by the prospects of meeting her or someone like her again. . . . Is this merely a description of a ludic playboy on the prowl for a sex object? It could be, but it need not be. For people who are concerned with persons as persons can experience such rich complexity of thought, emotion, and sensuality as much as anyone else; and so long as the object of one's affections shares one's views, an evening may be spent together than can be totally free of mutual exploitation.[13]

Perhaps Punzo could reply that he recognizes, with all ethicists, degrees of moral culpability, and that the two extreme images he advances are merely heuristic devices that describe the paradigms of morally licit and illicit sex. Under this interpretation, it is uncharitable to lump sexual libertines with deeply caring, but not maritally committed, couples.

This is a better interpretation of Punzo's doctrine, but it leads us to another set of questions: Why should deeply caring, but not maritally committed, couples be morally culpable to *any* degree? What arguments sustain the conclusion that *all* sex occurring outside of full marital commitment is illicit to at least some degree? Remember that Punzo is not appealing directly to many of the usual claims in support of a conventional outlook on sex: the need for stable families and a nurturing atmosphere for children, the fear of widespread venereal disease, the physical and psychological harm that often (usually?) accompanies frequent premarital sex, and society's presumed need to sustain its enduring traditions through strict control of erotic impulses. Rather, his argument rests heavily on the notions of "existential integrity" and "existential sharing." But at bottom, what do such phrases mean and imply?

At first blush, Punzo's argument seems question begging: to be morally permissible, sex must be preceded by marital commitment; marital commitment is required to ensure existential integrity and existential sharing; existential integrity involves persons' acceptance of their bodies as a dimension of their total personality; and existential sharing implies full exchange and division of the burdens, opportunities, and challenges of the parties' historical existence. Thus, morally permissible sex requires antecedent marital commitment because if the latter is lacking then sex is without existential integrity, which itself is another name for marital commitment!

But, surely, there is more to Punzo's argument than this series of circular definitions. He seems to have abrogated the Roman Catholic church's indivisibility principle and substituted his own inseparability maxim: humans cannot legitimately separate sexual activity from full commitment to their partner's total existence as a person through time.

Now, what presuppositions underlie and what arguments support the inseparability maxim? First, Punzo assumes that all sex that lacks the requisite marital commitment must involve "a 'depersonalization' of [the parties'] bodily existence, an attempt to cut off the most intimate physical expression of their respective selves from their very selfhood." This assumption is false. Not only does Punzo overlook the possibility of deeply caring sex between two people who lack marital commitment, but also the possibility of such people engaging in sex as a way of expressing and nurturing their mutual concern that could facilitate a subsequent joint marital commitment. Moreover, one can argue that deciding for oneself to engage in sex without marital commitment is not a depersonalization of bodily existence, but a conscious choice to express the self in one way rather than another. That is, such sex is not an animalistic reflex or instinctual response that necessarily denigrates what is unique in humans; it is itself conscious human expression and an aspect of self-making. Moreover, if the subject and object of genuine marital commitment—and thus of existential integrity and existential sharing—are persons in their existential completeness, and if persons in their completeness include sexuality, then those who vow mutual, marital commitment without having engaged in sex may ironically be accused, in Punzian fashion, of making such commitment without knowing each other in the full existential dimensions of their beings. Perhaps we can turn part of Punzo's argument on its head and conclude that premarital sex is a moral *requirement*!

Second, Punzo assumes that premarital sex must involve the objectification of the human body: fashioning one's body and/or the partner's body as an external object to be handed over totally to another to be used for the other's purposes. This assumption is also false. Punzo is, again, a prisoner of a false dilemma: either the profligate libertine or the chaste spouse. The objectification claim has currency only where one or both parties are being "used," where one or both are being regarded and treated as less than human. The paradigms of wrongful objectification include regarding one's partner as less than an equal subject of experience and as a mere means to one's ends. Punzo states boldly that premarital sex is morally impermissible because by definition it regards and treats humans as less than they are. This is a startling claim, particularly because experience yields illustrations of premarital sex that seem uncontaminated by the paradigmatic instances of wrongful objectification and that appear free of any other plausible charges of wrongful use. Punzo's wrongful objectification assumption has force only if his inseparability maxim has independent validity, but the objectification assumption is designed to *support* the inseparability maxim. Once again, Punzo's argument is ensnared in a web of stipulative definitions and vicious circularity.

Third, Punzo assumes that sexual activity is unique and that it must be liberated from the commodification inherent in contractual analyses and market rhetoric. This assumption is not clearly false, but it is certainly arguable. Ironically, Punzo here joins forces with the political left, which also decries the commodification of sexuality and its imprisonment in contractual and market rhetoric. Because Punzo lacks fervent leftist aspirations and thus harbors no desire to stigmatize capitalist contractual arrangements as inherently immoral, it is incumbent upon him to morally distinguish presently accepted wage labor contracts from sexual relations. This distinction might be made on the basis of the comparative risks involved; the degree to which the service performed involves constitutive attributes of personhood; the type of product which results from the service; the disposition of that product; the relative degree of power, need, and vulnerability between the contracting parties and the coercion that thereby results; or the comparative side effects and consequences.

Punzo alludes to the uniqueness of sex based on its identification with inalienable constitutive attributes of the parties. In this vein, he suggests that sexual acts are more fundamental to personal identity than ordinary wage labor. But more is needed here. To say that sexual acts are closer to personhood or considered more priceless or engender more distress if lost than personal services guaranteed by ordinary wage labor contracts is only to repeat in conclusory fashion precisely what must be proved. If what we do affects directly whom we are, one can certainly argue that the more enduring character of wage labor is more central and crucial to personal identity than temporary and relatively infrequent sexual activity. Moreover, Punzo must demonstrate that there is a *necessary* distinction between sexual contracts and wage labor agreements or, if not, what features of our culture militate a *contingent* distinction.

Much is commendable and instructive in Punzo's background vision: he explores the connection between constitutive personal attributes and human flourishing and highlights the dangers of market rhetoric and commodification. But he still needs to advance a fuller argument that permits us to distinguish between presumably legitimate wage labor and presumably illegitimate contractual analyses of sexual interactions. I am not claiming here that such distinctions cannot be made in a principled fashion, only that Punzo has not provided the required argument.[14] In sum, Punzo's three major assumptions in support of the inseparability maxim are either false, question begging, or themselves in need of further argument.

This brings us back to his invocation of existential integrity. In short, existential integrity demands unity in personal relations, a merging of all dimensions of self with another. Conversely, the deliberate separation of the physical dimension of self from the other dimensions of human personality implies the absence of existential integrity. Again, the wrongfulness of sex without marital commitment is that such sex transgresses this ideal.

For Punzo, existential integrity is an objective condition of being. As such, whether a person possesses existential integrity is independent from that person's own evaluations and feelings about the matter. Suppose we presented to Punzo a couple who consistently engage in sex without marital commitment. Both parties seem psychologically well balanced, reasonably happy and well adjusted, and no apparent harm of any sort has befallen them as a result of their sexual relationship. Moreover, the parties themselves concur with all of these findings and refuse to believe that they have compromised their respective existential integrities by virtue of their actions.

What would Punzo say about this? Presumably, he would insist that the parties are deluded: they fail to recognize their objective situation, namely their lack of complete existential integrity. Despite their feelings, subjective reports, and good faith beliefs, these parties have surrendered their respective existential integrities.

Typically, those who disparage nonmarital sex do so because they are firmly convinced that such actions are invariably accompanied by deception, promise breaking, or harm of some sort; or they may be swayed by a religious conviction that such actions transgress God's will and law; or they may fear that nonmarital sex threatens the stability of families or the well-being of children or the foundations of societal institutions. Punzo makes no such appeal. His is an especially daring thesis: even in the absence of the usual litany of horrors and regardless of the subjective evaluations of the parties involved, nonmarital sex is wrong because it *necessarily* contravenes existential integrity.

Unfortunately, Punzo's refreshing audacity is purchased at the steep price of credibility. Despite its invigorating brazenness, Punzo's thesis is likely to strike readers who do not antecedently agree with him as ultimately trivial: a series of stipulative definitions presented in a mutually self-supporting fashion that from the outset is immune from critical scrutiny and refutation. That is, his contentions about existential integrity, without a convincing independent argument in favor of his inseparability maxim, are advanced in a nonrefutable manner. Regardless of the apparent external evidence that no harm is present and in spite of the participating parties' sanguine analysis of their sexual relationship, Punzo will still maintain the wrongfulness of their actions. Moreover, the alleged wrongfulness is constituted by an abstract notion of existential integrity that does no more than invoke in conclusory fashion the very inseparability maxim it is presumably designed to sustain.

Finally, there remains a deeper philosophical problem with Punzo's argument that we have not yet considered. Suppose that my earlier criticisms are completely without persuasive and logical power. Suppose that sex without marital commitment does necessarily lead to some kind of existential fragmentation. Granting this, does it follow logically that such sexual interactions are *morally* impermissible? Unless we are morally required to perform only those actions which facilitate existential integrity, the most that can follow is that sex without marital commitment in such cases is strategically unsound or imprudent. The realm of the "moral" is not coextensive with the realm of what is in my "best interests." That is, one is not morally required to do all and only actions that facilitate one's best interests. Thus, the mere showing that "A" (engaging in sex only where marital commitment persists) is in the best interests of person "X" does not logically entail that A is morally obligatory for X, although it may well imply that it is prudently wise for X to honor A.

I am assuming here that Punzo does intend his argument to entail a moral prescription and not merely to embody a moral ideal. That is, I am assuming that Punzo is arguing that an antecedent marital commitment is a moral requirement of proper sexual behavior and not merely that such commitment is a nonobligatory ideal toward which to strive. On this issue, Punzo tells us:

> If one sees man's moral task as being simply that of not harming anyone, that is if one sees this task in purely negative terms, he will certainly not accept [my argument on sexual ethics]. However, if one accepts the notion of the morality of aspiration, if one accepts the view that man's moral task involves the positive attempt to live up to what is best in man, to give reality to what he sees to be the perfection of himself as a human subject, the argument may be acceptable.[15]

Which of the following, if any, is Punzo advocating: (a) Sex only with marital commitment is a nonobligatory ideal toward which to strive for those who aspire to human perfection; (b) Sex only with marital commitment is an ideal, but a morally obligatory one because striving for human perfection is itself a moral obligation for humans; (c) Sex only with marital commitment is a moral obligation *simpliciter*?

Punzo's meaning in the quoted passage is not clear. If he intends (a), he merely espouses a purely aspirational standard for those who subscribe to his vision of human perfection. Thus, those who do not meet this standard could not thereby be deemed morally deficient, and Punzo does not engage the debate with those, such as myself, who are arguing about moral *requirements*.

The more interesting interpretations are (b) and (c), which both advance sex only with marital commitment as a moral requirement. Advocates of (b) contend that there is a universal moral obligation to "perfect" ourselves by developing our excellences to their greatest potential; sex only with marital commitment is a necessary component of human perfection, at least for the overwhelming majority of humans who do not remain celibate through their lifetimes; hence, sex only with marital commitment is itself morally required, at least for noncelibates. Champions of (c) argue even more forcefully: independently of its alleged connection to human perfectibility, sex only with marital commitment is a moral requirement as such.

If Punzo advocates (b) or (c), we can return to the questions at hand: Supposing that sex without marital commitment does necessarily lead to some kind of existential fragmentation, how does it follow logically that such sexual interactions are morally impermissible? How can we argue legitimately from facts about existential fragmentation to evaluations of moral impermissibility?

One possible argument would be phrased thus: sex without marital commitment necessarily results in existential fragmentation; existential fragmentation contravenes a person's self-interest; each human has a duty, of some scope and weight, to pursue her or his self-interest; therefore, sex without marital commitment is morally wrong because it violates our duty to self. The thrust of this argument is that sex without marital commitment is literally self-denigration, a demeaning of the self by the self. Difficulties with the argument, however, are twofold. First, it is not at all clear that the resulting existential fragmentation is self-demeaning; and, second, duties to the self are notoriously problematic. What is the source of such a duty? If the duty exists, is it possible, as with most duties, for one party to discharge the other party's obligation? That is, is it possible for the self to let the self off the ethical hook? If that is impossible (because if it were possible it would eviscerate the force of the duty, given that an individual could fulfill or ignore the prescription at will), on what basis is the duty indefeasible and inalienable? What is the scope of such a duty? Given that we are not morally required to do all and only actions that facilitate our best interests, how can we limit the breadth of the duty yet retain its presumed power?

Another possible argument would be phrased as follows: sex without marital commitment necessarily results in existential fragmentation; existential fragmentation contravenes a person's interests; each human has a duty, of some scope and weight, to respect and facilitate the interests of others; therefore, sex without marital commitment is morally wrong because it violates our duty to others. The force of this argument is that engaging in sex without marital commitment transgresses the interests of the other party, regardless of whether it contravenes our own interests. But this argument is either unsuccessful or unnecessary. First, it assumes that although my consent to and understanding of the sex act may prevent the reviling of my interests, the other party's interests are nevertheless besmirched. But what can justify my taking my own self-determination as (at least sometimes) trumping the presumed violation of my interests endemic to sex without marital commitment yet denying that possibility for the other party? Second, if there is necessarily a transgression of interests (either the other party's and/or my own) in sex without marital commitment, that is a form of harm—and one need not be an aficionado of sex only with love and intimacy to advocate that the infliction of harm, other things being equal, is immoral. That is, virtually every moral theory embraces the basic proposition that we must not harm the interest of others unless overriding moral reasons are present. Thus, under this interpretation, the argument is unnecessary. Furthermore, because Punzo makes no direct appeal to tangible harm as a necessary consequence of sex without marital commitment, it is unlikely that this argument captures the spirit of his position.

A third possible argument, perhaps one closer to Punzo's intended meaning, would be constructed in this way: sex without marital commitment necessarily results in existential fragmentation; existential fragmentation contravenes a person's efforts to strive for perfection as a human subject; each human has a duty, of some scope and weight, to strive for perfection as a human subject; therefore, sex without marital commitment is morally wrong because it violates one of our moral duties. The allure of this argument consists in its imperative not to squander our talents and to develop actively our capacities. But upon what does this moral requirement rest? It cannot rest on the will of God, given that Punzo makes no such appeal. It cannot rest on the mere fact that recognizing such a duty is presumably in our self-interest, given what was said earlier about the relationship between self-interest and moral duty. It must rest on some independent moral principle that Punzo does not carefully specify. Moreover, such a principle fundamentally threatens at least one other paramount value: the individual's right of self-determination.

Even if such a principle could be advanced, we must take care that it coheres with sound moral practices and considered judgments. Mundane life experiences reveal a host of daily events that undoubtedly fall far short of honing perfection of human subjects but that are not as a matter of course stigmatized as immoral: viewing a mindless sitcom or cheering for our favorites in the World Wrestling Federation, expending vast amounts of time and money collecting baseball cards, organizing and participating in a women's fashion show, to name but a few. We must be wary of taking the seductive call to human perfection too seriously, lest this ideal preclude numerous (most?) activities which we enjoy on a regular basis. If we sanctify the quest for human perfection as a moral requirement we may well be constructing a standard of behavior beyond the reach and patience of even the Mother Teresas and John the Baptists among us!

Punzo might respond that these criticisms obfuscate the distinction between aesthetic and moral judgments. The television shows we view, the kinds of food we consume, the manner in which we exhaust our leisure time, Punzo might contend, are not of themselves moral issues. Although they are subject to evaluation and they do invite praise or condemnation of certain sorts, they are judged primarily as matters of taste. Moral issues, on the other hand, demand that a person confront "the character of his own being as a human subject. . . . He is faced with deciding what sort of person he will be."[16]

This is all true. But once we begin to brandish the slogan of "human perfectibility as a subject" too feverishly, we invite many choices that were previously considered to be merely aesthetic into the realm of the moral. For numerous aesthetic judgments do imply consequences for self-making.[17]

Given his own standards, Punzo must demonstrate that sex without marital commitment is "destructive of human freedom or not in keeping with the character of human subjectivity."[18] He sets the agenda for his own task when he states: "If it can be shown that [nonmarital sexual] unions involve the reduction of human subjects to the status of objects, the immorality of the unions has been established."[19]

The question is not, as Punzo often seems to imagine, whether matters of sexual interaction are aesthetic or moral.[20] Clearly, issues pertaining to such matters are moral. The real questions are these: What moral standards of evaluation are applicable to sex? Why should such standards be applied to sex? Is sex inherently different from other activities in the moral realm? If so, why?

The "morality of aspiration" to which Punzo subscribes requires careful and clear answers to all of these questions. Punzo's attempts to provide the required details, however, fail for the reasons adumbrated above. In sum, Punzo's approach overrates and universalizes the importance of sex only with marital commitment for existential integrity and psychological flourishing. First, it is clear that many people have not confined themselves to sex only with marital commitment, yet such people do not necessarily exhibit the effects of dehumanization and psychological disintegration so feared by proponents of this approach. Second, even if sex without marital commitment did lead to existential fragmentation, it does not follow that the sexual interactions were morally impermissible or that they necessarily involved wrongful objectification of humans. Finally, although love, commitment, and intimacy are important aspects of human personality, it is not clear that they are always primary. We engage in many worthwhile activities that are unaccompanied by love, full commitment, and intimacy. Why must sex be different? If it is claimed that sex is different because it is necessarily and deeply connected to human personality, further questions remain: Is that connection an ahistorical fact? Cannot pleasure, without love and intimacy, serve as a legitimate goal of sex for many people? Is the importance of sex for existential integrity a biological fact or merely a social construct of certain subgroups within society?

JOHN HUNTER

Hunter's approach to sexual ethics is much closer than Vincent Punzo's to a paradigm of a "sex with love" method. Moreover, Hunter is careful to concede that sex without love is not necessarily immoral, although it necessarily falls short of his moral ideal: "Sexual activity is not immoral nearly so often as some people would have us believe . . . some of our sexual activities may be regrettable without being immoral; but if anything is substandard in some nonmoral way, its avoidance will not be something we have a right to require of people, but will be a matter of preference, recommendation, encouragement."[21]

Obviously, this does not suggest that sex is merely prudentially unsound, but morally permissible, when it is accompanied by harm, deception, promise breaking, or exploitation. On the contrary, Hunter accepts the common catalog of wrong-making characteristics. He seems, then, committed to the proposition that sexual activity is not inherently different from and should be morally evaluated by the same criteria as other actions in the moral realm. His argument adds, however, the conclusion that sex without love is often accompanied by regret and an emptiness whose source is the unmet human need for intimacy. These ungratifying aspects of sex without love are spiritually impoverishing and, accordingly, frustrate ideal human interaction, even though they do not necessarily imply the moral impermissibility of the particular sex acts that engender them.

> When sex is impersonal, caresses come out as an expression of enthusiasm for caressing. If one does not know or care whether the other person is lonely, reads Dickens, likes cats or believes in God, caresses lose their character as expressions of affection. Then there is an emptiness in lovemaking that may be disturbing, and in the case in which one does know and does not like such things about a person, caresses take on the character of falsity.[22]

Hunter describes ideal sexual relationships as characterized by mutual caring for each other as complete persons. This implies liking not merely the other's talents, attributes, and appearance, but their personhood in its entirety: "If one mate could immediately be replaced by another equally congenial and there was no sense of a particular personal loss, then there was not an attachment to just this person. Each person was interested, not in the other person, but in that person's conversation, taste, cheerfulness, cooking ability or sexual compatibility."[23]

Ideal sexual relationships must include mutual trust, total mutual acceptance, and an intimacy distinguished by the sharing of one's innermost thoughts as well as one's body. Personal and intimate relationships are necessary, says Hunter, in order to liberate ourselves from isolation, estrangement, and lack of spiritual communication. In such relationships we come to self-knowledge and confront opportunities to reimagine and remake the self: "Wherever [personal intimacy] prevails, it releases us from constraints of caution and distrust, which are both thwarting in themselves and tend to make our lives arid. The intimate relationship enriches our lives, both by releasing a creativity of personal interaction, that has been inhibited, and by eliciting it from another person."[24]

Hunter understands, however, that it is easy to invoke but difficult to define "intimacy." Accordingly, he offers four generalizations to facilitate our understanding of that term. First, he states a replaceability criterion: "A test of whether a relationship is personal or not is whether anyone else having the same or comparable good qualities would do as well. A commercial relationship is usually impersonal, and there it makes no difference, as between honest and competent practitioners, whom we employ."[25]

Second, he adds cautiously that "the application of this test is complicated . . . by the fact that it may pain us to lose a friend, not because of a particular attachment to that person, but only because congenial connections can be somewhat rare, or because we have been particularly fortunate in a certain friendship."[26] In spite of this apparent disclaimer, he still insists that "the test may still be useful . . . either in the case in which we are fortunate in replacing one friend by another, or in the case in which, although we have enjoyed a friendship and it was not replaced by another, no loss was felt. In other cases, we may have to apply other tests."[27]

Third, Hunter distinguishes intimate relationships from impersonal affiliations on the basis of total acceptance: "A personal relation is objective, and an impersonal one subjective: in the latter case it is just to the extent that I find a person's qualities agreeable or congenial that I am interested, whereas in the former case I care about a person's tastes or hopes or fears *whatever they may be*, just because they are the person's. There is thus a quality of total acceptance about a relationship that is personal, a readiness to let the chips fall where they may."[28]

Finally, he underscores the role reciprocal trust plays in enhancing mutual self-esteem and the meaningfulness of our lives: "There are two related character traits that make for personal intimacy, one a disposition to trust other people, so that one will not fear to reveal oneself, and the other a tendency to inspire trust."[29]

Hunter also highlights the difference between requiring and recommending sex only with love and intimacy:

Personal intimacy is . . . an excellent thing, deserving of concern and much to be cherished and promoted, but we make a mistake if we treat it as a matter of moral concern. . . . Personal intimacy is therefore not something on which we have a right to insist. It may be regrettable but it is not sinful to relate to people in a generally impersonal way; and it may be excellent but it is not saintly to be caring, interested in and responsive to people.[30]

Given that he is not burdened by pretensions to innovative moral discoveries, on what basis can Hunter persuade us that sex only with intimacy is preferable to other forms of sexual interaction? At bottom, he draws two pictures of human relationships, one personal and the other impersonal, and he asks to which we find ourselves attracted. The impersonal depiction includes an easy congeniality: witty, pleasurable conversation that focuses on matters of little personal involvement (e.g., films, books, sports, news); tenuous affiliations that are often threatened seriously by tensions, disagreements, and disappointments; sex often accompanied by regret and lingering estrangement; mutual evaluation of and preoccupation with specific attributes and characteristics; and dispositions for self-concealing behavior and limited mutual trust. The portrait of personal relationships includes deeper self-revelation: intimate exchanges of the parties' innermost concerns; substantial attachments that accept heightened mutual vulnerability and risk as partly constitutive of the parties' union; sex accompanied by mutual understanding that more is at stake than merely the intensity of erotic pleasures; mutual acceptance of the nonreplaceability of the respective parties; and a spiritual openness crowned by dispositions to trust and inclinations to inspire trust.

Hunter's careful and insightful defense of sex only with love and intimacy—as prudentially sound, although not morally required—invites a summary of the litany of reasons that have been advanced in the literature by his ideological fellow travelers. Chief among these is the rich meaning that accompanies sex with love and intimacy. Lovers experience security and reciprocity, they sense mutual appreciation for the people they are, they entertain feelings of specialness, and they perceive sex as a human expression that transcends the accumulation of pleasurable sensations. Moreover, lovers may share an enduring relationship that goes beyond the gratifications of the bedroom and nourishes their total well-being. In this fashion, sex with love engenders an emotional security that eradicates or minimizes wrongful objectification of humans. Finally, it may be argued that lovers will be more forgiving and generous in the bedroom than nonlovers simply because the former have lasting attachments that exceed the pursuit of sexual pleasure.

Notice, however, that all these reasons originate with the same aspiration: the caution that we should not perceive sex qua sex as a major focus of our being. The arguments in favor of sex with love incline us toward a fuller outlook on our total prosperity. They counsel us to place sexual fulfillment within the detailed context of our lives. Thus, advocates of this approach are arguing that when all is said and done sex is merely one, and not the most important, dimension of our lives. They advise sex only with love for its salutary effects on our paramount needs: "For human beings the more powerful need is not for sex per se but for relationship, intimacy, acceptance, and affirmation."[31]

There are at least two issues here. The first centers on whether, from a prudential standpoint, sex with love is preferable to sex without love. The second focuses on whether an affirmative answer to the first question implies that humans should engage in sex *only* with love. Clearly, one could agree that sex with love is, all things considered, strategically preferable to sex without love, yet deny that humans should engage in sex *only* with love. Such a person could reason that the case against sex without love must include not only its relative inferiority to sex with love, but also an argument that sex without love is inherently unwise. Without the latter argument, a critic could contend that sex without love, even if it is prudentially inferior to sex with love, is still preferable to no sex at all!

Hunter, for example, does an admirable job of making the case in favor of sex with intimacy, but fails to highlight reasons why sex without intimacy is inherently unwise. Punzo, on the other hand, does advance arguments why sex without marital commitment is inherently unwise and even immoral, but his arguments have been judged earlier as unsound or incomplete.

Although it is difficult to disparage sex with love in relation to sex without love, a task that seems akin to criticizing lower taxes and later deaths, such efforts have been made.[32] Nonlovers experience adventure and shared risk, they sense mutual appreciation for freedom and nonpossessiveness, they entertain feelings of specialness as they exercise unique opportunities, and they perceive sex as an inherently valuable human enterprise that transcends instrumentalist concerns. Moreover, nonlovers may share enduring commitments to the inherent joy of sex and to their own independence, convictions that nourish their total well-being. In this fashion, sex without love engenders an emotional liberation that eradicates or minimizes wrongful objectification of humans. Finally, it may be argued that nonlovers will be more forgiving and generous in the bedroom than nonlovers simply because the former lack lasting attachments and thus are free from the psychological baggage and mundane bickerings endemic to lovers. Accordingly, sex without love between otherwise morally upright people need not conjure images of lascivious, wild-eyed predators who seek only the satiation of their excessive impulses at others' expense.

Notice the symmetry between the case made in favor of sex with love and the case made in favor of sex without love. Virtually every reason given in support of the former can be turned on its head and recast as a reason in support of the latter. This is no accident. The symmetry between the respective considerations in favor of sex with love and sex without love is the result of a fundamental conflict at the heart of human experience: our yearning for intimate connection with others and our recognition that others are necessary for our identity and freedom coalesce uneasily with the fear and anxiety we experience as others approach.[33] We simultaneously long for emotional attachment yet are horrified that our individuality may evaporate once we achieve it. These are conflicting impulses because our desire for close personal connections and our desire for radical individuality seemingly cannot be fulfilled simultaneously.

The security, intimacy, and enduring relationships of sex with love speak to our yearning for community, while the adventure and freedom of sex without love resonate in our need to assert individuality. Each type of sex tends to privilege one of the impulses of this fundamental conflict and to marginalize the other. The behavior corresponding to the privileged impulse is then treated as either a moral prescriptive or, more frequently, a sound prudential principle.

Many, perhaps all, of us do experience the dread of simultaneous attraction and repulsion at the approach of others. Moreover, this disharmony may never be fully reconciled once and forever, and so we find ourselves making uneasy compromises and adjustments during our life's journey. If this fundamental conflict is indeed so pervasive, its effects must surely resonate in matters so fundamental as sex.

But few, if any, of us experience the tension between individualism and community as *contradictions*. Do we truly desire, even for a moment, a total and unqualified individuality which would make us completely immune from external intrusion? Do we truly desire, even for a moment, a total and unqualified immersion into community such that we are indistinguishable from "the one"? In order to be contradictions, one of these extreme impulses must be true and the other false at any particular moment. It is more likely that these conflicting impulses are more akin to logical contraries: they cannot both be true, but both may be false at any particular moment.

In fact it is probably the case that we antecedently desire precisely with what we end up: a mixture of individualism and community, a measure of both the experience of specialness and uniqueness and the fulfillment of intimate connection with others. On a more mundane level, I may enjoy immensely the gustatory delights of fettucini alfredo but also take pride in my trim figure and low cholesterol level. My impulse was never to eat all and only fettucini, nor is my conflicting desire never to indulge in an iota of fat or cholesterol-producing food. Through use of judgment and a minimum of rational reflection I can satisfy both impulses more or less to the degree I antecedently desired. Accordingly, the fundamental conflict besetting humans is more of this sort than a dramatic existential crisis.

Having said this, does it then follow that we must or should engage in both sex with and sex without love, perhaps as a way of fulfilling each of our conflicting impulses to some degree? No, such a conclusion is too strong. After all, a person could choose a fully monogamous sexual existence, thus giving full privilege to the communitarian impulse, yet satisfy fully her individualistic impulse in the nonsexual aspects of her life. There is no reason that we can realize the benefits of the fundamental conflict only if we arrive at a clear compromise of the two impulses in every sphere of our existence. Moreover, a monogamous person might argue that she transcends the fundamental conflict in her relationship: much as one experiences when she is a member of a smoothly functioning team or club engaged in a common cause, the tensions between self and others retreat or evaporate.

Most of the sex-with-love literature is vivified by two false visions of social exchange: either a "unity of selves" image, in which two hearts "beat as one" and the distinction between self and other realizes final serenity, or a war of "each against every," in which independent marauders seek satisfaction of their ravenous sexual urges without regard for the humanity of their partners. The former image embodies a romantic craving, often fantasized but rarely, if ever, achieved. In fact, enduring love and intimacy are complicated bonds that may well depend more on shared experiences in struggling with life's crises than the more commonly invoked notion of "caring about a person's tastes or hopes or fears whatever they may be, just because they are the person's." The common notion strays too closely to an agapic love that either collapses into mere appreciation of an abstraction without qualities or is available only to the divine. On the other hand, the independent marauder picture rings true for relatively few people. Surely, it does not apply to all people who have engaged in sex without love.

ROGER SCRUTON

Scruton provides one of the most eloquent and ingenious contributions to this genre. Adopting an Aristotelian framework, Scruton arrives at conservative conclusions without using some of the less plausible conservative assumptions. Thus, he denies the following: that moral sex must be linked to procreative intent; that the essence of sexual desire is found in the depths of a perfected soul; that sexual desire is mere bodily appetite and thus ersatz yearning; that the mind and body are separate elements of personhood; that sexual desire transcends social settings and influences; that moral evaluation must appeal to the dictates of a supreme being; and that gender can be ignored when morally evaluating sex.

Instead, Scruton argues that sexual activity has a natural and specific role in human self-fulfillment. He portrays self-fulfillment as culminating in the highest type of flourishing, happiness.[34] Echoing Aristotle, Scruton takes flourishing to be "the activity of [human] *essence*: it is the successful employment of those capacities that are integral to [a person's] being."[35] An indispensable aspect of realizing one's essential nature is the cultivation of virtue, which is "the disposition to choose those courses of action which contribute to my happiness: which cause me to flourish as a rational being."[36] Scruton also reiterates the Aristotelian theme that happiness is predicated over an entire life, instead of in temporal slices. In that vein, he links happiness with personal responsibility, which "denotes a pattern of thought and feeling, whereby a person anchors himself, not in the moment, but in the stretch of time which is his 'life' "[37]

According to Scruton, sexual desire is intentional and interpersonal. Rather than aspiring to impersonal physical release, sexual desire seeks a response from a particular object of desire. It is a yearning for another person, a craving to unite with and to inspire the sexual desire of the other. Such desires are fulfilled only through experiences of shared sexual excitement in which the consciousnesses of both participants are centered on the pleasures of their bodies: the natural aim of sexual desire is only fully satisfied in erotic love. Thus, sexual desire that does not aim at spiritual union, embodiment, is ersatz desire. The consummation of sexual desire and love is an irreplaceable way for the participants to affirm each other's value. Moreover, sexual desire is a public phenomenon in the sense that it is artifactual and emerges within other human constructs such as societies and institutions.

Humans sexually desire not merely another person, in some generic sense, but an embodied person whose gender is partly constitutive of who he or she is for us: "Sexual desire is itself inherently 'nuptial': it involves concentration upon the embodied existence of the other, leading through tenderness to the 'vow' of erotic love."[38] Embodiment, then, is a form of union that transcends the physical link between persons that it includes. Members of the opposite sex are significantly different in physical and mental makeup, Scruton tells us. As a result, heterosexual relationships entail great risks of the unknown which encourage paramount values for human fulfillment: mutual commitment and fidelity.

> The opening of the self to the mystery of another gender, thereby taking responsibility for an experience which one does not wholly understand, is a feature of sexual maturity, and one of the fundamental motives tending towards commitment. This exposure to something unknown can resolve itself, finally, only in a mutual vow. Only in a vow is the trust created which protects the participants from the threat of betrayal. Without the

fundamental experience of the otherness of the sexual partner, an important component in erotic love is therefore put in jeopardy.[39]

Further, interpersonal union which implicates sexual desire focuses on the body of the other person in a unique and salutary fashion: "It is only when kisses and caresses become part of the aim of interpersonal union, and the true source of pleasure, that we are forced to see the other's body as truly him, and contact with his body as contact with him."[40]

But how is this linked with sexual morality? The role of sexual morality is to "unite [the personal and the sexual], to sustain thereby the intentionality of desire, and to prepare the individual for erotic love."[41] Scruton claims that mutual affirmation of personal worth is necessary for self-fulfillment, and self-fulfillment—the realization of a person's nature and telos—is an eminent moral value. His portrayal of sexual ethics consists of a series of inferences drawn from his visions of embodiment and personal fulfillment. Thus, a certain kind of sex is morally recommended, the kind that venerates human nature and facilitates self-fulfillment. Any sexual practice is deficient insofar as it reduces a party to something less than an embodied personality. Although sexual desire does not presuppose erotic love, it does provide a motive for love. Moreover, sexual activity *ought* to implicate love, which is a paramount human value: "Love is the fulfillment of [sexual] desire, and therefore love is its *telos*."[42]

Accordingly, Scruton assumes that a phenomenological description of human sexual experience bears prescriptive implications. He ratifies the conservative litany of proscribed sex.[43] Necrophilia and bestiality are perverse because interpersonal emotion and the requisite intentionality are impossible from a corpse or an animal. Masturbation is simply physical release that exists "to facilitate sexual gratification without the trouble of human encounter."[44] It creates a "compliant world of desire, in which unreal objects become the focus of real emotions, and the emotions themselves are rendered incompetent to participate in the building of personal relations. The fantasy blocks the passage to reality, which becomes inaccessible to the will."[45] Masturbation thereby manifests the defining feature of perversion in Scruton's view: aiming at a goal other than enduring spiritual union, turning away from the risks and rewards of interpersonal desire, invoking strategies of substitution which are inherently destructive of personal feeling, thwarting a life of personal fulfillment.[46]

Homosexuality exhibits flawed intentionality and interpersonality because it does not implicate the strangeness of the other gender and is thus accompanied by a diminished sense of risk: "In the homosexual act I remain locked within my body, narcissistically contemplating in the other an excitement that is the mirror of my own."[47] Incest is noxious because it violates domestic ties and responsibilities, thereby eviscerating rather than sustaining interpersonality. Incest "builds upon a pre-established interpersonal relation that is in fact incompatible with it . . . it destroys the interpersonal relation that exists between [the parties] while offering no commitment in its place."[48] Prostitution is lamentable not because the prostitute "gives herself for money, but [because] she gives herself to those whom she hates or despises,"[49] an act that vitiates any possibility of the intentionality and interpersonality required for self-fulfillment.

More strikingly, Scruton argues against premarital sex and fleeting sexual encounters. Refraining from premarital sex protects sexual desire from "obscene abuses"[50] and permits full interpersonality and intentionality to blossom, which smooths the way for ultimately fulfilling sex. Chastity is "justified in terms of the disposition from which [it] springs. It may be in the long-term interests of the rational agent that he acquire just this kind of control over his sexual impulses."[51] Fleeting sexual encounters or "one night stands" tend toward mere physical release and thus cannot transmit the mutual self-affirmation and interpersonality that Scruton prizes. Worse, variance from prescribed sex soon become habitual and impede us from self-fulfillment and happiness.

> People cannot easily see their sexual behavior as a sequence of isolated acts . . . a particular encounter . . . may reverberate through one's life, gathering to itself the significance of every subsequent longing . . . we all feel the promptings of lust, but the rapidity with which sexual acts become sexual habits, and the catastrophic effects of a sexual act which cannot be remem-

bered without shame or humiliation, give us strong reasons to resist them.[52]

What about lifelong chastity? We might expect Scruton to disparage it straightaway given his extravagant encomiums to sex and erotic love as necessary for human self-fulfillment and happiness. But he is not so inflexible. As stated previously, he lavishes praise on chastity as a proper restraint on sexual desire that safeguards sexual impulse from abuses, nurtures full intentionality, and facilitates erotic love. Regarding lifelong chastity he provides a less enthusiastic defense: "It is never obviously admirable, unless the outcome of a vow: unless, that is, it is an act of renunciation which is the inverse and the image of the vow of love, and which has its own troubles and ecstasies."[53]

There are at least two available interpretations of Scruton's sexual morality. A strong interpretation would argue that the human telos is self-fulfillment culminating in happiness; that humans have a moral obligation to strive for the human telos; that virtue, the disposition to select actions wisely, is necessary for self-fulfillment; that self-affirmation and affirmation of and by others are necessary for virtue; that erotic love is necessary for self-affirmation and affirmation of and by others, at least necessary for noncelibates; that sexual desire provides a motive and is necessary for its telos: erotic love; that sexual desire can realize its telos only if sexual activity exhibits the requisite interpersonality and intentionality compatible with erotic love; and, therefore, that sex only with the requisite interpersonality and intentionality ("sex only with love") is itself a moral obligation.

A weak interpretation would abrogate the premise that humans have a moral obligation to strive for the human telos. It would argue instead that sex only with love is the preferred moral ideal for humans, the ideal best able to facilitate the human telos. Striving for and achieving the human telos, although not strictly required from a moral point of view, is nevertheless the wisest and most appropriate course for humans to adopt. Accordingly, for the other reasons embodied in the strong interpretation, sex only with love is recommended as the wisest and most appropriate approach to sex.

The strong interpretation is beset by a variety of difficulties. From the outset, it is not clear that there is one human telos or what must constitute it. Although self-fulfillment and happiness will surely strike us as eminently worthwhile, it is not clear that these values are either superior to or more in line with our human nature than other eminently worthwhile values. Indeed, whether there is a persuasive and substantive conception of human nature is itself highly contested. Moreover, even granting that self-fulfillment and happiness constitute the human telos, it is not clear what generates our alleged moral obligation to pursue that telos. However laudatory such pursuits may seem to most of the Western world, why are self-affirmation, striving, and perfection of human capacities and desires moral obligations? Scruton's neo-Aristotelian call for perfectionism as a universal moral requirement rests on suspicious metaphysical underpinnings and mysterious connections between alleged facts about human nature and appealing values.

But I will suspend such criticisms for the sake of argument and stipulate, with the strong interpretation of Scruton, that we have a moral obligation to seek self-fulfillment and happiness. I will stipulate further that sex with love facilitates that pursuit. But it is not obvious that even if mutual self-enhancement requires love, such love must be *erotic*. Nor is it clear why sex without love would necessarily retard the pursuit of mutual self-enhancement, or that it is an inferior activity because sexual desire does not aim at enduring spiritual union. Surely Scruton's distress that "perversions" such as masturbation, premarital sex, and "one night stands" soon prove habitual and become substitutes for erotic love is misplaced. The empirical evidence is that many (most?) humans who have engaged in such actions can nevertheless achieve satisfying erotic love. Scruton succumbs here to one of the recurrent bogeymen of this genre: either sex fully satisfies pursuit of the human telos and is therefore morally sound, or sex necessarily retards that pursuit and is thus morally deficient. There is no middle ground.

That this dilemma is false is clearly demonstrable. Even if masturbation, premarital sex, and one night stands are, for the sake of argument, inferior to sex with love, it hardly follows that they necessarily lack value. On the contrary, they may well be "better than nothing": they may be inferior substitutes but nevertheless at times prudentially (and even morally) preferable to sexual abstention. Such actions usually do not become singular habits which henceforth preclude erotic love; in fact, they may even have an indispensable positive value of developing and exercising sexual capacities that are themselves necessary for erotic love.

The error that fuels Scruton's false dilemma is that sexual desire must aim at one function: fostering erotic love and its allegedly unique mutual affirmation that in turn promotes self-fulfillment. Again, although this may well seem laudatory, it hardly follows that sex without love must retard the preferred function or that sex of whatever stripe cannot have other prudentially and morally sound functions: achieving pleasure, expressing passion, experiencing adventure, among others. Such additional functions may also speak to important constitutive human attributes and they surely do not necessarily conflict with Scruton's preferred function of sex.

The error that fuels Scruton's anxiety that perverse acts degenerate quickly into immoral habits is another familiar, previously identified bogeyman of this genre: either the wise practitioner of sex only with love or the witless sexual profligate bent on self-destruction. In fact, the destination of self-fulfillment and happiness may have many acceptable routes. Scruton himself goes some distance in acknowledging this when he concedes that lifelong chastity, accompanied by a requisite vow and long-range project that makes a life meaningful and coherent, can realize the human telos. Carrying this concession a step further, there may be alternate ways for different people, who exhibit varying degrees of inclination toward risk and security, to experience life-affirming, self-fulfilling, happiness-inducing sex. Moreover, Scruton's harsh portrayal of sexual fantasies— as curbing one's ability to build rewarding personal relations—is overblown. Such fantasies are virtually universal among humans, and there is little reason to believe that fantasies have prevented fulfilling interpersonality or that fantasizers tend to act out their imaginings.

In the immediately preceding paragraphs, my argument has concentrated on Scruton's reductionist tendencies, which culminate in his insistence that moral sex has only one function. But he also manifests unhealthy doses of abstractness and ahistoricism as well. Ignoring for the moment my previous criticisms, we may still ask whether Scruton's mutually self-affirming and happiness-inducing heterosexual erotic love can occur under conditions of considerable class, economic, racial, and gender oppression. Curiously, Scruton never struggles with social conditions of oppression and how they might impede his preferred sexual prescriptions. Instead of attending to the powerful feminist argument that gender oppression reduces or even prevents the possibility of mutually self-affirming and mutually happiness-inducing heterosexual erotic love, Scruton flirts with some crude gender stereotyping.[54]

The weak interpretation of Scruton evades several of my criticisms: the grave difficulties which accompany the establishing of a moral requirement to strive for the alleged human telos; the false universalism which wrongly categorizes humans into only two sexual types; and the incredulous stigmatizing of all sex without love as necessarily immoral. These victories, resulting from the weak interpretation's renouncing the premise that humans have a moral obligation to strive for the human telos, are purchased at a stiff price: they domesticate much of the panache and sheer boldness of the strong interpretation.

Under the weak interpretation we must perceive sex only with love as one acceptable ideal—as one version of maximally fulfilling sex—among many. Here we would admit that no universal prescription for sex only with love can be written legitimately. We would now offer sex only with love as an appealing ideal that, once embraced, issued its own moral imperatives, but we would have to concede that there is no universal moral imperative to ratify the ideal itself.

Surely, even under the weak interpretation, the ideal of sex only with love will prove attractive to many people with compatible psychological makeups, preferred lifestyles, relative inclinations toward risk and security and toward individualism and community, and perceptions of the ultimate human good. For many people, adopting the ideal of sex only with love will be a wise and prudentially sound choice.

But this conclusion is hardly startling or even interesting. I do not know anyone who argues seriously that sex only with love is necessarily immoral. Thus, everyone concedes that sex only with love is morally permissible, and virtually everyone grants that it constitutes an acceptable moral ideal. Critics deny, however, that it is the only acceptable moral ideal and that sex only with love must be adopted by all noncelibates. The weak interpretation of Scruton's work is compatible with the critics' denials. Accordingly, the only remaining points of dispute would be the specific arguments Scruton advances in favor of his nonobligatory ideal and the number and types of people who should be drawn to that ideal. Such issues are most animated when they are intramural disputes within the sex-only-with-love genre.

In sum, sex with love and intimacy will remain an ideal for those of us who perceive our sexual behavior as part of a deeper aspiration: sharing the struggle with life's crises with a long-term partner, a mutuality which helps to satisfy the human longing for community. But this admission does not establish the prudential soundness of sex *only* with love and intimacy. This conclusion can only be founded on a showing that sex without love necessarily hinders future prospects of achieving the ideal, or is inherently fragmenting to the human spirit, or necessarily violates our self-interest in other ways, or leads inevitably to a demeaning of self or others. Such claims, however, are more easily proclaimed than proved. Moreover, we have seen that findings that sex with love and intimacy embodies an ideal and that sex with only love and intimacy constitutes sound prudential strategy still fall far short of establishing sex only with love as a moral prescription. Accordingly, while sex-with-love literature will always strike felicitously our romantic chords and our communitarian instincts, it has failed to demonstrate a convincing sexual imperative.

Dissatisfaction with traditional Western sexual morality has led to several different approaches. The idea of contract has often provided an alternative to traditional moralities, not only in regard to political obligation and justice, but also in regard to sexual morality. We now examine this approach.

4

THE SANCTITY OF CONTRACT AND THE HORROR OF EXPLOITATION
Libertarianism and Kantianism

Contractualist approaches contend that sexual activity must be morally assessed by the same criteria relevant to any other human activity. Hence they underscore the importance of mutual, voluntary informed consent and highlight the appropriateness of tolerating sexual diversity as a recognition of human freedom and autonomy. Some contractualists are influenced by a strain of Western thought which depicts sex as a valuable gift to be exercised boldly and frequently (e.g., Rabelais, Boccaccio, Kazantzakis); while other contractualists subscribe to an ancient view that sex should be savored in proper moderation (e.g., Homer, Aristotle, Montaigne).

I argue that libertarianism, the most radical form of contractarianism, sanctifies mutual agreement as morally self-ratifying and thus wrongly ignores numerous moral distortions that occur in the realm of contract: widely unequal bargaining power, prominent differences in psychological vulnerability, oppressive background circumstances, and impermissible commodification of constitutive human attributes. Hence, the libertarian rhetoric of voluntary exchange and free interaction disguises the morally significant formative environment in which choices are made. Moreover, attempts to add a principle of rectification to account for that formative environment and its past social inequities threaten to destroy the basic libertarian structure.

Contractarian attempts to ameliorate libertarianism's problems often make use of ideal methods of choice, such as Rawls's "original position." These methods aspire to transcend the tyranny of actual agreements as morally self-ratifying by establishing overriding, neutral moral principles. I argue, however, that such methods of choice must define their allegedly neutral vantage point specifically enough to generate determinate conclusions. But this involves a prior acceptance of the very social order that the ideal method purports to justify. Thus, ideal methods of choice invariably fail to justify their allegedly neutral moral principles.

Finally, I examine the work of Kant. I argue that his own writings on sexual ethics are plagued by strikingly wrong perceptions of the value of sex and unsubstantiated views on the inherent lack of value of nonmarital sex. Nonetheless, Kant's work sounds some unassailably correct notes for sexual ethics: the irreducibility of humans, the need for reciprocity, the importance of self-respect, and the commitment to renounce exploitation and commodification.

I conclude that libertarian-Kantian social theory provides the basic ground for a persuasive theory of sexual ethics. There are, however, a host of conceptual and practical difficulties with libertarian-Kantianism which militate against unbridled acceptance of that theory. Such difficulties lead me to turn in later chapters to leftist and feminist critiques of society for several reasons, including the felt need to give fuller content to notions such as "exploitation" and "mere use."

LIBERTARIANISM

A libertarian position often gains much initial acceptance because it is invariably proposed in those cultures that eagerly glorify the right of contract as necessary for the sanctity of human freedom. Starting from the axiom that persons are ends in themselves, possessors of rights, and the bearers of inherent dignity, libertarian contractualists are wary of moral theories that promote paternalistic measures to protect individuals from their own alleged poor judgment. Thus, the contemporary philosopher Robert Nozick writes:

> [Libertarianism] treats us as inviolate individuals, who may not be used in certain ways by others as means or tools or instruments or resources; it treats us as persons having individual rights with the dignity this constitutes. Treating us with respect by respecting our rights, it allows us, individually or with whom we choose, to choose our life and to realize our ends and the

conception of ourselves, insofar as we can, aided by the voluntary cooperation of other individuals possessing the same dignity.[1]

Libertarians, following John Locke (1632–1704), usually ascribe certain rights to humans based on our capacities and freedom in an imagined "state of nature": "Individuals in Locke's state of nature are in 'a state of perfect freedom to order their actions and dispose of their possessions and persons as they think fit, within the bounds of the law of nature, without asking leave or dependency upon the will of any other man.'. . . The bounds of the law of nature require that 'no one ought to harm another in his life, health, liberty, or possessions.' "[2]

Each of us thus has a series of natural rights which are accompanied by a set of natural negative duties: to refrain from harming, defrauding, coercing, and stealing from other humans. No external source, whether governmental or religious or social, has the legitimacy to decide what is in the self-interest of individuals. Such decisions are unwarranted paternalisms which condescendingly deny individual freedom and mock individual autonomy. Although Locke himself set limits to what a person could permit another to do to him, purists such as Nozick do not.

Locke . . . would hold that there are things others may not do to you by your permission; namely, those things you have no right to do to yourself. Locke would hold that your giving your permission cannot make it morally permissible for another to kill you, because you have no right to commit suicide. [Nozick's] nonpaternalistic position holds that someone may choose (or permit another) to do to himself *anything*, unless he has acquired an obligation to some third party not to do or allow it.[3]

The force of the term "anything" requires elaboration. Would such an unadulterated libertarian permit a person to sell himself into slavery as long as no (other?) negative duty was violated in the process? Would not such a sale destroy the future free exercise of the very capacity that libertarians aspire to venerate: that individual's autonomy? Again, there is intramural disagreement here. But the purest versions of libertarianism permit the transaction in question.

"[An important] question about an individual is whether a free system will allow him to sell himself into slavery. [Nozick believes] that it would. . . . It also would allow him permanently to commit himself never to enter into such a transaction. But some things individuals may choose for themselves, no one may choose for another."[4]

Applying libertarian philosophy to sexual relations results in the view that sex is morally permissible if and only if it is consummated with mutual and voluntary informed consent. Rather than focusing on a particular conception of the marriage institution, or a specialized understanding of the "proper" function of sex, or a natural law perception of the necessary link between sex and human personality, this view highlights the importance of human autonomy as reflected in the agreements we make. Proponents insist that the paramount values are individual freedom and autonomy. Thus it is tyranny to insist on a particular kind of sexual interaction or to prescribe a specific domain for acceptable sex. The test of morally permissible sex is simple: Have the parties, possessing the basic capacities necessary for autonomous choice, voluntarily agreed to a particular sexual interaction without force, fraud, and explicit duress? Accordingly, sex is impermissible where one or both parties lack the capacities for informed consent (e.g., underage, or significantly mentally impaired, or nonhuman); or where there is explicit duress (e.g., threats or extortion), force (e.g., coercion), or fraud (e.g., one party deceives the other as to the nature of the act or the extent of his or her feelings as a way of luring the other to accepting the liaison).

The most glaring weakness of this position is that it ignores numerous moral distortions that occur in the realm of contract: parties to a contract may have radically unequal bargaining power, they may display prominent differences in psychological vulnerability, one of the parties may bargain under the oppression of destitute circumstances, or the contract may treat important attributes constitutive of human personality as if they were mere commodities subject to market bartering. Such distortions call into question whether a particular contract is truly morally permissible. The existence of a contract is not morally self-validating. That is, once we know that a contract, arrived at through "voluntary consent," exists, there is still the further question: Are the terms of that contract morally permissible? The libertarian position can succeed only if voluntary contractual interaction comprises the totality of morality. The following illustrations are designed to call that assumption into question.

Rocco is a poor but honest barber's son whose family is in desperate need of the basic requirements of life. He tries a variety of ways to secure the money he needs but is unsuccessful. Banks draw their shades when they see him approaching; social service agencies disband voluntarily when they discover that Rocco has made an appointment with them; and even loan sharks, noticing that his legs are insufficient collateral, refuse Rocco's supplications. Finally, Rocco learns of the strange proclivities of his neighbor, Vito. Vito, a wealthy and sadistic chap, has a standing offer of $5,000 plus medical expenses to all who will allow him to chop off the middle finger of their right hand. In fact, Vito displays a handsome collection of various human digits mounted tastefully on the wall of his den. Rocco approaches Vito and asks him if the offer still stands. Vito brandishes $5,000 and exclaims, "Let's make a deal!" After negotiating minor aspects such as the type of axe to be used, whether or not Rocco's hospital room should be private, and Rocco's share of the proceeds Vito will realize from the admission fees he charges those who view his den, the contract is finalized and its terms consummated. Rocco is $5,000 richer and one finger poorer!

Even though the contract imagined was voluntarily agreed to in the absence of force, fraud, or duress, many still would insist that such a contract is immoral because Vito has exploited the dire circumstances, vulnerability, and outright desperation of Rocco's situation. Moreover, both parties treated part of Rocco's body as if it were a mere commodity subject to market forces. It might be objected that the libertarian can avoid such a counterexample because Vito did harm Rocco: he cut off his finger. But this objection is not persuasive because a libertarian seems to be committed to allowing *Rocco* to judge whether the loss of a finger, combined with a gain of $5,000, amounts to a "harm." For the most committed libertarians, consent vitiates harm, and thus they cannot claim here that Vito violated Rocco's negative right not to be harmed. Such libertarians have more faith in the value of individual freedom and autonomy than they have in a priori moral assertions.

But, still, some might think it unfair to trade on the melodramatic and gruesome features of the finger-chopping illustration. They might insist, perhaps as Locke would, that Rocco has no right to permit Vito to chop off his finger, regardless of the proffered compensation, because Rocco has no right to chop off his own finger. Such an action could be plausibly depicted as inherently wrongful self-mutilation. I suspect strongly, however, that Nozick's purer version of libertarianism is ultimately more consistent and more honest than this Lockean view, which may well disingenuously smuggle in nonlibertarian principles into its moral calculus, principles which could be extended, thereby corroding and gobbling up the basic libertarian structure. Be that as it may, let us consider another example.

Rosalia is a middle class college graduate who yearns to be an actress. She seems to have most of the necessary qualifications: she is physically attractive, possesses a measure of acting talent, and has excellent work habits and a keen intelligence. Rosalia takes a leave of absence from her tenured teaching position at a New Jersey high school and travels to Hollywood to pursue her dream. After numerous screen tests and a few minor parts, her first major stroke of good fortune arrives: she is one of three finalists for a major role in an important movie. After all three finalists undergo additional screen tests, Rosalia is called into the office of Angelo, the casting officer for the movie.

Angelo, not one to rest on formality and not graced by an abundance of class, makes the situation plain to Rosalia: any of the three finalists will do an excellent job in the role and the movie is a certain major success; all of the actresses possess the necessary talent for the role and preliminary surveys suggest that they are equal in audience appeal; consequently, Angelo has decided to cast the part on a special criterion. He asks Rosalia, as he has asked the other two finalists, if she will consent to have sexual intercourse with him. If she refuses this proposition, she will not receive the acting role. If she accepts the proposition, and if the other two finalists refuse, Rosalia will receive the role. If she accepts, and one or both of the other finalists also accept, Angelo will cast the role on the basis of which finalist pleased him the most. Angelo does not resort to explicit coercion, fraud, or threats of physical harm. If Rosalia decided to refuse his proposition she will not get the acting role, but she can lead her life as she did prior to the auditions.

If Rosalia accepts the proposition, despite the fact that Angelo repulses her, what would a libertarian say? Remember that Angelo makes no threat, utters no falsehood, makes no attempt to deceive

Rosalia about his method of casting. Angelo, it may be argued on libertarian maxims, merely offers Rosalia a contract of a certain sort. Once we agree that no negative duties are being violated, should Rosalia accept the contract's terms and the respective parties keep their part of the bargain, it seems that libertarians must ratify the morality of the transaction. After all, Rosalia is the best judge of her self-interest, and she has calculated that (1) having sex with Angelo and thus a chance to fulfill her acting dreams is a more valuable state of affairs to her than (2) refusing Angelo's crude entreaties and perhaps destroying forever her acting aspirations.

Critics of libertarianism would charge that Angelo has exploited Rosalia's great desire to become an actress; that both Angelo and Rosalia have wrongly commodified their sexuality; that Angelo has much greater bargaining power than Rosalia; and that Rosalia's acquiescence is in part due to the systematic oppression of women by men in our society, a condition that encourages such offensive barter. In short, critics would charge that an enormous power differential consumes the possibility for genuine exchange. But for her overpowering yearning to become an actress and the limited opportunities to fulfill that longing, Rosalia would have never consented to occupy Angelo's casting couch.

A committed libertarian would, however, be unconvinced. First, it should be clear that, unlike Rocco's situation, Rosalia's predicament is not the consequence of her lacking a necessity of life. Becoming a famous actress may be one of her greatest desires, but it is not, strictly speaking, a need. Second, the fact that desires such as Rosalia's almost always go unfulfilled is itself one of the reasons why their realization is so valuable. Third, in an important respect Rosalia's situation is no different from a host of mundane dilemmas we all find ourselves confronting: but for their lack of economic independence, numerous people would not labor at their current jobs; but for their deep desire for recognition, numerous writers and scholars would not suffer the hardships that accompany their craft; but for their lack of physical attractiveness or persuasive charm, many people would not be married to their current spouse. In sum, libertarians could point out that all the choices we make are affected greatly by our antecedent situation, but as long as that antecedent situation was not the result of explicit violations of natural negative duties, subsequent transactions must be evaluated on their own contractualist merits.

In this vein, Nozick is once again helpful:

> Some readers will object . . . that some actions (for example, workers accepting a wage position) are not really voluntary because one party faces severely limited options, with all the others being much worse than the one he chooses. Whether a person's actions are voluntary depends on what it is that limits his alternatives. If facts of nature do so, the actions are voluntary. (I may voluntarily walk to someplace I would prefer to fly to unaided.) Other people's actions place limits on one's available opportunities. Whether this makes one's resulting action non-voluntary depends upon whether these others had the right to act as they did.[5]

Thus my natural inability to fly unaided does not render my walking to the grocery store nonvoluntary, nor does my secret desire to marry Sophia Loren suggest that my actual marriage was a nonvoluntary action. It takes the consent of at least two parties to consummate a voluntary exchange, and should Sophia refuse my romantic pleas I have no legitimate complaint. Moreover, the fact that I embody minimum personal charisma and generally lack the personal qualities others find attractive does not vitiate the voluntariness of my marital choice. The general point is clear: that person P would prefer doing action X instead of action Y and that P labors under severely restricted opportunities and choices from the outset are insufficient to establish that Y was nonvoluntary and that P was wronged by Y. Libertarians are thus unconvinced by classic leftist illustrations of workers with severely restricted options who are presumably exploited because they consent to draconian employment terms: "Z is faced with working or starving; the choices and actions of all other persons do not add up to providing Z with some other option. . . . Does Z choose to work voluntarily? . . . Z does choose voluntarily if the other individuals . . . each acted voluntarily and within their rights."[6]

But libertarians are sometimes properly chastised for extracting transactions from their social context and for arguing as if contracting parties are merely abstract choosers rationally seeking their self-interest. Such criticisms are hurled by those firmly convinced that radical contractualism disguises several virulent sources of social oppression: the past and present subordination of some classes (e.g., women, blacks, workers) to other classes (e.g., men, whites, capitalist owners), the general effects of vast economic inequality, and the subjugation of virtually everything to impersonal market forces. Accordingly, critics may well contend that focusing on the present, carefully circumscribed, situations of Rocco-Vito and Rosalia-Angelo obscures the larger moral picture: What social circumstances facilitated Rocco's destitute circumstances? On what basis did Vito acquire his economic advantage? What contexts nurtured Rosalia's obsessive desire for recognition as an actress? What images of power sustain Angelo's calculated abuses? In these situations, are constitutive human attributes treated as mere commodities subject only to market influences? In general, to what extent, if any, are morally illegitimate class, gender, and economic inequalities at work here?

The libertarian rhetoric of voluntary exchange and free interaction can mask the morally significant formative environment in which choices are made. We must not myopically ignore the influences of the past on the choices of the present. We cannot ask simply: Have Vito and Angelo violated the natural negative rights of Rocco and Rosalia, respectively? Instead, we must peer more carefully into the character influences of contracting parties if we aspire to a more satisfying moral evaluation of the terms of their present agreement.

It is unfair, however, to charge that libertarians are unaware of such an attack. For example, in the area of economic distribution, Nozick acknowledges that past injustices must be recognized when assessing current distributions:

If past injustice has shaped present holdings in various ways, some identifiable and some not, what now, if anything, ought to be done to rectify these injustices? What obligations do the performers of injustice have toward those whose position is worse than it would have been had the injustice not been done? . . . How, if at all, do things change if the beneficiaries and those made worse off are not the direct parties in the act of injustice, but, for example, their descendants? Is an injustice done to someone whose holding was itself based upon an unrectified injustice? How far back must one go in wiping clean the historical slate of injustices?[7]

Nozick recognizes that one's current economic holdings are not necessarily just entitlements and that a present transaction is itself just only if the respective parties' assets are antecedently held justly. This complicates libertarianism in important ways. The good news for libertarians is that they can clearly elude the criticism that they wrongly ignore the past when evaluating present transactions. But there are at least two pieces of bad news for libertarians. First, it is difficult to construct an appropriate principle of rectification. Second, such a principle, once developed, threatens the libertarian structure.

There is a core of truth in the slogan ''behind every great fortune lies a crime.'' It may well turn out that an equitable and highly developed principle of economic rectification will require extensive application. Moreover, we must not ignore unassailable illustrations of historical injustice in our society: slavery, the disenfranchisement of women, religious intolerance, mistreatment of ethnic minorities. Such injustices did not come about benignly—through the voluntary collective choices of equally free moral agents—but had their genesis in clear violations of the natural negative rights so prized by libertarians: blacks were literally stolen from their homeland, women were prevented by law from access to many areas of the public sphere, and minorities were in many cases denied their civil rights. Such transgressions of negative rights do not merely affect one's subsequent economic holdings, but also one's mindset, class affiliation, and psychological vulnerability.

A highly refined principle of rectification, it would seem, requires attention not only to economic redistribution based on past transgressions of some people's negative rights, but also to precisely those far-reaching aspects of social context libertarians are sometimes chastised for ignoring. Because there is not now and has never been a time when equally free, rationally self-interested parties contracted in a social context uncontaminated by legal inequities, the effects of past oppression, and unjust economic holdings, libertarians must recognize a principle of rectification. But once acknowledged, this principle foreshadows the collapse of libertarianism into an insipid form of welfare liberalism, libertarianism's despised adversary.

Accordingly, libertarians seem trapped by an uninviting dilemma: either the Scylla of a moral evaluation flawed by its blindness to formative contexts, or the Charybdis of a principle of rectification that threatens to domesticate or even cannibalize the basic libertarian structure. While libertarians have identified important aspects of morality—notions of individual freedom and autonomy—they may be seen as having exaggerated them to the point where these aspects constitute the whole of morality. It is this exaggeration that ensures libertarianism's doom.

KANTIAN MODIFICATIONS TO RADICAL CONTRACTUALISM

It is possible to meet some of the objections to libertarianism by modifying the view. The most serious criticism leveled against libertarianism results from its sanctification of actual contracts. Nonlibertarians are convinced that the mere existence of an apparently voluntary agreement is insufficient to establish its moral credentials. Some philosophers, such as the contemporary thinker John Rawls, accept the power of free transactions, but recognize the need to supplement actual contracts with independent moral principles.

To discover such independent moral principles, Rawls resorts to a heuristic device designed to manifest the principles humans would select under ideal conditions of choice. He calls this starting point the "original position": "Principles of justice for the basic structure of society are the object of the original agreement. They are the principles that free and rational persons concerned to further their own interests would accept in an initial position of equality as defining the fundamental terms of their association. These principles are to regulate all further agreements."[8] Rawls hopes that such independent moral principles will enhance adequately the libertarian worship of free contract: the original position must embody contractual bargaining from an impartial vantage point of true equality as each chooser, although trying to advance her own self-interest, must take into account the needs of others.

Rawls contends that legitimate moral principles must ameliorate the effects of the "natural lottery," the vastly different genetic gifts and social circumstances with which people are endowed at birth.

He reasons that if we know our own constitutive attributes—our age, sex, race, religion, intellectual capacities, and so on—our choices in the original position will tend to favor those characteristics. Thus, in the original position we must be shrouded by a "veil of ignorance" that precludes choosers from knowledge of their particular constitutive attributes.[9]

In the original position, Rawls maintains that people would be guided by a "maximin" strategy when selecting principles that will help determine the distribution of social goods: "The maximin rule tells us to rank alternatives by their worst possible outcomes: we are to adopt the worst outcome of which is superior to the worst outcomes of the others."[10]

In the original position, shrouded by a veil of ignorance, and employing a maximin strategy, what principles of justice would humans select? Rawls proposes two principles in lexical order. The first is the liberty principle: "Each person is to have an equal right to the most extensive total system of equal basic liberties compatible with a similar system of liberty for all."[11] The second is the difference principle: "Social and economic inequalities are to be arranged so that they are both (a) to the greatest benefit of the least advantaged, consistent with the just savings principle, and (b) attached to positions and offices open to all under conditions of fair equality of opportunity."[12] The liberty principle has priority over the difference principle in that liberty cannot be restricted in the service of extending economic benefits.

We need not investigate the acceptability of Rawls's two principles of justice, nor need we argue about the plausibility of the maximin strategy. The more important question concerns the relationship of conclusions about particular moral principles to hypothetical methods of selection. Ideal methods of choice, such as the original position, must define their allegedly neutral vantage point specifically enough to generate determinate conclusions. In so doing, they exclude certain moral, epistemological, and metaphysical intuitions and privilege others. But this involves a prior acceptance of the very social order that the ideal method purports to justify. Accordingly, practitioners of such methodologies are reminiscent of magicians who put the rabbit *in* the hat.

Rawls recognizes that "for each traditional conception of justice there exists an interpretation of the initial situation in which its principles are the preferred solution.''[13] He argues, however, that his version of ''justice as fairness'' expresses our considered moral judgments better than the available alternatives. Having said this, in what sense can he maintain the pretension to a neutral derivation of moral principles required to constrain actual contracts?[14]

Rawls's influential work, although failing to provide the foundation of the ideals of equality and impartiality, is the culmination of a Kantian tradition that exalts the value of humans as ends in themselves. Despite the limitations of Rawls's original position, it is still in this tradition that the proper modifications to libertarianism may be located.

IMMANUEL KANT

Kant (1724–1804) gave the most detailed classic expression to the inherent moral standing of humans. The constitutive elements of Kantianism are well known: morality based on a ''categorical imperative''[15] reflecting a practical reason that finds benevolent motives unnecessary;[16] morality identified as rationality imposed on humans by the terms of their existence;[17] the notion of ''duty'' exalted as the fundamental moral concept; and the universality of moral judgments founded on the impersonal equality of humans.[18]

For our purposes it is not necessary to explain and critique fully the details of Kantianism. Instead, I will extract one of Kant's most powerful ideas, the inherent value of human subjects, and show how that ideal provides a salutary supplement to radical contractualism. Although Kant's theory is rarely accepted in its entirety, his veneration of individual human dignity resonates strongly in the Western moral tradition.

One way of supplementing libertarianism is to incorporate the Kantian principle that ''it is morally wrong for persons to treat others merely as a means to their own ends.'' Kant's maxim suggests that individuals are culpable if they objectify their victims: if they treat others as mere objects or tools to be manipulated and used for the users' own purposes. One of the worst acts that one person can inflict upon another is to recognize and treat the other as something less than the other really is: to recognize the other not as an end, not as an equal subject of experience. Arguably, treating important attributes constitutive of human personality as if they were mere commodities susceptible to market transactions is one example of exploitation in this broad sense.

Kant uses his maxim to defend a conventionalist account of sexual morality: sex without love is wrongful commodification; marital commitment is necessary for licit sex; and uses of sexuality for unnatural purposes are crimes against human nature. His explanations of these three positions merit attention.

Sex without love is wrongful commodification because it objectifies humans: "A love that springs merely from sexual impulse cannot be love at all, but only an appetite. Human love is good-will, affection, promoting the happiness of others and finding joy in their happiness. . . . Sexual love [on the other hand] makes of the loved person an Object of appetite; as soon as that appetite has been stilled, the person is cast aside as one casts away a lemon which has been sucked dry."[19] Kant identifies the wrongness of such objectification with the denial of inherent human value: "As soon as a person becomes an Object of appetite for another, all motives of moral relationship cease to function, because an Object for another a person becomes a thing and can be treated and used as such by every one."[20] Underlying Kant's identification of sex without love as wrongful commodification is his strikingly negative perception of the value of sexuality as such. He conjures images of avaricious, predatory males and passive, victimized females who engage in sex because of uncontrolled inclinations and needs.[21]

We can redeem sexuality and preserve precious human dignity only by recognizing restraints on our behavior. Humans are not free to treat their bodies as commodities because human bodies are not property, they are part of human selves: "The underlying moral principle is that man is not his own property and cannot do with his body what he will. The body is part of the self; in its togetherness with the self it constitutes the person; a man cannot make of his person a thing."[22] Kant concludes that we are not merely self-interested parties who negotiate under conditions of full libertarian freedom; instead, we are all bound by the constraints of rationality and, thus, morality. Accordingly, the presence of fully informed, mutual consent is insufficient to establish the moral permissibility of sexual behavior: "A man is not at his own disposal. He is not entitled to sell a limb, not even one of his teeth. But to allow one's person for profit to be used by another for the satisfaction of sexual desire, to make of oneself an Object of demand, is to dispose over oneself as over a thing and to make of oneself a thing on which another satisfies his appetite, just as he satisfies his hunger upon a steak."[23]

For Kant, sexuality can atone for its pursuit of the satisfaction of desire only by taking place under special circumstances: "The sole condition on which we are free to make use of our sexual desire depends upon the right to dispose over the person as a whole—over the welfare and happiness and generally over all the circumstances of that person."[24] Kant suggests that two people can efface the wrongful commodification inherent in sex and thereby redeem their own humanity only by mutually exchanging "rights to their whole person." The implication is that a deep, abiding relationship of the requisite sort ensures that sexual activity is not separated from personal interaction which honors individual human dignity: "But how am I to obtain these rights over the whole person? Only by giving that person the same rights over the whole of myself. This happens only in marriage. Matrimony is an agreement between two persons by which they grant each other equal reciprocal rights, each of them undertaking to surrender the whole of their person to the other with a complete right of disposal over it."[25]

Now, talk about the "complete right of disposal" over the person of another seems peculiar. Normally, we speak of "disposing" only when talking about property or things. So how can the mutual right of disposal over the other restore the moral permissibility of sex?

> If I yield myself completely to another and obtain the person of the other in return, I win myself back; I have given myself up as the property of another, but in turn I take that other as my property, and so win myself back again in winning the person whose property I have become. In this way the two persons become a unity of will. Whatever good or ill, joy or sorrow befall either of them, the other will share in it. Thus sexuality leads to a union of human beings, and in that union alone its [morally permissible] exercise is possible.[26]

Although Kant's talk about giving oneself up as property and winning oneself back as a person by taking the other as property is distasteful and too reminiscent of mutual exploitation, his major point is a classic one: Mutual devotion ensures respect for personal dignity.

Although he regards all sex without marriage as a transgression of sound reason, Kant identifies specifically three types of sex acts as crimes against nature: "Uses of sexuality which are contrary to natural instinct and to animal nature are [crimes against nature]." First, he calls masturbation an "abuse of the sexual faculty without any object, the exercise of the faculty in the complete absence of an object of sexuality. The practice is contrary to the ends of humanity and even opposed to animal nature. By it man sets aside his person and degrades himself below the level of animals."[27]

Second, he stigmatizes homosexuality as "contrary to the ends of humanity; for the end of humanity in respect of sexuality is to preserve the species without debasing the person; but in this instance the species is not being preserved . . . but the person is set aside, the self is degraded below the level of the animals, and humanity is dishonored."[28]

Third, he labels bestiality an act that "degrades mankind below the level of animals, for no animal turns in this way from its own species. All [sex crimes against nature] degrade human nature to a level below that of animal nature and make man unworthy of his humanity. He no longer deserves to be a person."[29]

Kant generates his conclusions on sexual ethics from his general maxim about human objectification and commodification, a supplementary view of what is necessary for the integrity of the self, and a firm conviction that humans lack the rightful authority to negotiate contractual terms that include human constitutive attributes. He is, however, often under the mystifying spell of a false dilemma we earlier unmasked: either the libertine who values sex inherently for pleasure and who assiduously evades all concern for others, or the chaste practitioner of sex only where full marital commitment is antecedently in place. He thus fails to recognize sexual relationships that fall short of mutual surrendering of "the whole of one's person to the other with a complete right of disposal over it," yet retain reciprocity of concern and respect. Moreover, his portrayal of the impermissibility of contracting about human constitutive attributes consists only of repeated assertions that such bartering reduces the self to a thing, necessarily severs the bodily from the integrated whole person, runs contrary to human nature, and thereby constitutes wrongful commodification. Kant relentlessly pounds home these themes by reiterating them in conclusory fashion.

Numerous objections can be raised to Kant's conclusions. First, the vast differences between contracting to permit someone to cut off one's arm for a fee and agreeing to engage in nonmarital sex with another: the former is a permanent physical mutilation which is reparable only by artificial limb, the latter, depending on the circumstances, need not cause permanent physiological or psychological damage; the former precludes, or renders more difficult, a host of subsequent human activities that require a full set of limbs, the latter, depending on the circumstances, need not be accompanied by deleterious consequences; thus the former has a finality about it, in terms of future activities and permanent loss, that the latter usually lacks. (Here I have waived an appeal to the libertarian principle that, in the final analysis, we *do* have the moral freedom to barter our limbs.) Accordingly, it is not clear that nonmarital sex, like limb-selling, is wrongful commodification.

Kant, of course, would not be swayed by my appeal to the consequences of the respective acts. He views nonmarital sex as inherently, not merely instrumentally, wrong. But on what can he base his position? Apparently on his notion of the human self. He distinguishes the empirical self from the transcendental self. The empirical self belongs to the sensible world and is known by introspection and through determination by the laws of nature. The transcendental self, however, embodies the human will, which is free from determination by empirical causes and which submits only to moral laws founded solely on reason. These moral laws ultimately determine, among other things, conclusions on sexual ethics.

These moral laws are themselves drawn from Kant's categorical imperative. But the categorical imperative historically has been chastised as form without content: an abstract formulation that cannot yield substantive moral conclusions without a specific, antecedent moral vision. Accordingly, it is reasonable to view Kant's categorical imperative as the moral precursor to Rawls's political original position: a device that cannot justify our basic moral judgments, because to generate conclusions it must presuppose such judgments.

If this analysis is correct, then Kant has not established persuasively his conclusions on sexual ethics. We are thus free to admire

Kant's salutary effect on radical contractualism, yet disagree with his portrayal of sexual ethics. Surely Kant strikes the correct note with his paeans of praise to the irreducibility of humans, the need for reciprocity, the importance of self-respect, and the commitment to abrogate exploitation. Such convictions will lead us to search for a sexual ethic which is Kantian in structure but which strays somewhat from Kant's specific moral conclusions on sexual behavior.

KANTIANISM WITHOUT KANT

Over fifteen years ago, I sketched a sexual ethic that embodied such aspirations.[30] This position acknowledged explicitly that the morality of sexual activities is evaluated by the same rules and principles generally relevant for assessing human actions. There was no attempt to conflate the domains of the "moral" and "prudent": to claim that an act is morally acceptable does not imply that it is advisable to pursue. That is, the morality of an action is not the only criterion we should use when deciding whether to pursue it. An act may be morally permissible but strategically unsound and ill-advised because it is not in a person's best long-term interests, or because it is offensive to our tastes, or because it distracts us from more worthy endeavors.

Starting from the Kantian maxim that "it is morally wrong for someone to treat another merely as a means to his ends," I argued that when we engage in sex this maxim is even more important because paramount feelings, desires, and drives are involved. Kant's maxim does not preclude treating others as means to our ends, because, after all, we often require the cooperation of others to fulfill our goals. It is not morally permissible, however, to treat others *merely* as a means to our goals by regarding them as inferior subjects of experience.

The next stage of the argument portrayed sexual interactions as contractual. That we engage in sex is, in part, a recognition that we are not self-sufficient. Sex may be seen as a voluntary agreement by the parties to satisfy the expectations of each other. As such, reciprocity is at the core of sex. When two people voluntarily consent to a sexual liaison, they create mutual obligations based on their respective needs and expectations. We interact with others sexually in order to fulfill certain desires that we cannot fulfill by ourselves (e.g., reproductive urges, desire for pleasure, yearning for love and intimacy, longing for validation by others, and the need for security, as well as less laudatory drives such as aggression, submission, and domination).

The final stage of the argument noted that promise breaking, deception, and harming are paradigm cases of immorality. Compelling special circumstances may in particular cases vitiate the wrongfulness of these actions, but we assume the burden of persuasion when we claim that in a specific situation lying, for example, is morally permissible. If it is true that sex implicates contractual relationships, then any failure to satisfy the terms of the agreement is, other things being equal, morally wrong.

The argument seemingly resonated warmly in libertarian bosoms. But Kant's maxim requires that we recognize the important insight that eluded libertarians: contracts are not morally self-validating. Thus the apparently voluntary consent of the parties is insufficient to establish moral merit. One's choices can be distorted by a host of exploitative dimensions: wrongfully taking advantage of another's limited alternatives, desperate situation, or dire needs; manipulating another into consent through use of unequal bargaining power; and undermining the informed consent of another through economic coercion. My approach to sexual ethics suggested these paradigms as partially constitutive of "exploitation" broadly defined as "treating someone as a mere means." Thus, after we determine the existence of a voluntarily formed contract, there is always a further question to be asked: Are its terms fair, and were they transacted without exploitation? Under this rubric, sex is morally impermissible if and only if it involves deception, promise breaking, illicit force, or exploitation.

Philosophers, trained in the art of counterexample and reflexively salivating at the prospect of unsettling "if and only if" formulations, are drawn irresistibly to numerous questions: What if a sex act met the tests of the analysis but, if consummated, would cause serious and irreversible harm to a child? What if a sex act met the tests of the analysis but, because of extraordinary circumstances, would cause social upheaval that would adversely affect numerous innocent third parties? Given that deception, promise breaking, and even force and exploitation are morally permissible in certain carefully circumscribed nonsexual situations, why is that not so in sexual situations? Does the analysis truly want to insist truculently that deception, promise breaking, force, and exploitation are *never* permitted in morally licit sex? And that their absence *ensures* the morally permissibility of sex?

Although it is framed in philosophers' favorite stylized jargon of necessary and sufficient conditions, the analysis morally evaluated only sex acts taken in themselves. It did not purport to consider all other morally relevant features of the choices at issue: third-party effects, wider social consequences, and extraordinary contexts. The problem I faced when composing the essay was a familiar one to philosophers dealing with applied ethics. Moral issues are exceedingly complicated and ineffable; they can almost never be captured in all of their complexity by a single principle. Even mediocre philosophers can imagine possible examples where, because of extraordinary circumstances or third party effects, a principle framed in terms of necessary and sufficient conditions must crumble. But to avoid entirely principles framed in terms of necessary and sufficient conditions enfeebles moral philosophy.

As a result, my approach to sexual ethics invited numerous criticisms, some of which I was aware of at the time I wrote. For example, some readers cringed at the coldness of the approach. Why is the realm of contract applicable to such an intimate area? Unlike business contracts, sexual contracts are rarely spelled out or subject to protracted negotiations. How do we know when a contract is in place and what reasonable expectations can be formed?

Imagine the following exchange of letters by Mary and John, a pair of prospective paramours.

Dear John,

Although I aspire to self-sufficiency, experience has confirmed what I have long suspected: the presence of sexual drives whose nature requires the participation of another for their satisfaction. We have known each other for a time sufficient for me to extend to you the following offer.

Pursuant to my need to satisfy erotic urges, I hereby request your participation in an act of sexual intercourse on Friday, July 26, in my bedroom. As consideration for your participation, I promise to satisfy your similar urges.

I hope that you will accept the terms enunciated herein. Please respond no later than Wednesday, July 24, after which time my offer expires.

Yours in lust,
Mary

Dear Mary,

I have received your offer and, after serious review of its terms, find it too vague. To wit, you have failed to specify the nature and length of the sexual transaction at issue. Will our intercourse be no-frills, such as the "missionary position," or will it include acrobatic positions? Will oral or anal sex be part of our transaction? Will we spend the night together or part company immediately following the consummation of the terms of our contract? Will I be extended an option for future contractual arrangements? Will my acceptance of your offer in any way limit my freedom to contract sexually with other parties? Should either of us be dissatisfied with the other's effort or success in fulfilling the contract, what avenues of regress will be available?

I know, Mary, that we hold ourselves generally to high moral standards and that we share a libertarian-Kantian approach to sexual ethics. You will therefore understand that reasonable expectations are paramount in sexual exchanges. Lacking explicit answers to my queries, I am unable to form the requisite reasonable expectations. Accordingly, although my passions are aflame and my yearning for you is profound, I must reject your offer as presently constituted. I am, of course, open to further negotiations.

Yours in moral sex,
John

This exchange of letters may seem both peculiar and amusing. These reactions stem from the seeming inappropriateness of the correspondence. Doesn't that inappropriateness suggest that sex is not a contractual arrangement from the outset?

Not really. Although sexual contracts are not as formal or explicit as corporate agreements, we are guided by the concept of reasonable expectation. Where important doubts are present, parties should proceed cautiously and may ask specific questions about the other's expectations: when in doubt do not overestimate what the other party has offered and seek a more explicit overture if appropriate. Such questions need not be posed as formally or clumsily as John's missive to Mary. The contractual nature of sex emerges from the requirements of mutual consent and satisfaction of mutual needs and desires. Although prized feelings of intimacy are often involved that render the consenting parties emotionally vulnerable, this may illustrate only that sexual contracts are the most important agreements we make.

Another misgiving about my analysis was that one could engage in morally permissible sex, as defined by the applicable standard, yet not serve one's long-term best interests. Doesn't the radical separation of prudence from morality strike a false note? How can sex be morally permissible yet contrary to our best long-term interests and happiness?

Although we assume that always acting morally engenders a measure of happiness, the connection is not guaranteed. Achieving happiness is hostage, among other things, to a variety of physical and material dimensions (e.g., health, satisfaction of certain biological needs, and a sufficient amount of good luck) that moral action in itself does not provide. Thus the concepts of "morality" and "happiness" are not necessarily coextensive.

However, even with the qualifications and responses discussed above, my basic analysis of sexual ethics was incomplete and troubling. First, "exploitation" is not a self-executing concept. The content of expressions such as "use another as a mere means," "commodify illegitimately constitutive attributes of self," and "objectify another" must be supplied by a more general social and political theory. Critics are correct in thinking that libertarian-Kantians use such phrases too often as talismanic incantations whose magical meanings are intuitively obvious to all. Certainly, the position advocated here considers the following cases illustrative of exploitation: taking advantage of another's limited alternatives, desperate situation, or dire needs; manipulating another into consent through use of unequal power; and undermining the voluntary or informed consent of another through deception or various forms of physical or economic coercion. But even these explanations of "exploitation" need further specification. Moreover, when arguing that one party has taken advantage of another, advocates of this approach must make fine distinctions between "justified persuasion," "unjustified manipulation," and "implicit economic coercion." Arguably, any two parties will always be unequal in rhetorical skill, argumentative technique, and personal charisma. Are these attributes the source of inherent domination and ideological distortion, or merely the legitimate instruments of rational persuasion?

Furthermore, my libertarian-Kantian analysis conjured the specter of abstract bargainers rather than real people. It lacked attention to concrete social reality and actual power-differentials in our society. There are at least two aspects of this problem. First, libertarian-Kantians analyze the behavior of the sexual parties irrespective of gender. This gender-neutral analysis obscures the power disparities between men and women and the often different meanings sex embodies for them. The effect is to silence women's voices and to marginalize their ideological perspectives. Second, libertarian-Kantians analyze the behavior of sexual parties irrespective of class. This class-neutral analysis obscures economic and social disparities between the relatively affluent and the relatively disadvantaged. The effect here is to legitimate implicitly current social contexts and to accept as necessary and natural the economic, sexual, and familial arrangements in place.

These difficulties compel consideration of more general issues about social relationships. As possible antidotes to the maladies of class-neutral and gender-neutral libertarian-Kantian analysis, we now turn to Marxism and feminist theory.

PART 2
THE LEFTIST CRITIQUE
Politics, Economics, and the Depravity of Conventional Wisdom

5

THE PROSTITUTION IN CAPITALIST MARRIAGE
Marxism

Marxism criticizes other approaches to sexual ethics on the basis of an analysis of the nature of personal relationships and denies the possibility of genuinely equal sexual relationships in the kind of society prevalent in Western capitalism.

Classical Marxism conceives the bourgeois family as founded on the unremitting basis of capitalism: private gain. The rhetoric of commodities pervades the family, as women, lacking access to the public sphere, are forced to link themselves to men for financial reasons. Accordingly, sex *within* capitalist marriage is viewed as a form of prostitution. Only the destruction of the capitalist system and the establishment of communism can redeem sexuality by providing the requisite conditions of economic and social equality.

Marxism's examination of the formative environment of "uncoerced" agreements proves an antidote to some of the excesses of radical contractualism. Nevertheless, I argue that Marxism embodies an overly sanguine picture of sex within the proletarian class, an astounding naiveté regarding the phenomenon of nonmonogamous sex and its relation to economics, and a crude reductionism which stubbornly traces all oppression to an economic genesis.

SEXUAL ETHICS

The classical Marxist critique of Western sexual relationships is sketched by Karl Marx (1818–1883) and Friedrich Engels (1820–1895) in their *Communist Manifesto* and in Engels's *The Origin of the Family, Private Property, and the State*. The Marxist critique observes that in bourgeois families wives provided cheap domestic labor and socially necessary tasks (e.g., care of children and the elderly) and were expected to produce identifiable and legitimate heirs for the orderly transfer of capitalist property, while husbands provided lodging and board in return. This exchange presumably explained the need for conjugal fidelity on the part of women and provided an economic basis for the existence of male prerogatives within the family.

> On what foundation is the present family, the bourgeois family, based? On capital, on private gain. In its completely developed form this family exists only among the bourgeoisie. . . . The bourgeois family will vanish . . . with the vanishing of capital. . . . The bourgeois sees in his wife a mere instrument of production.[1] . . . Remove the economic considerations that now force women to submit to the customary disloyalty of men, and you will place women on an equal footing with men. All present experiences prove that this will tend much more strongly to make men truly monogamous. . . . The supremacy of man in marriage is simply the consequence of his economic superiority and will fall with the abolition of the latter.[2]

Thus, classical Marxism conceives the bourgeois family as founded on the unremitting ground of capitalism: private gain. Because bourgeois women in a capitalist society were excluded from the public workplace, they were forced to tie themselves financially to men. The emotional and personal attachments seemingly at play in marital sex in fact reduce to a series of commercial interactions where purportedly reciprocal contractual benefits are exchanged. Accordingly, the rhetoric of commodities pervades even the inner, private sanctum of capitalist life.

> Monogamy arose through the concentration of considerable wealth in one hand—a man's hand—and from the endeavor to bequeath this wealth to the children of this man to the exclusion of all others. This necessitated monogamy on the woman's, but not on the man's part . . . the impending social revolution will reduce this whole care of inheritance to a minimum by changing . . . the means of production into social property . . . with the transformation of the means of production into collective property the monogamous family ceases to be the economic

unit of society. The private household changes to a social industry. The care and education of children becomes a public matter.[3]

Engels retained an overly romantic vision of the proletarian marriages of his time, sanguinely insisting that such unions escaped the crass commercialism and inequality of bourgeois families. He tended to ignore causes of oppression that were not directly and obviously attributable to economic sources. Because material inequalities were not striking in proletarian families, the amount of private property was insufficient to promote deep interests in inheritance, and proletarian women often worked outside the home, Engels concluded that "the material foundations of male dominance have ceased to exist [in proletarian families]."[4]

His disdain for bourgeois marriage, however, recognized few bounds. He sometimes described women's role in such marriages as akin to slavery and thus a rank below even the downtrodden proletariat wage laborer: "This [bourgeois] marriage of convenience often enough turns into the crassest prostitution—sometimes on both sides, but much more generally on the part of the wife, who differs from the ordinary courtesan only in that she does not hire out her body, like a wageworker, on piecework, but sells it into slavery once for all."[5]

Here Engels turns the Christian argument on its head: sex *within* the bourgeois family is a form of prostitution (in a pejorative sense) and is thus immoral because its genesis is the economic exploitation of the deprived by the powerful and its result is the commodification of the attributes constitutive of women's innermost selves: "What is considered a crime for women and entails grave legal and social consequences for them, is considered honorable for men.[6] . . . By changing all things into commodities, [capitalist production] dissolved all inherited and traditional relations and replaced time hallowed custom and historical right by purchase and sale, by the 'free contract.' "[7]

Classical Marxism protests, however, that in a capitalist society the notion of "informed consent" is contaminated by the underlying need for economic survival. Reports of "mutual agreement" and "reciprocal benefit" may be illusions emanating from the false consciousness[8] of capitalist materialism.

In order to make contracts, people must have full freedom over their persons, actions and possessions. They must furthermore be on terms of mutual equality. . . . Marriage according to bourgeois conception was a contract, a legal business affair, and the most important one at that, because it decided the weal and woe of body and spirit of two beings for life. At that time the agreement was formally voluntary. . . . But it was only too well known how this consent was obtained and who were really the contracting parties [the families of the respective parties].[9]

The solution to the maladies of the bourgeois family is the socialization of housework, the full inclusion of women in the public arena, and, most important, the dismantling of the capitalist framework which nurtures class division and economic exploitation[10]: "The full freedom of marriage can become general only after all minor economic considerations, that still exert such a powerful influence on the choice of a mate for life, have been removed by the abolition of capitalist production and of the property relations created by it. Then no other motive will remain but mutual fondness."[11] Engels cannot describe fully the details of sexual relations in a communist society, but he does underscore the preconditions of truly moral sex:

a race of men who never in their lives have had any occasion for buying with money or other economic means of power the surrender of a woman; a race of women who have never had any occasion for surrendering to any man for any reason but love, or for refusing to surrender to their lover from fear of economic consequences. . . . They will follow their own practice and fashion their own public opinion about the individual practice of every person—only this and nothing more.[12]

Engels, however, at times gives the clear impression that people under a communist structure would not be prone to the promiscuity, adultery, and sexual perversions endemic in capitalist regimes: "Since sexlove is exclusive by its very nature—although this exclusiveness is [under capitalism] realized for women alone—marriage founded on sexlove must be monogamous."[13] Because under communism marriage will be founded only on sexlove, it follows that relations will be monogamous because marriage will be founded on pure motivations. Clearly, Engels betrays here an incredible naiveté regarding the phenomenon of love and sexuality. Even under conditions of full economic and social equality and in the presence of mutual "sexlove," neither monogamy nor fidelity is fully ensured. Moreover, talk of the natural exclusivity of sexlove suggests an essentialism[14] that Marxists otherwise diligently avoid and stridently berate when invoked by non-Marxists.

Perhaps we should not make too much of this. It is probably better to downplay Engels's essentialist leanings and to underscore his willingness to concede the open possibilities of sexual relations under communism.[15] In any event, we can fairly describe a classical Marxist approach to sexual relations: sex is morally permissible only if the parties share a measure of equality, are not motivated by (conscious or subconscious) economic needs, and do not wrongly commodify their persons—all of which in turn require the elimination of capitalism.

EXPLOITATION AND SEXUALITY

How does Marxism's analysis of exploitation[16] apply to sexuality? Will eliminating the economic pressures enveloping capitalism ensure that sexual relations will be free and uncoerced? Within capitalism can two people have nonexploitative sexual relations if they are economic equals? Is the possibility of wrongful commodification eliminated once capitalist exchange disintegrates?

Presumably, Marxists suggest that once capitalism falls, or at least by the time communism is in place, many currently fashionable employment contracts and sexual relations will disappear.[17] As the coercive economic forces which underlie such agreements crumble, so too will the agreements themselves. Thus, Marxists take the relevant economic forces as necessary conditions for, among other things, the exercise of certain disapproved sexual relations such as prostitution. The elimination of necessary conditions must, therefore, imply the jettisoning of disapproved sexual relations. The problem with this interpretation is twofold: first, it may saddle Marxism with a substantive (ahistorical?) theory of human nature, which is required for Marxism to project confidently specific human activities once capitalism has evaporated; and second, it reveals Marxism's stark reductionist tendency to trace all social ills to economic causes.

Perhaps a better interpretation would take capitalist economic forces as sufficient conditions for those sexual relations of which Marxists disapprove. Under this interpretation, the presence of capitalist relations of production ensures that certain sexual maladies will occur, but the elimination of capitalism does not guarantee the disappearance of disapproved sexual relations: at the end of capitalism the forms that sexual relations will take is up for grabs. This interpretation comports better with the openness to human possibilities often displayed by Marxism, but has the disadvantage of domesticating somewhat Marxism's critical bite. Under this interpretation, capitalist economics cannot be identified antecedently as the sole cause of dysfunctional sexual relations, nor can socialist relations of production be identified as the magical elixir ensuring cure. This interpretation salvages, however, the Marxist claim that capitalism must be eliminated if economically free and psychologically salutary sex is to be possible.

But what can we do about sex within capitalism? Suppose Vittoria and Dominic are economic equals, both attorneys who hold comparable rank, experience, ability, earnings, and prestige. From a Marxist perspective, both are capitalists of a sort and thus exploiters, and both are attorneys and thus types of economic parasites. But is Dominic an exploiter of Vittoria? Is Vittoria an exploiter of Dominic?

Most non-Marxists would say, of course, that we do not have enough facts to answer adequately such questions. Lacking information about general societal conditions and the specifics of the parties' personalities and dealings, any proffered answers are lame. As for the Marxist, she might be tempted to say that the apparent absence of exploitive economic relations at least holds open the possibility of uncoerced, thus permissible, sex. After all, Engels's cheerful portrayal of proletarian sexual relations was founded on the alleged economic equality of the participants.

But Dominic and Vittoria are not members of the proletarian class, and the answer is not so clear in their case. Their economic equality is not the same as absence of economic power and coercion, as is presumably the case in proletarian relations. Dominic and Vittoria both have a measure of economic power that members of the proletariat lack. Do their comparable economic powers in effect cancel each other out and render their relationships coercion free? Or do two strong economic powers multiply the possibilities for exploitation? Is economic equality paramount for uncoerced sexual relations? Or is absence of economic power?

Our ability to answer is complicated by the fact that Engels's excoriation of bourgeois marriage is so encompassing and his appreciation of proletarian marriage so naive. Moreover, in the capitalism of his day we would find few Vittorias with economic power and influence comparable to their male partners. With all such disclaimers in mind, I prefer to interpret Marxism as conceding the *possibility* of uncoerced sex between Vittoria and Dominic as long as they truly share a measure of equality, are not motivated by economic needs vis à vis each other, and do not wrongly commodify their persons by treating each other as mere instruments of mutual benefit. This interpretation, to be sure, reneges on the stipulation that the elimination of capitalism is required for the possibility of uncoerced, free sexual relations. Under an advanced form of capitalism unknown to Marx and Engels, however, a form in which some women have comparable economic power to their male partners, there is the possibility for nonexploitive sexual relations.[18]

In any event, the classic Marxist critique of bourgeois sexual relations depends heavily on the notions of exploitation and commodification. It is clear that Marxists take libertarian consent and mutual use as insufficient to vitiate exploitation. Libertarian notions of consent ignore pernicious class divisions and economic inequalities, while mutual use—each party knowingly and reciprocally using the other for personal benefit—multiplies, rather than erases, impermissible exploitation. The Marxist aspiration to a communism which transforms and transcends the capitalist polarities of individuality and community precludes the use of one human by another.

RECIPROCITY AND MUTUALITY

It is therefore somewhat misleading to talk of Marxist sexual analysis in terms of reciprocal exchanges of benefits. Reciprocity connotes equal sacrifices or transfer of equal benefits. As such, reciprocity invokes a type of quantification that conjures images of libertarian contractualism. Marxist sexual relations are better portrayed as presupposing equality as an antecedent condition of mutuality, where the parties give and accept what they need without regard for the aggregate amount of benefits and burdens exchanged.[19]

Pious paeans to mutuality must always be carefully scrutinized, however, because where inequalities precede a relationship, the call for mutuality almost always results in the subordination of the socially disadvantaged party. That is why full social equality must be a prerequisite for mutuality, a prerequisite that is obviously a major obstacle. Still, mutuality may well embody our highest hopes for sexual relations.[20]

By highlighting social context, Marxism astutely points out that sexual relations must not be abstracted from the totality of our lives. Marxism portrays the ills of sexual relations as resulting not from wrongful acts by individuals, but from the political and social institutions allied with a particular economic structure, capitalism. But the doctrine tends to focus myopically on the relations of economic production in a society. Perhaps the most glaring omission in Marxism's analysis of sexual relations is one that generally pervades its argument: the failure to recognize clearly that economic class division is not the sole source of human oppression. By reducing the cause of all social maladies to wrongful productive relations and prescribing the transformation of capitalist economic arrangements as the omnipotent cure, Marxism leaves itself vulnerable to charges that it ignores other sources of human oppression such as racism, sexism, religious intolerance, and age discrimination. If, as one might suspect, these various forms of oppression cannot all be traced to one specific cause, then it is unlikely that economic reforms, which may be at the root of some forms, can remedy all social ills. Thus, the magic elixir of political revolution may be less dynamic than Marxists imagine.

Moreover, our observation of the actual practices of those countries purporting to be socialist confirms that Marxism's crude reductionism is faulty. Socialist regimes in practice have fallen far short of gender-equal utopias.[21] In this same vein, Marxism ignored the sexual division of labor: the biological function of women as childbearers and their social function as childrearers. The sexual division of labor is reflected in the traditional distinction between the public sphere of important social activity, the realm of male prerogatives; and the private sphere of essential but less highly regarded and compensated family activity, the realm of female performance. The abolition of private ownership of the means of production may thus be insufficient to liberate women from male oppression.[22] Accordingly, some feminists, denying the analogy of husband-wife to employer-employee, would argue that the primary source of women's oppression is not capitalism, but men. These thinkers highlight the differences in the alienation and exploitation accompanying traditional Western marriage and the alienation and exploitation accompanying capitalist employment.[23]

SEXUALITY AND WAGE LABOR

This argument raises an interesting question: Is sexual activity different from other human activity such as labor? By assimilating the exploitation and alienation accompanying the alleged prostitution in bourgeois marriage and the institution of prostitution generally, to the exploitation and alienation accompanying wage labor under capitalism, classical Marxism suggests that the wrongness afflicting sexual relations is the same as that afflicting employment relations. Lacking control of their working conditions and having limited, equally debilitating economic options, women in bourgeois sexual relations and workers under capitalism are denied freedom. Lacking the freedom and creative control needed to realize their inherent value, they are subtly coerced to accept the terms set by the economically advantaged. Under such conditions, sexual relations and wage labor necessarily produce the hostile estrangement that defines alienation and the radically unequal allocation of value that characterizes exploitation. At least under capitalism, Marxists seem to conceive of sexual relations in much the same way they envision wage labor.

If my analysis is correct, then Marxists and libertarians paradoxically join forces. Both groups refuse to distinguish sexual relations from other human activities such as labor. Libertarians, in effect, permit the commodification of virtually everything as long as everyone's natural negative rights are respected. Marxists prohibit the commodification of virtually anything, because under capitalism certain classes lack the conditions of freedom. Libertarians perceive utopia as featuring a minimal noncoercive state which enforces limited security needs and polices violations of negative duties; under such perfect contractualist conditions we need not fear commodification, because transactions will reflect only free choices of individuals pursuing their life's aspirations. Marxists envision utopia as featuring material abundance and a minimal central authority; an extensive government is unnecessary, because conditions of scarcity, which engender social conflict, have evaporated and the means of economic production are owned collectively. Under such perfect creative conditions we need not fear commodification, because people will have no need to barter their persons or their labor; economic transactions will reflect collective deliberations by the producers themselves and personal choices will be uncontaminated by economic pressures. In a curious way, libertarians and Marxists, although defining their respective utopias in strikingly different ways, search for the same thing: the conditions under which truly free choice can flourish. Moreover, both are open to human possibilities: once conditions of free choice are in place, neither view prescribes the specific details of what humans would be like or what humans must seek.

It must be noted, however, that Marxism's counsel on the similarity between wage labor and sexual relations is not unambiguous. We have already seen several classical Marxist inclinations that can be used to argue that sex is ultimately different from wage labor: the essentialism that sanguinely predicts the end of promiscuity, adultery, and sexual perversions under communism; the economic analysis that allegedly explains the absence of "sexlove" among the bourgeois despite that class's preoccupation with sex; and the anticontractualism that systematically and constantly mocks libertarian principles and ideology. One could argue that rather than aligning themselves with the libertarian principle of free choice and ideology of pure process, Marxists are better served by arguing that under capitalist relations of production, sexual relations are no different from employment transactions, but that under communism, sexual relations will be different from labor because in a classless society the true nature of sexlove and intimacy can flourish. Such a position would underscore that sexual malfunctions—prostitution, widespread infidelity, perversions—emerge from the economic malfunctions of capitalism. Once these economic contradictions are soothed, then eliminated by communism, sexual relations will thrive and manifest their inherent qualities of mutuality and love.

Although such an approach may be available, Marxism would be well advised to ignore it. The essentialism that underlies the "sex is different from other activities" approach is a two-edged sword: on one hand, it permits Marxists to label certain sexual acts as antecedently impermissible, as automatically stigmatized before knowing the other details of communist society. This has the advantage of currying favor with those who, for whatever reasons, are firmly convinced that prostitution, adultery, and promiscuity are inherently wrong. Thus, it tends to contrast the mutuality and love of communism with the crassness and pervasive commodification of capitalism.

On the other hand, the "sex is different from other activities" approach coalesces uneasily with other strengths of Marxist doctrine. First, the approach blemishes Marxism's general inclination to accept radically open human possibilities, to avoid blueprints and prescriptions for human activity under communism, and to luxuriate in human creativity under conditions of economic freedom. Second, the essentialism of the approach, with its substantive conception of the inherent nature of sexuality, repudiates Marxism's tendency to embrace only a "thin" theory of human nature, a notion of "species-being" which merely expounds the centrality of creativity and uncoerced labor for human flourishing. Third, Marxism's notion of species-being appeals to the constitutive quality of human labor, its integral connection to human self-identity. For Marxism, if anything is a nonfungible, constitutive attribute of self, it is work, not sexuality.[24] Thus any appeal to the unique, constitutive character of sex, an appeal often made by the "sex is different from other activities" approach, may run afoul of Marxism's emphasis on the primacy of uncoerced labor for human identity.

Fourth, although the "sex is the same as other activities" approach may paradoxically place Marxism on the same path as libertarianism, as we have previously observed, the "sex is different from other activities" approach paradoxically locates Marxism on the same path as political conservatism: adherence to essentialism about sex, commitment to the inherent impermissibility of certain sexual acts, reliance on the necessity of specific types of human relations, belief in carefully circumscribed, proper function(s) of sex, and thus dedication to the limitation of free sexual expression.

Fifth, those who argue that sex is different from other activities often appeal to certain features of sexual relations, such as the linkage of genitalia or other body parts, that distinguish sex from wage labor. Yet such a distinction is not as clear as it seems. For example, Alan Soble argues that "the observation that bodies come into their most intimate contact during sexual activity might even have suggested to [Marxists] that "sex is different." This observation, however, is shortsighted. Breathing the air in coal mines involves an "invasion" of the body, and there are services that involve intimate insertion of body parts: dentistry and medicine (gynecology and proctology). The Marxist cannot in this way drive a wedge between sexual activity and ordinary labor."[25]

But accepting the libertarian "sex is the same as other activities" approach is also accompanied by at least three problems. The first is that Marxism, although it retains its ability to excoriate capitalism for its commodification fetishes, renounces the inherent impermissibility of certain sex acts and thus relinquishes some of the power of its attack on specific sexual expressions within capitalism. Moreover, Marxism cannot antecedently preclude prostitution, promiscuity, and adultery from communist society. This problem is mollified, however, by the Marxist contention that communist society defeats general conditions of exploitation and alienation. The second problem is that the "sex is the same" approach nurtures Marxism's unfortunate inclination to reduce the causes of all oppression to economic sources, thus obscuring the (at least partially) noneconomic genesis of racism, sexism, and other wrongful discriminations. This problem is ameliorated somewhat by a conceptual possibility open for some Marxists: retain the "sex is the same" approach but concede that not all oppression has fully economic origins. The identification of sexual with other malfunctions need not be linked to their allegedly common origins. The point here would be that sex is the same as other activities not necessarily because its distortion can be traced to the same social causes as other activities, but because sexual relations have no inherent structure and do not necessarily make special claims on our personal identities. The third, and far more serious, problem is that Marxism severs its link to the numerous feminists who subscribe to the "sex is different from other activities" approach.

Many feminists distinguish sexual from other activities, including wage labor, on the centrality of sex to our identity. For example, Carole Pateman argues that "sexual services, that is to say, sex and sexuality, are constitutive of the body in a way in which the counseling skills of the social worker are not. . . . Sexuality and the body are . . . integrally connected to conceptions of femininity and masculinity, and all these are constitutive of our individuality, our sense of self-identity."[26]

Feminists often claim that sexual acts, particularly those involving reproduction, are more fundamental to personal identity than nonreproductive labor, but this seems to beg the question. To say that reproductive acts are "closer to personhood"[27] or "considered more priceless"[28] or "engender more distress if lost"[29] than personal services contracted in ordinary wage labor is only to repeat in conclusory fashion precisely what must be proved. If what we do affects directly who we are, it is certainly arguable that the more enduring character of wage labor is more central and crucial to personal identity than temporary sexual activity.

Moreover, feminists must be cautious in invoking the inherent difference of reproductive activity. They must avoid resting their case on an overly sentimental view of motherhood and the maternal bonds that allegedly develop during the gestational period. Such a view would be especially ironic when advanced by feminists who otherwise ridicule the purported maternal instinct as merely a social artifact of male-dominated society.

I will return to this problem in later chapters. For now, it is enough to observe that the case for sex being an actively different from others because of features that are allegedly constitutive of human identity, though it has much initial appeal, is not easily established. Is reproductive activity accompanied by less chance of gender oppression than sexual activity generally? Is the connection women allegedly now make with sexuality and personal identity a necessary feature of human nature? Or is it a contingent feature of male-dominated society? Must sex be closer to personhood than wage labor?

When identifying Marxism with the "sex is the same as other activities" approach to sexual ethics, I have highlighted certain instincts it shares with libertarianism: openness to human possibilities once proper conditions of choice are in place, refusal to specify in full detail what humans must be like and what they must do under such conditions, and general respect for experimentation and innovation. These, combined with its commitment to a "thin" theory of human nature and to the primacy of labor, not sex, as constitutive of human identity, incline Marxism toward the "sex is the same as other activities" approach. But to say that Marxism requires the "sex is the same" approach overstates the case. We have already noted several passages from Engels, especially his veneration of the inherent qualities of "sexlove" and his optimistic, although tentative, predictions of sexual relations under communism, which can be used to support the "sex is different from other activities" approach. Thus my interpretation of Marxist sexual ethics on this issue reveals my tentative and contestable conviction that Marxism is better served by accepting the "sex is the same as other activities" approach, and my equally contestable judgment that the convergence of libertarianism and Marxism in certain important respects need not destroy the deeper uniqueness of either perspective. (Ultimately, I will argue that although sexual contracts are not necessarily and inherently different from ordinary wage labor agreements, the two types of commitments are contingently different for many of the reasons feminists cite.)

But we should not mask the quandaries and predicaments that clearly afflict Marxism. To those who lack antecedent political commitment to classical Marxist doctrine, the base–superstructure model seems fragile, the notion of false consciousness appears too malleable, and visions of a final society which transcends the conflict of individualism and community exhibit necessitarian illusions that Marxists themselves otherwise ridicule. Still, Marxism provides a mediating alternative to the harsh reductionism of libertarianism and to the abstractness of Kantianism. Marxism pours specificity into the general notions of exploitation and alienation, it demands that we examine concrete social reality when evaluating human relationships, and it jolts us into interrogating appeals to the consent of the underclasses.

Perhaps Marxism needs more subtlety in pressing such influences. Marxism replaces the contractualists' ersatz vision of abstract rational bargainers with its own faulty version of abstract class members respectively exploiting and being victimized. Marxism, while eluding the singlemindedness plaguing contractualists, succumbs to a different variety of reductionism: the translation of all oppression to an economic genesis. As such, Marxism requires an antidote for its own excesses.

Feminism, with its commitment to unraveling gender oppression, its conviction that not all domination has economic origins, and its counsel that preoccupation with class issues often obscures women's perspectives, merits fuller examination as a possible remedial influence.

6

THE POVERTY OF CONTRACT
Feminist Rejoinders to
the Status Quo

The feminist movement is richly diverse and has a long history. I will not try to chronicle that history or describe every strain of feminist thought, as such a task is beyond the scope of this work and has already been undertaken successfully by other writers.[1] Instead, I hope to adumbrate the philosophical framework, to highlight the spirit that animates feminism, and to consider seriously the challenges feminism launches against classical Western thought in the context of sexual ethics.

Despite much internal disagreement among feminists, some elements of a new sexual ethic emerge: sex is morally permissible only if the traditional roles of male dominance and female submission are absent, women are not politically victimized by their sexuality, and women have the capacity and real power to control access to and define themselves.

I argue that a man and a woman can be economically equal, but socially unequal—unequal in terms of political influence, prerogatives within the family, reproductive roles, and general social status. Thus, social inequalities, although often correlated to economic oppression, are neither reducible to nor defined by economic inequalities.

Moreover, I argue that heterosexuals can create their own liberating subcontexts even within a general social context that is seriously flawed. Thus, the general oppression of women as a class does not imply that all heterosexual relationships and sexual encounters are necessarily immoral.

Although a varied movement, feminism is vivified by several general themes: a deep suspicion of socially constructed gender roles, a demand for the full inclusion of women in the public sphere, a call for an end to power differentials between males and females, and a distrust of claims venerating current social practices as necessary or inevitable. At its most general level of classification, feminism is committed to ending the oppression of women. Feminism hopes to accomplish this by explaining the causes and raising our consciousness of women's subordination, and by exploring possible solutions and engaging in practical activity aimed at liberating women from political and social subjugation.

At the heart of these hopes and activities is feminism's firm conviction that political and social life is thoroughly permeated by a gender bias that invariably undermines the power of women as a class. As a precondition of accomplishing its practical task, feminism begins by focusing on the importance of women's experiences and the inability of much of traditional Western thought to account for those experiences. Indeed, feminists argue, mainstream (male) theorizing is inclined strongly to deny or marginalize women's personal narratives, particularly in two areas of special concern to women: motherhood and sexuality. Women, therefore, are often alienated because of the dissonance between their subjective experiences and dominant social theory and practice.

To sharpen feminism's general themes and manifest the currency of feminism's heterogeneity, I will concentrate on feminist responses to the following questions: What is human nature? What is women's oppression? What is the solution to women's oppression? What is an appropriate conception of sexual ethics?

In addressing these questions, I will avoid the usual labels affixed to feminist thinkers: liberal feminist, Marxist feminist, radical feminist, socialist feminist, existentialist feminist, psychoanalytic feminist, feminism unmodified, and so on. Although such labels provide efficient ways of referring to various feminist thinkers, they suffer at least three defects: the modifiers bear too much psychological and political baggage that often hinders fresh analytic assessment, the modifiers may suggest wrongly that feminism is merely derived from and parasitic on these other movements, and the obsession to categorize may itself be part of the larger social problem that feminists aspire to unsettle. Accordingly, I will address the relevant questions simply by presenting them in unadorned fashion and analyzing a variety of responses feminists have made.

IS THERE A WOMEN'S PERSPECTIVE?

Prior to examining the questions relevant to our inquiry on sexual ethics, we must consider another fundamental question: Is there a unique and irreducible "women's perspective"? Is there a "women's point of view" which can serve as a critical and external standpoint from which to evaluate the status quo?

I do not find the thesis that there is a "women's perspective" a helpful analytic instrument. On one hand, advocates of the thesis may intend only to highlight the ways women's voices and experiences have been hitherto marginalized, and even pushed off the page, in our culture. Moreover, the thesis may underscore the importance of certain reproductive and sexual phenomena experienced exclusively by women. This weak version of the feminist thesis is laudatory, indeed unassailable, but does not require the invocation of a mysterious "women's perspective." On the other hand, advocates may intend a stronger thesis: men and women are trapped in separate and unequal realities, incommensurable points of view that ensure radical conflict between the sexes. This strong thesis is uncommonly interesting, but thoroughly problematic.

First, the "women's perspective" implicitly demeans social, economic, ethnic, racial, and religious differences among women. By talking about women qua women, the strong thesis wrongly assumes that other differences among women are irrelevant.[2] Furthermore, feminists who brandish "women's perspective" often assume that they speak for all ("real") women, or all right-thinking and thus worthy women, or all politically correct women. This assumption is, ironically, redolent with the arrogance of the false imperialism that feminists otherwise accuse dominant men of embodying: an allegedly pernicious objectivism that mocks and trivializes contrasting viewpoints.

Second, the "women's perspective" is too facilely taken as self-ratifying: "men's perspective" is thoroughly contaminated with patriarchal aggression and domination, while "women's perspective" germinates from women's experiences and is thus purified and morally superior. Under this corollary, as Jean Grimshaw notes, the two perspectives are commensurable: "man's perspective" is morally self-invalidating, the mirror of patriarchal oppression, and "women's perspective" captures the moral ideal as it emanates from the experiences of the victim. This characterization may strike numerous critics as naively reductionist; even worse, it may need the support of an essentialism that proclaims that "women are somehow naturally virtuous and men naturally wicked."[3] Again, the irony is striking: feminists otherwise view appeals to essentialism as false metaphysics, and they observe that such appeals have traditionally served to disadvantage and oppress women.

Third, advocates of the "women's perspective" may backtrack to the incommensurability corollary: the different perspectives of the two sexes simply do not speak in the same tongue, hence veridical communication is impossible. But the incommensurability corollary is fragile in the face of political experiences between the sexes where communication does take place. Moreover, if we take incommensurability too seriously, we descend into false necessity: women and men can never speak the same language and, accordingly, can never resolve questions of sexual oppression through communicative means. Only armed insurrection, evolutionary metamorphism of the human species to androgyny, or political revolution remain as possible paths to social equality for women.

Fourth, advocates of the strong thesis may retreat from charges of false imperialism by accepting the validity of multiple female realities. Thus, they would abrogate talk of one "women's perspective" and speak instead of various "women's perspectives." This strategy, however, would still beg the question of what morally ratifies "women's" viewpoints and not those of "men." Further, this strategy might still have to be supported by either essentialism or an overly sanguine perception of victims' experiences as self-ratifying. Finally, Grimshaw argues that "the assumption of multiple female 'realities,' all of which are 'valid' and none of which have any claim to be regarded as more adequate than any other, cannot provide a way of conceptualizing things such as oppression, exploitation, the domination of one social group by another."[4] Insofar as feminism aspires to conceptualize precisely such notions, this strategy fails.

I must emphasize that none of the above manifests any inherent defect of feminist theory as such. If persuasive, my critique serves only the limited purpose of stigmatizing a minor and unnecessary rhetorical device employed by some feminists. As we will now see, the absence of this rhetorical device does not prevent feminists from advancing rich and unsettling critiques of the social and political status quo.

WHAT IS HUMAN NATURE?

Debates about human nature are often described wrongly as conflicts about a rigid universalism, under which humans are depicted as biologically determined and beyond change, and a radical plasticity, under which all aspects of personality are up for grabs and totally subject to social conditioning. Instead, such debates are better understood as concerning the underlying explanations of human behavior and the social consequences attending those explanations.[5]

Rationality

Some feminists argue that the distinguishing and most valuable feature of human nature is rationality. Individuals are thought to be logically and ontologically prior to collectives. All fully functioning humans possess an equal capacity for rationality, although their exercise of the capacity may vary significantly.

This view is accompanied often by a conviction that humans, existing under conditions of material scarcity, are motivated primarily by self-interest. Further, it is argued that women are as ''human'' as men and thus have an equal capacity for the full exercise of reason. If this elementary fact has been obscured, it is because carefully circumscribed social roles have defined the sexes.

Feminists who subscribe to such a view of human nature are most concerned with establishing the conditions under which individuals, regardless of sex, can enjoy the freedom to realize their full creative potential. This aspiration is often accompanied by a prescription for ''androgyny.''

> Members of the androgynous society would be physiologically male or female, but they would be unlikely to show the same extreme differences in 'masculine' and 'feminine' psychology as those characteristics are currently defined. That is to say, there would not be the current extreme contrast between logical, independent, aggressive, courageous, insensitive, and emotionally

inexpressive men and intuitive, dependent, compassionate, nurturant, and emotional women. Boys and girls would receive the same educational opportunities and no attempt would be made to impose those character traits that are considered traditionally to be masculine or feminine.[6]

The call for androgyny is founded in part on a practical consideration: if all humans embodied androgyny, then invidious discrimination could no longer occur on the basis of gender. Some feminists advocating this view counsel "monoandrogyny"—a synthesis of the best characteristics of the current masculine and feminine gender types. Others advise "polyandrogyny"—a pluralism of personality types, some exhibiting the prevailing male model, others manifesting the prevailing female model, and still others displaying a mixture of the prevailing models. Under polyandrogyny, however, these three models of personality would be embodied roughly equally by biological males and biological females.

Accepting the "humans are essentially rational" approach to human nature is accompanied by several conceptual and political dangers. First, denying differences between men and women in their abstract essence often suggests gender-blind laws and policies that tend to aggravate the unequal social power of the sexes. While biological men and biological women taken abstractly may well comport to this approach, actual men and women have been subject to extensive and continuing social differentiation which must be taken into account. Accepting gender neutrality too often translates practically into the further sanctification of male standards, further marginalizing women's experiences and reinforcing the values of the dominant, and presumably oppressive, social order. The ahistoricity of gender neutrality masks the reality of gender conditioning.[7]

Second, the radical individualism of the rationality approach hides the social nature of all humans and the ways in which women form an identifiable class. Alison Jagger quotes Naomi Scheman in support of this criticism: "Scheman concludes that humans have 'emotions, beliefs, abilities and so on only in so far as they are embedded in a social web or interpretation that serves to give meaning to the bare data of inner experience and behavior.' For this reason, Scheman claims that the [rationality approach's] conception of human individuals as existing outside a social context is logically as well as empirically impossible. It is a conceptual as well as an empirical truth that human interests are acquired only in a social context."[8]

Third, the rationality approach glosses over the importance and ramifications of women's distinctive role in human reproduction. Technological advances have not fully liberated women from the burdens of pregnancy and, to the extent that such burdens are inversely proportional to the accumulation of social power, failures to acknowledge real differences between men and women tend to jeopardize women further.

Conscious and Purposeful Activity

Most feminists argue that there is no substantive or "thick" human essence. Instead, humans create themselves through their labor in particular social settings. This approach accepts the ontological primacy of communities and portrays humans as having deep needs for creative expression. Practical action, rather than rational speculation, is primary for human flourishing.

This is, of course, the basic Marxist framework I explained in the previous chapter. Rosemarie Tong describes its appeal to many feminists as

> its promise to reconstitute human nature in ways that preclude all the pernicious dichotomies that have made slaves of some and masters of others. Marxism also promises to make people free, a promise that women would like to see someone keep; and, indeed, there is something very liberating about the idea of women and men constructing together the social structures and social roles that will permit both genders to realize their full human potential.[9]

This "thin" conception of human nature proscribes the search for universal, biological tendencies, and, instead, prescribes understanding humans by attending to their activity in particular economic and social contexts. The current maladies of women are due to economic relations of production that alienate and perniciously divide. The liberation of women, it is argued, will follow the fall of advanced capitalism, which is the source of all oppression.

Most feminists disparage appeals to "thick" theories of human nature. For example, Alison Jaggar argues that a historical and dialectical conception of human biology sees human nature and the forms of human social organization as determined not by our biology alone, but rather by a complex interplay between our forms of social organization, including our type of technological development, between our biological constitution and the physical environment that we inhabit. . . . We cannot say abstractly that biology determines society, because we cannot identify a clear, non-social sense of ''biology'' nor a clear, non-biological sense of ''society.'' The thesis of universal biological determinism cannot be stated coherently.[10]

Despite Marxism's amicable reliance on a thin theory of human nature, I have argued in the previous chapter why feminists should not embrace it in its unadulterated forms: they marginalize women's reproductive and sexual concerns; they wrongly reduce all oppression to one cause; they fail to account for women's oppression in noncapitalist regimes; they divide women into the classes of ''bourgeois'' and ''proletariat'' instead of recognizing the commonalities that unite women as a class; and they assume gender-blind categories that obscure women's role in reproduction, while simultaneously assuming the constancy of that role.

Plasticity

This approach is animated by the basic Marxist framework but recognizes the limitations of Marxism's unadulterated forms. Thus it amends Marxism to facilitate feminist concerns: the primary class division is between men and women, and the relations of procreation, instead of the relations of economic production, comprise the base of society. The base, in one way or another, determines (or affects greatly or limits radically) the superstructure of society. In this fashion, the subordination of women becomes the primary form of oppression in a society, and only by overthrowing the dominant relations of procreation can unalienated sexual relations occur.[11]

At the heart of class division, according to this view, are the biological differences between men and women. This account permits us to explain the pervasive oppression of women by men that transcends the economic structures of various societies. Regardless of the economic structure in place, reproductive differences between men and women remain. Marxism's error is in misconceiving the fundamental class division along economic lines. In fact, say advocates of this approach, the fundamental class division is biological.

The power of this approach, from a feminist perspective, is its locating the subordination of women as the primary form of class oppression. Many feminists are drawn to the view that oppression of women by men is fundamental in one or more of the following ways: that the oppression of women occurred temporally first; that it causally sustains other forms of oppression; that it must be eradicated first; that it constitutes a conceptual model for understanding oppression as such.[12]

The weaknesses of the plasticity approach lie in its seemingly necessitarian foundations: If biological differences form the core of women's subordination, does that suggest that the oppression of women is inevitable and nontransformable? Alternatively, if the liberation of women requires a massive biological revolution then the plasticity approach will strike many as utopian, i.e., impractical, or undesirable.[13] Moreover, beyond promoting biological revolution, the plasticity approach may facilitate feminist passivity in that biology, not men nor economics nor hierarchy, is viewed as the cause of women's oppression. Thus, the prescription of the plasticity approach may be eyed suspiciously by feminists who advocate social and political struggle above all.

Separate and Unequal

Some feminists argue that men and women perceive the world in different ways. Because the male perspective is dominant, women's ways of knowing and experiences are marginalized. Human nature is thus separate and unequal. Male ways of knowing are reflected disproportionately in dominant social ideologies, while women's ways are disparaged as emotionalism or irrationalism. The remedy, say advocates of this approach, is for women to celebrate their own natures instead of striving to conform to male ideologies and aspirations. The pernicious hierarchies of the patriarchy have obscured basic differences between men and women by portraying women's perspectives as ersatz versions of reality.

Sometimes the "separate and unequal" approach refers to the well-known work of Carol Gilligan as an illustration of the differences between male and female perceptions. In *In a Different Voice*,[14] Gilligan states that young girls and young boys deal with moral problems differently: boys are more legalistic ("the ethics of rights"); girls are more sensitive to preserving the relationships involved in given situations ("the ethics of care"). Gilligan argues that the ability to integrate the ethics of care with the ethics of rights indicates mature moral development.[15]

More generally, Gilligan concludes that women's conception of self differs radically from men's conception of self. When asked, men respond by portraying the self as individual, autonomous, predominantly rational; women conceive the self as more interdependent and gaining its identity from participation in a wider subjectivity.[16]

The separate and unequal approach is undeniably correct that women's experiences are not taken as seriously as men's experiences and that a relatively small group of males has a disproportionate voice in setting the terms of social existence. But its reliance upon the "different voices" of men and women and their "different ways of conceptualizing the world" bears closer examination. Are such differences truly "natural"? Or are they manifestations of the different roles and social conditioning men and women have assumed in the public and private spheres, respectively? Is "women's voice" merely the effect of women's social subordination?

Feminists have criticized the different voices approach on a number of grounds. Ann Scales, for example, is unconvinced that the required incorporation of the two voices can occur in our current genderized realm: "By trying to make everything too nice, incorporationism represses contradictions. It usurps women's language in order to further define the world in the male image."[17] Catharine MacKinnon pays lip service to the "strong and elegant sensitivity" in Gilligan's work, but is firm in distancing herself from it: "What is infuriating about [Gilligan's work] . . . is that it neglects the explanatory level. *Why* do women become these people, more than men, who represent *these* values? . . . the answer is clear: the answer is the subordination of women . . . calling [the ethics of care] hers is infuriating to me because we have never had the power to develop what ours really would be."[18]

The biological determinism, or metaphysical essentialism, that underlies the separate and unequal approach also troubles many feminists. Such notions have historically been used to oppress women. Women have been viewed as possessing certain characteristics, such as passivity, nurturing inclinations, and emotionalism, that have been cited as justification for their predominant role in the private sphere. The separate and unequal approach seems to accept clear metaphysical distinctions between male and female and then strives, when it goes beyond Gilligan's prescriptions, to valorize "female thinking" while deprecating "male thinking." A critic may well argue that this approach has assimilated too easily basic patriarchal (dualistic) thinking. Because women currently do not think and experience in an unalienated context, descriptions of how women react are contaminated. To accept such descriptions as definitive of "women's perspective" may be self-defeating.

Furthermore, there is a temptation to obscure racial, religious, ethnic, and socioeconomic differences among women by perhaps overemphasizing the alleged commonalities among all women. This tendency makes such feminists vulnerable to the charge that they are replicating another form of patriarchal thinking: projecting their own aspirations, yearnings, and self-identity—predominantly white, well-educated, relatively advantaged—as universal characteristics, in this case as the essential features of "woman."

Finally, the separate and unequal approach often depicts men harshly.[19] To the extent that such portrayals assume the biological determinism of "man's nature," they fall prey to the conceptual difficulties cited previously. It is more reasonable to conclude that men and women alike are subject to the historical-dialectical interplay of biology and socialization.

Social Practices

This approach tries to synthesize the stronger aspects of other feminist positions: it refuses to accept fixed, universal, nontransformable human characteristics; it accepts the important influences of procreative and other social practices on human identity; it refuses to minimize the historical differences between men and women; it focuses on the different social activities engaged in by men and women as a way of explaining socially constructed gender roles; and it identifies the resulting male and female "character structures" as major collaborators in the perpetuation of women's subordination.[20]

The social practices approach explicitly disavows two influential portrayals of human nature: abstract, attributeless individualism, which recognizes no differences between men and women, and biological determinism, which clings to inherent, fixed differences between men and women. Instead, the social practices approach acknowledges real distinctions between men and women but denies their biological foundations. Such distinctions will not vanish by mere fiat or by aspiration alone, but they are gradually transformable by changes in the social practices that occasioned and sustained them.

Because of this stance, the "social practices" approach does not view the subordination of women by men as a monolithic phenomenon. No particular economic structure, no particular social practice (such as relations of reproduction), no particular human biological feature can be identified as *the* cross-cultural cause of the oppression of women. Instead, the subordination of women has a variety of causes which are often culture specific. Thus, the social practices approach abrogates crude reductionism.

The power of the social practices approach lies in its rejection of the determinism, reductionism, and universalism that plague other feminist approaches. But the liberation of the approach from such conceptual quagmires is accompanied by a different, perhaps equally unsettling, series of questions: If women's oppression has no universal cause, what can account for its presence in all or nearly all cultures? If such causes are culture-specific, does this present the international feminist movement with constantly moving and radically localized targets? Once we acknowledge class, ethnic, racial, and religious differences among women, do we implicitly deny the possibility of "women's perspective"? Do we tacitly admit the impossibility of a truly unified class of "women"? Given that it is analytically true that men are as different from women as women are different from men, can the social practices approach explain the almost universal subordination of women by men? Can the approach explain the absence of the subordination of men by women?

WHAT IS WOMEN'S OPPRESSION?

Feminists are united in claiming that the oppression of women is an almost invariable feature of social life. They disagree, however, as to the focus and nature of that oppression. The following represent a number of explanations, some of which are mutually compatible and others not, of the paramount features of women's oppression.

Economic Disparity

Even if women earn parity in the formal rights held by men, they are still disadvantaged as a class because of their lack of economic equality. Some feminists argue that the equal and effective exercise of formal rights clearly depends on relative economic equality. Equally clear, they contend, is that extending suffrage to women, permitting women to own property, encouraging the fuller inclusion of women into the public sphere of the workplace, and similar grants of formal rights are insufficient.

The facts of economic disparity between men and women are striking and well documented. A report by a committee of the United Nations states: "While women represent half the global population and one-third of the [paid] labor force, they receive only one-tenth of the world income and own less than 1 percent of the world property. They are also responsible for two-thirds of all working hours."[21]

Moreover, in our country, even when women do enter the public workplace, they encounter several economic realities. First, substantial inequalities exist between male and female wages for the same job.[22] Second, the jobs designated generally as "women's work" earn less than jobs filled mainly by men. This is true even in the professions.[23] Third, some studies support the position that employers often set wage levels for certain jobs only after deciding whether those jobs will be filled by men or women.[24] The effect of such wage discrepancies is the creation of two separate and unequal labor markets.[25]

Such economic disparities extend to marriage and divorce.[26] A study conducted by Philip Blumstein and Pepper Schwartz concluded that "in three out of four of the types of couples . . . studied [all types of couples except lesbians] . . . the amount of money a person earns—in comparison with a partner's income—establishes relative power."[27]

As striking as this information is, economic disparities intensity when couples divorce. Lenore Weitzman's study concluded that "for

most women and children divorce means precipitous downward mo-
bility—both economically and socially. The reduction in income
brings residential moves and inferior housing, drastically diminished or nonexistent funds for recreation and leisure, and intense
pressures due to inadequate time and money . . . divorce increases
female and child poverty and creates an ever-widening gap between
the economic well-being of divorced men, on the one hand, and their
children and former wives on the other."[28]

The clearest reason for the "ever-widening gap" is that divorce
settlements often cannot divide equitably, if at all, the divorcing
couple's greatest economic resource: career assets.[29] The recognition
of this reality may exert additional pressure on women to remain in
and submit to oppressive marriages.[30]

The economic disparities between men and women and the material and social consequences accompanying women's separation
from men contribute to the wider perceptions that the proper function of women is man's nurturer and the proper self-image for
women is sex object. In this fashion, through economic leverage and
ensuing political inequality, and with the connivance of their socialization to particular works and roles, women are oppressed cross-
culturally by men.

Although the facts of economic disparity are unassailable, the
more fundamental question remains: Given that it is analytically
true that men are as different from women as women are from men,
why do women suffer disproportionate oppression?

Women's Reproductive Role

Some feminists sense paradox in the oppression of women. On one
hand, the phenomenon of the subordination of women by men is a
universal (cross-cultural) reality. On the other hand, the world ex-
emplifies a variety of economic structures. It would thus seem that
women's oppression cannot be explained adequately by the alleged
requirements of one especially pernicious economic structure, such
as advanced capitalism. But if that is the case, the most obvious alternative is appeal to biological determinism: there is something inherent to men and/or women which facilitates the subordination of
the latter by the former. The problems with such an appeal, however,
are twofold: first, its essentialism undercuts feminism's incessant

claims that socially created, not biologically ordained, roles are at the center of women's oppression; and second, its essentialism fosters an inevitability and a fatalism that reinforces social passivity. It simply is not clear that adherents to biological determinism can consistently advocate the required transformation to which feminists aspire.

One way out of this paradox is offered by Ti-Grace Atkinson.[31] She abrogates appeal to the maladies of advanced capitalism because she senses its inadequacy as an account of a cross-cultural phenomenon. She also refuses the consolations of biological determinism because she perceives it to be inimical to social transformation. Instead, she advances an argument that hinges on recognizing women's role in reproduction as a difference between men and women that has been hitherto viewed as biologically determined, but that can now be transcended.

Atkinson argues that there is only one inherent, not socially created, biological or psychological difference between men and women: women can conceive and bear children, men cannot. All other roles and traits attributed to the two genders are socially created for particular political purposes. Specifically, men, from the earliest times and cross-culturally, imposed restrictions and social definitions on women by exploiting the relative physical and psychological vulnerabilities that accompanied women's childbearing and child-caring functions. This exploitation conjures and sustains the more general differentiations between men's work, characteristics, and political role and women's work, characteristics, and political role.

Because she is firmly convinced that traditional male and female role characteristics are the result of and reinforce political oppression, Atkinson advocates the elimination of traditional roles and their replacement by an androgynous human personality. But given her earlier observation of the one not socially created difference between men and women, reproductive capacity, how is that possible? It is reasonable to assume, and Atkinson seems in fact to do so, that reproductive differences translate into further social differences. Yet she champions a sexually undifferentiated human personality in the face of that assumption.

Atkinson's answer to this puzzle is striking. Two major social transformations are necessary to realize sexually undifferentiated human personality: first, a biological and technical revolution that eliminates sexual reproduction in deference to extrauterine conception; and second, the elimination of the human sex drive, whose prevalence is dependent on its current role in reproduction. Atkinson assumes that human sexual inclinations are not instinctual or biological in the sense of necessary and beyond change. She claims that the sex drive itself is dependent on its reproductive and political functions. Because we now have the technological capacity to conceive and incubate outside the female womb, it is possible to push science further and make extrauterine reproduction the norm instead of the exception. Atkinson assumes that widespread heterosexual desire is a function of the need to reproduce to survive as a species. Once humans are liberated from uterine reproduction, sexual desire itself will wither away. These events would permit the emergence of undifferentiated human personality and would signal the termination of gender oppression.

Remarkably, Atkinson embraces a politically conservative premise—the function of sex is reproduction—to help establish a politically radical conclusion—sexual love is yet another socially created mechanism by which men oppress women.

> The most common female escape [from their subordinate status] is the psychopathological condition of love. It is a euphoric state of fantasy in which the victim transforms her oppressor into her redeemer: she turns her natural hostility towards the aggressor against the remnants of herself . . . and sees her counterpart in contrast to herself as all powerful (as he is by now at her expense). The combination of his power, her self-hatred, and the hope for a life that is self-justifying . . . results in a yearning for her stolen life . . . that is the delusion and poignancy of love. "Love" is the natural response of the victim to the rapist.[32]

The strengths of Atkinson's methodology are its ability to account for the cross-cultural phenomenon of gender oppression, its rejection of biological determinism accompanied by abject fatalism, and its insistence that what Atkinson takes to be the main source of women's oppression can be transcended. The weaknesses of her method, however, are numerous and glaring: she assumes that sexual activity has only one sustaining function: procreation; she concludes that the elimination of sexuality and erotic love are required for social equality; she places her faith in science and technology, two disciplines that have been controlled historically by men to the disadvantage of women; and she abrogates hope that social equality is possible in the presence of any gender differences. As such, Atkinson's liberation of women is purchased at an inflated price: the end of men and women, the death of eroticism, the sanitation of conception and birth. Even if such transformations are factually possible, and it is by no means clear that they are, the price may be too high for both women and men.

Atkinson's method, however, opens the way for other arguments. Feminists can take her basic assumption that women's reproductive role is the main source of cross-cultural gender oppression, but reject the specific fashion in which Atkinson remedied the problem. One could argue, for example, that even if women's reproductive role is biologically determined, it does not follow that gender oppression is inevitable. Such an argument refuses to accept fatalism as a necessary implication of biology. It may be possible to accept uterine conception as the usual human reproductive method, but resist the further consequences and inequities that method has wrought on women. Atkinson's main failure may be her inability to see transformative possibilities that fall short of biological androgyny but still nurture gender equality in the presence of difference.

If this analysis is correct then we have discovered another way to evade the paradox posed at the beginning of this discussion: concede a limited biological determinism of reproductive roles, identify reproductive roles as a fundamental culprit in the subordination of women, but refuse the conclusion that such roles necessitate cross-cultural gender oppression. Such an argument concedes that reproductive roles have hitherto collaborated in the oppression of women, but resists Atkinson's call for a technological revolution involving extrauterine conception and incubation. Instead, it may be possible to restructure reproductive roles to ameliorate the socially pernicious effects they have historically produced. Perhaps by reimagining and remaking traditional family roles, and by emancipating women from male entrepreneurial and political privileges, women can continue their biological role in reproduction, yet elude the political subordination that has historically accompanied that role.

Patriarchy

Many feminists insist that the quest for *the* source of women's oppression is misconceived. Given the varieties of economic systems, social conditions, and political climates extant in the world, it would be miraculous if just one cross-cultural fact could account for the many ways women are oppressed. Moreover, the biological role women assume in reproduction is insufficient to account for the total system of domination that is patriarchy. Specific reasons for the social subordination of women to men can be found only by examining particular cultures. Instead of facile reductionist answers, which purportedly identify global causes, feminists should search to identify the numerous ways patriarchy emerges and how it sustains women's oppression in various cultures.[33]

This approach begins by locating the specific differences that characterize the class of women and distinguish women from other politically subordinate groups. But the approach continues by relentlessly unmasking the ideological superstructure that emerges from and reinforces patriarchal privilege. Accordingly, what is paramount is not the mere fact that women have a different reproductive role from men, but the accompanying ideology which defines "women" by that role: to be a woman is to be a mother, or to at least exemplify "motherly" attributes such as nurturer, sustainer, provider of domestic services. Because a disproportionate number of men enjoy decision-making and policy roles in all aspects of our society, men usually determine appropriate standards of conduct for the activities that define women. As such, feminists often stigmatize motherhood under patriarchy as unfree.[34] Moreover, women's value, especially from their teens through their thirties, is closely tied to their sexual attractiveness. In this fashion, through functional definition and political legitimation, and with the connivance of socialization, men usurp control of the bodies of women.

Patriarchal ideology, depending on its dominance, is irresistible in setting the boundaries of "womanhood." It helps shape the different socialization of boys and girls and helps frame the different self-images of the genders. In its most pernicious form, it is internalized by women and constitutes part of our collective "common sense." Many feminists insist that sexuality itself is a main focus of the patriarchal oppression of women.

Sexuality

Shulamith Firestone points out that "normal" sexual relations and erotic love conceal class disparities. Erotic love can be viewed under Firestone's analysis as the opiate of women: "Love requires a mutual vulnerability that is impossible to achieve in an unequal power situation. Thus 'falling in love' is no more than the process of alteration of male vision—through idealization, mystification, glorification—that [temporarily] renders void the women's class inferiority."[35] Because of the vastly unequal balance of social power constituting it, love's illusions and effects are soon dispelled. "Love means an entirely different thing to men than to women: it means ownership and control; it means jealousy . . . it means a growing lack of interest, coupled with a roving eye. Who needs it?"[36]

Elizabeth Rapaport explains Firestone's position in this way:

> The mutual self-respect which is necessary for healthy love is impossible where neither men nor women regard women as genuine and autonomous persons. They cannot, therefore, be mutually wide open to each other. Men do not see a person worthy of the effort. Women's self-concept precludes seeing themselves as having any personal substance and worth to reveal. They hope to gain substance and worth through the love of men. . . . All men are in a sense idealized in female eyes. They all possess the value of being self-sufficient, authentic, human subjects which women concur in believing is not true of themselves.[37]

Some feminists argue that women are literally the sexual slaves of men. Such thinkers refuse to accept rape and prostitution as aberrational; instead they contend that these horrors constitute sexual paradigms. Hence, Catharine MacKinnon's analysis:

> Compare victims' reports of rape with women's reports of sex. They look a lot alike. Compare victims' reports of rape with what pornography says is sex. They look a lot alike. In this light, the major distinction between intercourse (normal) and rape (abnormal) is that the normal happens so often that one cannot get anyone to see anything wrong with it. Which also means that anything sexual that happens often and one cannot

get anyone to consider wrong is intercourse, not rape, no matter what was done.[38]

Many men would resist this conclusion and point out a clear difference between rape and (normal) intercourse: the presence of mutual, informed consent in the latter. Further, they would question why women would acquiesce to (normal) intercourse if the experience is so irredeemably unsatisfying and even horrifying. MacKinnon advances a partial response:

Women also widely experience sexuality as a means to male approval; male approval translates into nearly all social goods. Violation can be sustained, even sought out, to this end. Sex can, then, be a means of trying to feel alive by redoing what has made one feel dead, of expressing a denigrated self-image seeking its own reflection in self-action in order to feel fulfilled, or of keeping up one's stock with the powerful.[39]

MacKinnon takes "male" to be a social and political, not a biological, notion. As such, what is male is severed from any claims of necessity or inherency. Moreover, she issues the "standard disclaimer"[40] that the male perspective is not shared by all and only (biological) males, "although most men adhere to it, nonconsciously and without considering it a point of view, as much because it makes sense of their experience (the male experience) as because it is in their interest."[41] Here she underscores the hegemonic function of the male perspective which claims and takes itself to be nonsituated and universal.

Because it is the dominant point of view and defines rationality, women are pushed to see reality in its terms, although this denies their vantage point as women in that it contradicts (at least some of) their lived experience. Women who adopt the male standpoint are passing, epistemologically speaking. This is not uncommon and is rewarded. The intractability of maleness as a form of dominance suggests that social constructs, although they flow from human agency, can be less plastic than nature has proven to be. If experience trying to do so is any guide, it may be easier to change biology than society.[42]

According to MacKinnon, the issues pervading definitions and de-terminations of rape provide one illustration of the intersection of the centrality of sexuality and the male quest for abstraction and ob-jectivity. She tells us that the law places primacy on the issues of consent, on the existence of prior social interaction as an indicator of consent, and on distinguishing rape from normal sexual encoun-ters. But in so doing, the law ignores the general societal condition of male domination and the social meaning of gender, marginalizes the victims' perspective, and presupposes a standard of criminality which reflects the meaning of the act to perpetrators.

MacKinnon emphasizes that the social meaning of sexuality is radically different for women and men, while dominant moral the-ory and law wrongly assume that sexuality's social meaning can be captured in gender-neutral terms. She views rape from victims' expe-riences and asserts that sexuality is a "social sphere of male power of which forced sex is paradigmatic."[43] Thus, she does not radically separate normal heterosexuality from violent rape. Under condi-tions of general male domination, she believes that it is difficult to distinguish the allegedly normal from the violently aberrational: "Where the legal system has seen the intercourse in rape, victims see the rape in intercourse. The uncoerced context for sexual expres-sion becomes as elusive as the physical acts come to feel indistin-guishable."[44] She takes special umbrage at the widespread legal ex-emption of marital rape and the law's use of prior social interaction as an indicator of consent which contraindicates rape: "*Women* ex-perience rape most often by men we know . . . women feel as much, if not more, traumatized by being raped by someone we have known or trusted, someone we have shared at least an illusion of mutuality with, than by some stranger."[45]

Beyond the issue of consent, MacKinnon vilifies the way the law distinguishes rape from mere sex by the level of force used: "The law does this by adjudicating the level of acceptable force starting just above the level set by what is seen as normal male sexual behavior, rather than at the victim's, or women's, point of violation . . . rape is a sex crime that is not a crime when it looks like sex . . . assault that is consented to is still assault; rape consented to is intercourse."[46] Thus, for MacKinnon, whether consent and an acceptable level of force are present in an encounter are not truly variable factual issues which have objective solutions in specific cases. She questions whether these are from the outset meaningful concepts, given the social meaning of gender and the pervasiveness of male dominance. MacKinnon also reiterates that "forced sex as sexuality is not exceptional in relations between the sexes but constitutes the social meaning of gender . . . to be rap*able*, a position which is social not biological, defines what a woman *is*."[47]

A properly feminist approach, MacKinnon insists, must begin in the meaning of sexual encounters from women's point of view. The wrongness of rape (and given the current situation, virtually all other heterosexual sexual encounters?) stems from its subordination of women to men. Under the present conditions of male dominance, legally contested interactions will or will not be deemed "rape" depending on whether men's or women's meaning wins out. But the law defines rape in terms of the mental state of the assailant: What did the perpetrator actually understand at the time of the encounter? What would a reasonable man have understood under the circumstances? Did the perpetrator have a mens rea such that his act is properly viewed as criminal? Thus, "man's perceptions of the woman's desires often determine whether she is deemed violated."[48] Yet under present conditions, "men are systematically conditioned not even to notice what women want."[49] Moreover, the law invokes its usual pretensions to objectivity and to the existence of a single, objective state of affairs that must and can be unpacked by the available evidence. In resolving such questions, judges systematically employ shared beliefs from the dominant male culture to animate legal norms with determinate meaning and legitimacy.[50]

The sexual objectification of women in our society is most starkly apparent, says MacKinnon, in how women are socially defined and in how gender neutrality is employed to marginalize women's perspective: "To be sexually objectified means having a social meaning imposed on your being that defines you as to be sexually used, according to your desired uses, and then using you that way. Doing this is sex in the male system."[51]

MacKinnon warns that what passes for women's consent to sexuality is in fact a combination of the effects of socialization and resignation to a lack of valuable alternatives: "Women are socialized to passive receptivity; may have or perceive no alternative to acquiescence; may prefer it to the escalated risk of injury and the humiliation of a lost fight; submit to survive. Also, force and desire are not mutually exclusive under male supremacy. So long as dominance is eroticized, they never will be. . . . Sexual intercourse may be deeply unwanted, the women would never have initiated it, yet no force may be present."[52]

She does not insist, however, that heterosexual relations are *inherently* defective. MacKinnon holds out at least a theoretical possibility for a general social equality which would redeem sexuality: "Inequality because of sex defines and situates women as women. If the sexes were equal, women would not be sexually subjected. Sexual force would be exceptional, consent to sex could be commonly real, and sexually violated women would be believed."[53]

Perhaps the strongest and most unsettling feminist critique of sexuality and erotic love is advanced by Andrea Dworkin in her uncompromising book, *Intercourse*.[54] Dworkin underscores and extends other feminist attacks by amplifying three alleged dimensions of "normal" heterosexual relations: inequality, exploitation, and noxious possessiveness.

The most striking aspect of Dworkin's work is her understanding of sex as *fundamental* to women's subordination. Thus, she does not take sexual inequalities and exploitation as merely the consequences of other oppressive features of patriarchy.

> The woman must be reduced to being [a] sexual object to be pleasing to men who will then, and only then want to fuck her; once she is made inferior in this way, she is sensual to men and attracts them to her, and a man's desire for her—to use her—is experienced by him as her power over him . . . equality requires not ever having been reduced to that object of sensuality in order to be used as a tool of men's desire and satiation in sex . . . [A woman's] inferiority will be created and maintained through [sexual] usage of her for enjoyment. *No rights to hold government office or other public positions of civil or professional power will change her status as long as she is exploited in sex.*[55]

She draws no clear distinction between rape and (normal) intercourse: "The normal fuck by a normal man is taken to be an act of invasion and ownership undertaken in a mode of predation: colonializing, forceful (manly) or nearly violent; the sexual act that by its nature makes her his."[56] Dworkin is not merely saying that men usually assume a dominant role in intercourse—thrusting, penetrating, and initiating. She views intercourse more vividly as the possession of women by men, as the most thorough obliteration of whatever humanity women embody in a patriarchal society.

> Fucking, in which both the man and the women experience *maleness*, essentially demands the disappearance of the woman as an individual; thus, in being fucked, she is possessed: ceases to exist as a discrete individual: is taken over . . . the fuck tends toward the class assertion of dominance. Women live inside this reality of being owned and being fucked: are sensate inside it; the body learning to respond to what male dominance offers as touch, as sex, as love . . . women feel the fuck—when it works, when it overwhelms—as possession; and feel possession as deeply erotic; and value annihilation of the self in sex as proof of man's desire or love . . . sex itself is an experience of diminishing self-possession, an erosion of self.[57]

Dworkin presses home the uniqueness of sex in creating, reflecting, or reinforcing class inequality. Intercourse is one experience that subjugates and binds women as a class that does not bind other subordinate groups. She readily acknowledges, however, that women have collaborated in their own oppression. By assimilating their value as determined by sexual attractiveness, by substituting intercourse for true freedom, by internalizing the ideology of the dominant male class, and by accepting their own inferiority as appropriate, women have conspired in their own objectification.[58]

An unavoidable question emerges: Does Dworkin take the alleged ills of sexual intercourse to be inherent and irredeemable? Or does she foresee at least the possibility that under different social conditions heterosexual relations could be transformed and equally valuable for both sexes? The answer is not clear. At times, Dworkin is uncompromising in her denunciation of heterosexual relations: "It is clear that reforms do not change the intractability of women's civil inferiority. Is intercourse itself then a basis of or a key to women's continuing social and sexual equality? . . . intercourse and women's inequality are like Siamese twins, always in the same place at the same time."[59] At other times, though, Dworkin apparently entertains at least the theoretical possibility that intercourse can be redeemed: "If intercourse can be an expression of sexual equality, it will have to survive—on its own merits as it were, having a potential for human expression not yet recognized or realized—the destruction of male power over women."[60] In sum, it is safe to say that Dworkin is, at best, less than sanguine about the prospects for sexual equality in intercourse, and, at worst, convinced that intercourse and women's oppression are constantly and hopelessly conjoined.

Economics and Dominance

Some feminists take pervasive male dominance as part of the ersatz economic base of society. This is not merely the view that women must have access to positions of power and privilege hitherto reserved for men; it is not simply a call for economic equality. Instead, this view perceives the economic base, which includes, among other social practices, childbearing, childrearing, and sexuality, to be inherently and fatally flawed. Thus, equal economic access for women will not cure social alienation and exploitation; it will at best only disperse those effects more equitably between the sexes. Only complete social transformation, it is argued, can truly result in social equality.[61]

This view is influenced by the Marxist observation that economic structures are fundamental to ideologies that justify and sustain class oppression. But, unlike Marxism, this approach includes sexual and reproductive relations as part of the economic base. This view is also influenced by those feminists who point out pervasive economic inequalities between men and women. But, unlike their more moderate sisters, advocates of this approach refuse to see salvation in equal access to extent positions of power. The "economic and dominance" approach concurs with those feminists who identify patriarchy as ubiquitous, but insists that patriarchy can be dismantled where the will and social resources to do so exist. This approach agrees with those feminists who view heterosexual relations suspiciously, but hopes that sexual relations are transformable once social and economic conditions are reimagined and remade.

WHAT IS THE SOLUTION TO WOMEN'S OPPRESSION?

The following are a variety of responses to women's oppression. The range of answers includes: the total separation of women from men, in-

cluding a female boycott of heterosexual relations; the decommodi-
fication of the female body; a biological revolution to liberate
women from the fundamentally unequal tasks of childbearing and
rearing; economic independence of women from men; pay for those
women who provide domestic and socially necessary services, compensation comparable to the wages earned by men in the public
sphere; obliteration of the distinction between "men's work" and
"women's work"; and full access for women to the public sphere,
particularly those prestigious positions that define political and social power.

This is clearly not an exhaustive list, nor are the various solutions
necessarily mutually incompatible There is, of course, a link between what a perspective takes to be the source of women's oppression and what it takes to be the proper remedy for that malady. Feminists who aspire to transform women's subordination by men will
select a number of the following suggestions and develop a coherent
political strategy for social change.

Equal Pay and Equal Access

It is unassailably correct that women have not historically enjoyed
equal access to the public sphere. As a result, they have had disproportionately little say in setting the terms of social existence. Moreover, the relegation of women to the private sphere has placed
women in a relatively disadvantaged situation with regard to control
of their marital and sexual situations. More subtly, the overwhelming presence of men in positions of economic, political, and social
power nurtures ideological domination where male perspectives
present themselves as objective standards. Thus, women who celebrate differences from men will to that extent fail to meet prevailing
standards of "merit" and "value."

One solution to such problems is equal pay and equal access for
women. An optimal baseline, for example a goal of 50 percent of positions of power occupied by women, is set. Then policies are required to
facilitate that goal. These often include temporary affirmative action
measures: preferring women candidates over equally qualified male candidates for jobs; preferring qualified women candidates over even more
qualified male candidates. The quest for economic parity, it is argued,
must start in equalizing access to public spheres of power. Moreover, ec-

onomic parity must be reached for those jobs that are currently held disproportionately by women in relation to comparably skilled jobs held disproportionately by men.

Advocates of equal access and equal pay also tend to embrace the professionalization of domestic labor.[62] Thus, work preparation, care for the infirm, child care, laundry, housecleaning, and food preparation will be done by external institutions.[63]

The view that women should be accorded equal access to the public sphere is no longer radical, although some of the policies accompanying that view remain controversial. The call for comparable pay for comparable work, for example, is still often perceived as impractical because of the difficulties of determining comparability in the skill levels, demands, and value of products of vastly different industries. Furthermore, comparable pay must often take into account starkly different levels of supply and demand. Likewise, affirmative action programs are often stigmatized for advancing the interests of those in the protected class who were least disadvantaged by past oppression while harming the interests of the those in the unprotected class who were least advantaged by past oppression. Such criticisms generally spring from defenders of the status quo.

But there are other criticisms offered by feminists who reject equal access and equal pay as insufficient or even undesirable. First, they are not sufficient because they do not, by themselves, alter reproductive and sexual relations, nor do they ameliorate what some take to be the inherent limitations of capitalist economics. Also, proponents of equal access and equal pay tend to obscure noneconomic sources of women's oppression, the entire patriarchal system which serves to marginalize women's voices, and to measure women by predominantly male standards. Second, paeans to economic parity can be viewed as coopting the women's movement: by "buying off" relatively few women and permitting their inclusion into male sanctums of social power, the patriarchy ensures the taming of the latent revolutionary impulses of the women's movement.

Furthermore, it is unclear that the professionalization of domestic labor will liberate women. It may well free relatively advantaged women from often unwelcome domestic drudgery, but only at the expense of an underclass of women who serve as professional domestics. As an empirical matter, we can expect that women, and not men, would disproportionately assume such roles. The imagery of happy-go-lucky domestic specialists "working at what they enjoy" is worse than disingenuous, given how feminism otherwise disparages "free" choices in constricted contexts.

Altering the Family Structure

Beyond equal access and equal pay, feminists such as Susan Moller Okin argue that we must alter the traditional family structure. Okin points out that families are the first and main locus of socialization. We learn to relate to one another, assimilate gender roles, and form long-range aspirations from the models we observe and the expectations that are expressed in our immediate social setting. Thus, the best way to learn the principles and hopes of a genderless society is by the theory and practice of our families. Furthermore, exemplars of genderless families can branch out and help transform larger society.[64]

The most effective way to implement this program, says Okin, is through the genderless family. The vulnerability of women and children can best be remedied by the obliteration of standard gender roles: men and women must share work equally in the public and private spheres, including reproductive labor.[65] Such remedies must facilitate the end of gender. Okin envisions a society in which being a male or a female is no more relevant than "one's eye color or the length of one's toes";[66] where childbearing would not necessarily be linked to childrearing; where "it would be a cause for surprise, and no little concern, if men and women were not equally responsible for domestic life or if children were to spend much more time with one parent than the other."[67]

To achieve such changes, of course, requires numerous reforms in the public sphere. These reforms are necessary for a host of reasons: to remove the excuse that men make more money in the public sphere than do women, and that thus it makes economic sense for a wife to agree to assume major responsibility for the domestic sphere; to crush the public sphere's assumption that its workers have someone at home to manage domestic concerns; to wipe out the economic vulnerability of women who divorce; to alleviate the unappealing choices now confronted by career women who desire a family; and to begin the long process of undermining gender stereotypes that currently become part of our socialization from birth.

Okin advances several specific reforms in this vein. I will mention only a few. Pursuant to her prescription for genderless families, she advocates that law and social policies must not assume general sexual differentiation:

> [Employers] should . . . be required to make positive provision for the fact that most workers, for differing lengths of time in their working lives, are also parents, and are sometimes required to nurture other family members, such as their aging parents. Because children are borne by women but can . . . be raised by both parents equally, policies related to pregnancy and birth should be quite distinct from those relating to parenting. Pregnancy and childbirth . . . should be regarded as temporarily disabling conditions like any others, and employers should be mandated to provide leave for all such conditions. . . . Parental leave during the postbirth months must be available to mothers and fathers on the same terms, to facilitate shared parenting.[68]

Schools, too, must educate children about the politics of gender: "Children need . . . to be taught about the present inequalities, ambiguities, and uncertainties of marriage, the facts of workplace discrimination and segregation, and the likely consequences of making life choices based on assumptions about gender."[69]

Okin recognizes, however, that many couples would still choose relatively traditional marriages with division of labor based on established gender roles. Under such circumstances, she counsels the elimination of the economic dependence of the domestic partner on the salaried partner who labors in the public sphere. Thus, she champions a revision in business practices when one partner works in the public sphere while the other assumes domestic burdens: equal legal entitlement to all earnings.

> The clearest and simplest way of doing this would be to have employers make out wage checks equally divided between the earner and the partner who provides all or most of his or her unpaid domestic services. In many cases, of course, this would not change the way couples actually manage their finances; it would simply codify what they already agree on—that the

household income is rightly shared, because in a real sense jointly earned.[70]

Okin further addresses the economic inequities suffered by women who divorce and how the recognition of these inequities often compels women to remain in unfulfilling marriages.

Both postdivorce households should enjoy the same standard of living. Alimony should not end after a few years . . . it should continue for at least as long as the traditional division of labor in the marriage did and, in the case of short-term marriages that produced children, until the youngest child enters first grade and the custodial parent has a real chance of making his or her own living. After that point, child support should continue at a level that enables the children to enjoy a standard of living equal to that of the noncustodial parent.[71]

Traditionalists, particularly wage-earning men who disagree vociferously that salaries are "jointly earned," will resist Okin's conclusions. Business entrepreneurs will also assail the added transaction costs of many of her suggestions. But Okin's advice is refreshingly realistic in that it does not require measures that are, practically speaking, impossible to implement. Moreover, she speaks from within a liberal tradition that places primacy on the role of socialization, education, and legal reform. She also understands that many couples will refuse her counsel, yet she advances recommendations to ameliorate the vulnerabilities of women and children in traditional family settings. In sum, she manifests a pluralism and pragmatism that permit her views to receive an extended hearing from a wide audience. Okin explicitly recognizes the need to fuse theory and practice. Accordingly, her position is especially stimulating and appealing.

My fawning approval, however, will be scorned by more radical feminists. Has Okin solved the problem of oppression based on reproductive labor? Has she understood the inherent exploitation and alienation of capitalist economics? Will her program take too long and thus be subject to cooptation by dominant ideologies? Can her theory account for the cross-cultural aspects of women's oppression? Instead of a strength of her theory, does her pluralism reflect a tacit and meek capitulation to the political status quo, a surrender that ensures the collapse of her wider vision?

Those, unlike myself, who find Okin's vision too domesticated may be drawn to the more disruptive aspirations of Ann Ferguson. She describes "revolutionary family-communities" in this way:

> Alter childbearing inequalities between men and women . . . challenge the sexual division of labor . . . break down the possessive privacy of the two primary sets of relationships in the American patriarchal family: the couple and the parent-child relationship . . . equalize power as far as possible between parents and children . . . eliminate the base for heterosexism . . . break down elitist attitudes about the superiority of mental and professional work to manual work . . . deal with racism and classism . . . introduce economic sharing in the family-community.[72]

Okin and Ferguson share a paramount assumption: the family is a potentially reformative or revolutionary force. To change basic family structure is to prefigure and stimulate wider societal regeneration.

Biological Revolution

I have already noted Ti-Grace Atkinson's call for a biological and technical revolution. Locating the source of women's oppression in their reproductive functions, which exist cross-culturally, Atkinson prescribes a biological and technical revolution which eliminates sexual reproduction in deference to extrauterine conception. She also speculates that such a revolution would eventually be followed by the elimination of the human sex drive whose prevalence is allegedly dependent on its current role in reproduction.

I have already listed the most obvious objections to Atkinson's proposal. But it is useful to add that Atkinson may suffer from the ills of false necessity: a belief that unless women fully transcend their collective reproductive role, they will necessarily be oppressed by men. She also appears to assume falsely that liberation from reproduction and sexual desire must translate into equality for women. Yet oppression has numerous sources—racial, religious, ethnic, socioeconomic—that persist even in the face of gender equality. Moreover, if the price for gender equality for women and men is a biological asexuality achievable only after hundreds of years, there may be little incentive for existing people to begin what they cannot even hope to achieve in the lifetimes of their immediate descendants. Thus, the realization of Atkinson's prescription may well seem too abstract even for those who accept her theoretical account.

Eliminate Capitalism

Marxism trumpeted what it took to be the underlying cause of class oppression: capitalist relations of production that are no longer suitable for the efficient and effective employment of advanced technology. For Marxists, the fact of women's oppression was a microcosm, or ancillary effect, of the oppression of the working class by the capitalist class. Class oppression will wither away if and when its functions and purposes disappear. Under Marxism, class oppression is functionally explained by the structural needs of capitalism. Thus, class struggle can end if and only if capitalism crumbles and is replaced by a socialism that serves as a transition to the "final form" of social arrangement: communism.

Some feminists are committed Marxists and accept this basic framework with only limited alterations. More commonly, however, feminists are attracted to Marxism's basic strategy of identifying functional explanations for oppression social relations and describing the underlying causes of radical political inequality, but they also perceive that the subordination of women to men occurs in noncapitalist economic settings. Even if Marxism can explain women's oppression in capitalism, and even if Marxism heralds the reconstitution of human nature and the effacement of noxious dualisms, it provides an inadequate description of the cross-cultural aspects of women's inferior status. Moreover, such feminists bristle at Marxism's suggestion that women's oppression is of secondary importance to the general oppression of workers. Instead, they argue that women's oppression, because it is cross-cultural and all-pervasive, is paramount. Finally, Marxism wrongly venerates the public sphere— it is only through unalienated and creative labor that humans realize their species-being—but marginalizes the sphere of intimate relations as fully dependent.[73]

As a result, feminists of this perspective assert a conception of society's economic base as that myriad of social relationships that frames the production of life's necessities: the production of people, the various phenomena of sexuality, and the production of services and goods. These relationships of production are not merely permeated with the projections of capitalism, but they are also redolent with the distortions of patriarchy (male domination). Accordingly, the dismantling of capitalism may well be a necessary condition for women's liberation, but it is not a sufficient condition. Patriarchy, too, must be defeated if women are to transcend their debilitating shackles. Under this view, the call for socialism must be accompanied by some of the other remedies that unsettle the traditional sexual division of labor listed in this section. The abolition of both class and gender are required for social transformation, in this view.

Lesbian Separatism

Because they connect perceptions of the proper kinds of sexual activity with wider views of the proper forms of politics, the most radical feminists scorn the kinds of sexual activity commended in centrist regimes: married, heterosexual, monogamous, reproductive, private, in well-defined relationships, and so on. Such feminists insist that this carefully defined sexual activity directly facilitates the general political subjugation of women. In *Lesbian Nation*,[74] Jill Johnston champions a separatist position and endorses lesbianism as a way of making a political statement and evading oppression by men. Under her view, women must undermine the domination and power of men in all relevant contexts, the most important of which is sexual activity.

In fact, Charlotte Bunch insists that heterosexuals are ersatz feminists and that women are inextricably bound to patriarchal control to the extent that they are sexually intimate with men: "The very essence, definition, and nature of heterosexuality is men first . . . For the Lesbian-Feminist, [sex] is not private; it is a political matter of oppression, domination, and power . . . lesbianism is a threat to the ideological, political, and economic basis of male supremacy."[75]

The lesbian separatism advocated by feminists such as Johnston and Bunch goes well beyond disparagement of heterosexuality. By controlling access to themselves, women transcend the numerous and insidious ways the patriarchy defines, uses, and trivializes them. In this vein, Marilyn Frye pleads for a separatism "from men and from institutions, relationships, roles and activities which are male-defined, male-dominated and operating for the benefit of males and the maintenance of male privilege—this separation being initiated or maintained at will, *by women.*"[76] By removing themselves from energy-draining, demeaning heterosexual relations, feminists presumably can better establish class solidarity.[77]

Some feminists, such as Ti-Grace Atkinson, point out that lesbian *sexual* activity is not necessary for political separatism from men: "It is this commitment, by choice, full-time of one woman to others of her class that is called lesbianism. It is this full commitment, against any and all personal considerations if necessary, that constitutes the political significance of lesbianism . . . [Women married to men] claim the right to private lives; they are collaborators."[78] Separatists underscore that the way women engage in sexuality and how they use their bodies has political significance as great as that flowing from how women use their intellects and their time.

But it is unlikely that lesbian separatism will ever constitute a majority of feminists. First, it is unlikely that sexual preference is simply a matter of political choice and thus alterable by act of will alone. There is increasing evidence that whether one is heterosexual or homosexual is influenced greatly by genetic factors outside our immediate control. One cannot change her sexual preference in the same fashion that she can change the color of her shirt or the category of books she reads. Thus, embracing abstract political principles is an unlikely genesis for radical changes in sexual activity. Second, even if sexual preference is fully alterable by will, the reinforcing effects of numerous years of heterosexuality are difficult, and in some cases impossible, to cast off. Third, the political separatism advanced by Atkinson, a movement that does not require lesbian sex, still provides sexual choices that will seem uninspiring to most women: either lesbianism or chastity. Fourth, the separatism movement fails to confront the patriarchy as much as it isolates and shields women from male dominance. A critic can reasonably charge that separatism does not constitute true political struggle, but is, instead, a flight from battle. Fifth, lesbian collectives will still have to grapple with various divisions among women themselves: ethnic, racial, religious, age, economic, educational, and so on. Thus, lesbian separatism will not necessarily end all oppressive hierarchy and division, even if it could succeed in isolating its proponents from one type of class struggle.

Reproductive Freedom

Some feminists stress the need for women to have genuine control over their reproductive lives. Sensing that patriarchy as a cross-cultural phenomenon must be rooted in the different reproductive roles of women and men, these feminists explicitly avoid conjuring a universal definition of reproductive freedom and, instead, strive for local approaches. Thus, they insist that reproductive freedom is needed for women wherever they may be, but understand that material possibilities and social conditions vary from culture to culture.

If there are common cross-cultural threads binding the call for reproductive freedom, they are the feminist conviction that widespread, not piecemeal, social transformations are necessary, and that imposed social roles are anathema.[79] In 1979, the Committee for Abortion Rights and Against Sterilization Abuse outlined a program for reproductive freedom applicable to Western capitalist regimes:

> the universal availability of good, safe, cheap birth control . . . adequate counseling for *all* women and men about *all* currently existing methods . . . adequate abortion services and an end to involuntary sterilization . . . good public childcare centers and schools; decent housing, adequate welfare, and wages high enough to support a family . . . quality medical, pre and postnatal and maternal care . . . an end to the cultural norms that define women in terms of having children and living with a man . . . people's right to raise children outside of conventional families . . . a transformation of childcare arrangements so that they are shared among women and men . . . all these aspects of reproductive freedom must be available to *all* people.[80]

This feminist challenge to the traditional reproductive division of labor and to childrearing implicates enormous economic transformations. Although the challenge is raised in the context of Western capitalist regimes, it is unclear whether a state which accepted and enacted this program could remain capitalistic. Surely, the program would require redistribution of wealth and resources to a degree uncomfortable with the capitalism we know. Either a socialist regime would be necessary to facilitate this program or capitalism would have to reinvent itself quite radically. Proponents of this type of reproductive freedom will cheer this conclusion, while those who are less sanguine about the prospects for fundamental transformations in capitalism will disparage the program as utopian and thus unrealizable. Even critics, however, may appreciate at least some aspects of reproductive freedom as both realizable and desirable.

WHAT ARE SEXUAL ETHICS?

What, then, do feminist perspectives consider morally permissible sex?

Heterosexuality Is Inherently Flawed

Some feminists contend that heterosexuality is by its very nature immoral. Andrea Dworkin, for example, sometimes affirms or comes close to affirming this position. She points out that social reforms have not redeemed male-female sex and suggests that intercourse itself is a basis of or a key to women's continuing social and sexual equality.

Ti-Grace Atkinson advocates a biological revolution that, in her view, would make heterosexuality obsolete. She takes the different reproductive roles of men and women to be the only true biological difference between the sexes, and she insists that only the elimination of this difference can ensure social equality. Thus, artificial childbearing is necessary as a first step toward eliminating the main function of intercourse: reproduction. Presumably, once its function has passed, intercourse will wither away as both women and men evolve biologically toward androgyny.

Lesbian separatists, such as Charlotte Bunch, sometimes suggest that heterosexuality is inevitably tied up with patriarchal domination. Hence, only by casting off heterosexuality can women truly be feminists and escape from the suffocating web of male domination. Embracing this position on sexual ethics presupposes at least one of the following background beliefs: (1) Men are constituted, in terms of excess aggression or surging testosterone, such that they are biologically geared for oppressing women. A major component of this cross-cultural male oppression of women is intercourse and sexuality. (2) Differences in reproductive roles, reflected in part by differently constructed genitalia, necessarily translate into social hierarchy and class division. (3) Heterosexuality is necessary (and sufficient?) for patriarchy.

The first background belief is animated by an essentialism which many women view suspiciously. Appeals to "human nature" and "inevitable biological construction" have been invoked historically to deny women access to the public sphere and to full realization of their human rights. Thus, essentialism can be plausibly seen as an important weapon of the patriarchy. By carefully delineating differences in the alleged inherent characteristics of the sexes, patriarchies have been able to "justify" different social roles for women and men. This role differentiation, many feminists charge, is at the heart of class oppression. By consecrating its own version of essentialism, the heterosexuality-is-inherently-flawed advocates may be ironically mimicking the erroneous methods of their tormentors. The advocates of this position portray men as incapable by nature of anything other than oppression and exploitation. Thus, this position is flawed because while it begins in general disparagement of the idea of an ahistorical human nature, it ends in reliance on precisely that notion.

The second background belief is hostage to false necessity: regardless of changes in the socioeconomic infrastructure and transformations in localized social practices, biology determines social status. This belief refuses to see any possibility that women can continue to conceive children, yet cast off the yoke of their oppression. A critic may well argue that this belief disenfranchises women from an exhilarating power which men lack—the creation of life—in service of a dubious agenda: the long-term evolution of the species toward biological androgyny. Even those women who accept the two peculiar assumptions supporting this position—that heterosexuality has only one function and that a boycott of heterosexuality must lead to androgyny—have reason to pause and wonder whether this abstract goal for future generations is worth their radical and identity-threatening transformation now.

The third background belief takes an aspect of patriarchal domination, current sexual relations, as a cause of women's more general oppression. Are women oppressed generally because of heterosexuality? Or is heterosexuality less than optimal because it operates in patriarchal contexts? Or are current heterosexual practices linked dialectically to the patriarchy—linked, not as cause-effect or effect-cause, but as mutually reinforcing and (somewhat) independent? The dialectical interpretation strikes me as the most plausible portrayal of the relationship between heterosexuality and women's oppression, but the causal interpretation—women are oppressed generally because of heterosexuality—seems to be the view energizing the third background belief. Why would someone be drawn to this causal interpretation? She could be enticed by her deeper allegiance to one or both of the first two background beliefs, or she might be convinced that sexual practices, whatever their form, are primary in determining social hierarchy.

I have already stigmatized the first two background beliefs as gravely problematic. Moreover, it is clear that class division and oppression need not be dependent on sexual practices: race, ethnicity, religion, economics, occupation, and geographical locale have been employed by oppressors of various kinds at different times. Accordingly, for these reasons of theory and for reasons of practice, the heterosexuality-is-inherently-flawed view of sexual ethics is destined to remain an interesting but unpersuasive fringe position.

Heterosexuality Is Socially Flawed

Some feminists are attracted to the view that heterosexuality is morally flawed, but suspicious of all essentialist claims. Accordingly, they argue that heterosexuality is socially flawed, but allow that massive social transformations might redeem future heterosexual relations.

At times, Andrea Dworkin apparently entertains at least the theoretical possibility that intercourse can be redeemed: "If intercourse can be an expression of sexual equality, it will have to survive . . . the destruction of male power over women."[81] Catharine MacKinnon also holds out at least a theoretical possibility for a general social equality that would salvage heterosexuality: "If the sexes were equal, women would not be sexually subjected. Sexual force would be exceptional, consent to sex could be commonly real, and sexually violated women would be believed."[82]

We must be clear, however, on the strength of claims of the heterosexuality-is-socially-flawed position. This view insists that all, or virtually all, male-female sexual relations are morally defective. No accompanying yearning or emotion, such as love or sexual desire itself, expiates these otherwise tainted liaisons. Heterosexual love, for example, is often disparaged as the "experience of [women's] diminishing self-possession, an erosion of self."[83] Furthermore, no accompanying social institution, such as marriage, can atone for the moral contamination of heterosexuality: "Intercourse [in marriage] distorts and ultimately destroys any potential human equality between men and women by turning women into objects and men into exploiters."[84] The heterosexuality-is-socially-flawed position perceives sexual relations and patriarchal domination as mutually sustaining, but it concedes that radical social transformation could morally repair heterosexuality.

At least three relevant comments invite examination here. First, subscribers to this position tend to depict women as powerless victims. They see women as (literally) overwhelmed by men, the false consciousness emanating from patriarchal ideologies, and a social structure not of their making. They scoff at the notion of consent and maintain truculently a stipulative definition that rules a priori that all (or virtually all) male-female relations under present social conditions are morally bankrupt. In so doing, they may well demean women and, ironically, conjure the very stereotype they would otherwise revile: helpless, unempowered females subject to all-powerful males who have ruthlessly exploited women's childbearing capacity.

Taken literally, such feminists suggest that virtually all women are incapable of informed consent because they have been victimized by extended conditioning by male-dominated society. This concession, however, is too general and could be used as a justification for even more paternalism: If women are truly incapable of informed consent, then why should they not be subject to the same benevolent despotism afforded other groups, such as children and the mentally incompetent, who also lack that capacity? Moreover, if a woman does report satisfaction and fulfillment from her heterosexual relations, should her report be stigmatized automatically as arising from false consciousness just because it differs from the fundamental doctrines of feminists of this political persuasion?

By disenfranchising women from the abilities to choose and to create pockets or minicontexts of heterosexual empowerment even in a general context of patriarchy, the heterosexuality-is-socially-flawed position sustains the false necessity that individuals cannot transcend (at least occasionally) their social contexts. There is a kind of classism *uber alles* at play here: the two sexes are inextricably imprisoned in their respective class roles and thus incapable of casting off their socially created "womanness" and "manness" to create, as individuals, their own salutary relationship within a society that is admittedly flawed.

Second, this position, like several feminist positions, gives the mistaken impression that men stalk the earth as empowered beasts of prey, gorging themselves at life's bounty while usurping the value embodied and created by women. Such a portrayal strikes certain men as laughable, not because these men minimize the oppression suffered by women, but because the portrayal exaggerates the power of many men. Relatively few men truly enjoy and exercise the prerogatives of social and economic policy-making. While it is unquestionably true that such policymakers are overwhelmingly male, it is also true that this group constitutes a minuscule percentage of men in our society. Moreover, men, as a class, labor under some uniquely distasteful conditions. Does the following description invoke images of a master race of men who are unambiguously savoring the fruits of social power?

> Men commit suicide at a rate of four times that of women. Men between ages 18 and 29 suffer alcoholism at three times the rate of women. Men account for more than 90% of arrests for drug violations. Real wages for men under 25 have declined during the past 20 years, and 60% of all high school dropouts are males. More than 80% of this country's homeless are males. Men's life expectancy is 10% shorter than women's.[85]

Third, blanket condemnations of heterosexuality discount too radically women's experiences. While it is true that in a flawed society such as ours the notion of consent is not self-validating, neither is it self-invalidating. There are vast differences, at least of degree and probably of kind, between heterosexual relations embodying and those lacking mutual consent. While I concede the panache of a slogan such as "women see the rape in (normal) intercourse," the motto, if taken literally, mocks the phenomenological distinctions between rape and (normal) sex. Instead of unmasking the alleged oppression in (normal) intercourse, it is more likely that this slogan wrongly minimizes the horror of rape. Many women will insist that they know the differences between love and submission, consent and force, and life-enhancing and life-diminishing heterosexual relationships. They know the differences because they have experienced the differences.

Accordingly, the heterosexuality-is-socially-flawed position is too extreme to accommodate women's experiences; it fosters the false impression that individuals are constituted entirely by one class membership: their sex; and it thus reduces complex social phenomena to simplistic generalizations.

Heterosexuality and Economic Parity

In a capitalist society, and virtually all other societies, money talks. We have already outlined the host of social inequalities between the sexes that are connected to vast economic disparities: distortions in bargaining cultivated by unequal power, the dependence of women on men, inequalities of prerogatives in the home, and the feminization of poverty.

The heterosexuality-and-economic-parity approach to sexual ethics could be construed in at least four ways. In descending order of strength, these interpretations are as follows: (1) a necessary condition for morally permissible heterosexuality is that women as a class have economic parity with men as a class; (2) a necessary condition for morally permissible heterosexuality is that an individual woman have economic parity with the individual man with whom she interacts sexually; (3) the presence of economic disparity in a heterosexual interaction conclusively establishes a moral tarnish, whose degree varies, and this taint implies that the interaction must be less than morally ideal, although it may still be morally permissible; and (4) the presence of economic disparity in a heterosexual interaction creates a rebuttable presumption of moral taint.

The first interpretation is the strongest in that it requires the most social transformation and in the absence of that transformation views all heterosexuality as immoral. Its weakness is similar to the main problem besetting the heterosexuality-is-socially-flawed position: it presupposes that the two sexes are inextricably imprisoned in their respective class roles and thus incapable of transcending their socially created "womanness" and "manness" to create, as individuals, their own salutary relationship within a society that is admittedly flawed. Furthermore, by making economic parity between the classes a necessary condition of morally permissible sex, this interpretation impugns all current heterosexual relations as wrong, without regard for variation and degree. Thus, this broadbrush approach fails to attend to contextual and experiential differences. At best, this approach must be supplemented by a fuller theory of sexual ethics that embodies moral criteria to distinguish degrees of immoral behavior. At worst, the approach reduces to a suspicious essentialism: where there is economic disparity, individual humans by nature are incapable of mutually invigorating relations. Finally, this approach problematically reduces all oppression to economics.

The second interpretation liberates its advocates from classism, but reinstates the requirement of economic parity on an individual level. Any particular heterosexual interaction or relationship where the parties are economically disparate is stigmatized as immoral. This interpretation suggests a "mix with your own kind" perception of sexual activity: a woman should select her bedmates from her own economic class. Because of the disparity in current salaries between men and women performing the same job, a woman with a relatively prestigious position may earn no more than a man with a more common position. Does this imply that a woman lawyer making a certain amount of money should enter into sexual relations only with those of similar salary? If so, more senior male lawyers might be off moral limits to her, while the male construction worker down the street, who makes a salary equal to the woman lawyer, is considered morally acceptable (insofar as we judge on the basis of economics alone).

This point may not be striking, but it flares in a more general direction: this interpretation, much like the first, insists that economic disparity, even on the level of couples, *must* translate to immoral relations. Again, couples are imprisoned by a false necessity that demands that they are unable to transcend, even for a few moments, their economic context regardless of their (noneconomic) constitutive attributes. As such, this interpretation betrays a pernicious reductionism: it defines individual men and women solely by their financial status.

The third interpretation is more subtle. It states that economic disparity inherently manifests moral deficiency in a sexual relationship, at least in those that are heterosexual. The degree of deficiency will vary with the degree of economic disparity and with other contextual factors such as respective education levels, influence in the public sphere, allocation of burdens in the private sphere, and so on.

This interpretation softens somewhat the claims of its two predecessors. Here the moral deficiency need not automatically imply that the heterosexual relationship is immoral on balance, but only that it is less than ideal. It is at least conceivable that other contextual factors can morally outweigh the taint of economic disparity, at least in instances where economic disparity is mild. Still, the third interpretation insists that the taint remains; that is, even where other contextual factors permit us to judge a sexual relationship as morally permissible on balance, the relationship is viewed as irredeemably contaminated in terms of economic criterion. Thus, such relationships necessarily stray from the moral ideal even when they are otherwise morally laudatory.

By viewing economic parity as less than a necessary condition of morally permissible sexual relations, the third interpretation evades the stronger criticisms presented against its two predecessors. But it nevertheless reinstates economic parity as a necessary condition of morally ideal heterosexuality. As such, it is still subject to interrogation: Does this interpretation perceive too rigidly the importance of economic parity? Why cannot couples transcend their economic disparity, through other contextual factors and their own constitutive attributes, and experience morally ideal sexual relations? Why is economic disparity a sort of original and eternal sin whose presence automatically disqualifies a couple from the moral ideal? In sum, the third interpretation is plausible and will be accepted by many thinkers, but the questions posed remain unsettling.

The fourth and final interpretation is the mildest of the heterosexuality-and-economic-parity approaches to sexual ethics. It says that the presence of economic disparity in a heterosexual interaction creates a rebuttable presumption of moral taint. Thus, economic disparity does not necessarily stigmatize a heterosexual relationship as morally impermissible or less than morally ideal. This interpretation does not isolate economics as a fully autonomous criterion. Instead, this interpretation evaluates sexual relations holistically and offers the possibility that the prima facie moral taint of economic disparity can be redeemed *fully* by other contextual factors. It acknowledges what the other three interpretations discount: the experience of transcendence in which human personality, through passion, spirituality, or indefatigable will, can escape its externally imposed social context and liberate itself from culturally determined notions of the possible and impossible.

Accordingly, under this interpretation we must view economic disparity suspiciously but not rigidly. The presence of economic disparity between a relatively advantaged male and a relatively disadvantaged female creates a presumption of moral taint, but that presumption can be rebutted by other relevant criteria of moral assessment. It is, then, at least possible that the couple, although economically disparate, can establish morally ideal sexual relations. Thus, economic disparity is not an original and eternal sin, but a prima facie moral blemish.

It should now be clear that the theory of sexual ethics urged in the following chapters subscribes to the fourth interpretation of the heterosexuality-and-economic-parity approach. While the third interpretation remains a viable perspective, I am more deeply persuaded by the appreciation for transcendence embodied by the fourth interpretation.

Heterosexuality and Social Parity

There are a variety of social inequalities that are at least somewhat autonomous from economic inequalities. A man and a woman can be economically equal, but socially unequal—unequal in terms of political influence, prerogatives within the family, reproductive roles, and general social status. Thus, social inequalities, although often correlated to economic oppression, are neither reducible to nor defined by economic inequalities.

The heterosexuality-and-social-parity approach to sexual ethics can be construed in at least four ways. Paralleling the interpretations of the heterosexuality-and-economic-parity approach, these inter-

pretations, in descending order of strength, are as follows: (1) a necessary condition for morally permissible heterosexuality is that
women as a class have social parity with men as a class; (2) a necessary condition for morally permissible heterosexuality is that an individual woman have social parity with the individual man with
whom she sexually interacts; (3) the presence of social disparity in a
heterosexual interaction establishes conclusively a moral tarnish,
whose degree varies, and this taint implies that the interaction must
be less than morally ideal, although it may still be morally permissible; and (4) the presence of social disparity in a heterosexual interaction creates a rebuttable presumption of moral taint.

Analyses and criticisms of these four interpretations also parallel
those offered in the section on heterosexuality and economic parity.
Thus, I embrace the fourth interpretation as the most persuasive,
while conceding that the third interpretation remains plausible and
reasonable. Social disparities, however, are often far-reaching, numerous, and intractable. Accordingly, social disparities may well be
more suspicious than economic disparities, and the presumption of
moral taint here may be even more difficult to rebut than economic
disparities, which stand alone.

Liberating Subcontexts Are Possible

The fourth interpretations of the previous two approaches to sexual
ethics, interpretations which hold out the practical possibility of re-
deeming the presumed moral taint of economic or social disparities,
presuppose that heterosexuals can create their own liberating subcontexts even within a general social context that is seriously
flawed. Thus, under this approach, the general oppression of women
as a class does not imply that all heterosexual relationships and sexual encounters are necessarily immoral.

Christine Swanton, Viviane Robinson, and Jan Crosthwaite subscribe to the view that liberating and morally permissible subcontexts can transcend broader patriarchal oppression. They adumbrate
the attitudes and skills necessary for men to treat women with
proper respect:

The man must view the woman as someone who has needs, intentions and wishes of her own, and as having a right equal to

his to fulfillment of those needs, intentions and wishes, even though they may be in conflict with his . . . treatment of the woman with proper respect requires the man to be open-minded about the possibility that [his antecedent] views may be mistaken or incomplete. Such an attitude of open-mindedness can be contrasted with an attitude . . . in which the correctness and appropriateness of one's views are treated as self-evident. . . . The man must see it as important that both parties have the opportunity to make a free and informed choice about whether and how they engage in any proposed interaction.[86]

These attitudes must translate into the following interpersonal skills:

The man must attempt to establish agreement whether implicit or explicit, about the focus and purpose of the interaction . . . The man must bring to the interaction a degree of openness about his views which enables the woman to make responses based on fact rather than misperception. . . . The man must disclose and test his views in a facilitative manner that encourages the woman to express any disagreements she has with them. Facilitative strategies include frequent invitations to the woman to express her own views, especially if they are likely to differ.[87]

The three authors describe in detail their notions of "relevant information," "informed consent," "interpersonal effectiveness," and "treating women as sex objects." It is not necessary, however, to delineate their position more fully to perceive that at their most general description, liberating heterosexual subcontexts require that the traditional roles of male dominance and female submission are absent, women are not politically victimized by their sexuality, and women have the capacity and real power to control access to and define themselves.

In the remaining chapters of this book, I will include, among other things, this general liberal-feminist description of transcendent heterosexual subcontexts as a necessary component of a new framework for sexual ethics.

PART 3
IN SEARCH OF UNDERSTANDING

Mediating Tensions between Leftist and Mainstream Theories

7

TOWARD SYNTHESIS
Sexual Morality in Five Tiers

I now introduce an alternate framework for sexual ethics, which I call "sexual morality in five tiers." My theory owes much to the classical and contemporary views of sexual morality discussed in the first six chapters. This debt is both negative—by identifying and avoiding the limitations of the other theories, I can realize a richer and deeper vision—and positive—by highlighting and dissecting the more persuasive aspects of the other theories, I can perceive the most fruitful avenues for synthesis.

I begin by identifying six common errors exemplified in moral theory and explaining how they apply to sexual ethics. I then critically analyze the "baseline theory" which purports to capture the meaning of sexual exploitation. I continue by explicating my preferred view, "sexual morality in five tiers." Finally, I conclude by examining some illustrations of sexual interactions and evaluating them by the methods of my preferred view.

SIX COMMON MISTAKES

The classical and contemporary views of sexual morality discussed earlier all make one or more of the following six errors:

1. Reductionism

This mistake involves subduing a complex phenomenon into only one of its numerous aspects. The core of this error is the wrongful aggrandizement of one contextual feature as dispositive of moral worth and the wrongful relegation of other contextual features to the scrap pile of irrelevancy.

Examples of erroneous reductionism are easily identified: some natural law theorists concentrate solely on procreative intent in a marital setting; the most fervent love and intimacy advocates focus totally on the presence of the requisite interpersonal commitments and emotions; libertarians concentrate only on the presence of mutual agreement; classic Marxists are obsessed with economic structure as the source of all oppression; and some feminists seize on patriarchy as an automatic contaminant of heterosexual relationships. Predictably, when these theories engage each other and dispute conclusions, each inevitably accuses other positions of being excessively doctrinaire and overlooking important factors of moral assessment. These accusations are mutually accurate, because all those theories are, indeed, guilty of erroneous reductionism.

The solution to the problem of reductionism demands that no single feature is sufficient to establish the moral credentials of sexual interactions, although I hold open the possibility that particular sexual relations may manifest a single defect serious enough to establish their immorality. Thus, numerous contextual features must be assessed when we determine the morality or the degree of immorality of sexual relations.

2. Abstractness

We philosophers are especially prone to the error of abstractness. At times, we are lured into this mistake nonconsciously. We begin by identifying parties as ''X'' and ''Y'' and citing the features of their relationship or interaction we deem relevant, then we announce moral conclusions after we evaluate those features. The problem is that there are no Xs or Ys in the world. In the context of sexual ethics, there are only real people with numerous constitutive attributes, most of which are relevant for a truly complete moral assessment of their relationships. When we generalize all people to Xs and Ys, or all men to Xs and all women to Ys, we cannot do justice to particularity and concreteness. Such generalizations lead to false stereotypes: all people yearn for love and intimacy; sex without intimacy must be psychologically fragmenting; women aspire to security in a relationship, men are swashbuckling sexual adventurers; men are patriarchal pariahs, women experience self-validating, veridical normative visions based on their systematic victimization.

Hence, the error abstractness clouds our vision of numerous real social differences: sex, race, economic status, subjective importance placed on sex, actual reaction to sexual propositions, and socialized attitudes. The solution to the error of abstractness requires more and subtler attention to the constitutive attributes of the respective parties and resistance to generalized characterizations that obscure particularity and thereby retard accurate moral assessment.

3. Ahistoricism

Closely related to the error of abstractness is the mistake of ahistoricism. This mistake takes many forms, but two are keenly important in sexual ethics: first, the pretension that we can discover a universal, timeless sexual ethic that is impervious to social and temporal change; second, the sham that even if a universal sexual ethic eludes us, we can still apply our current dominant ethic without regard for its historical genesis.

The first form exudes a false imperialism that assumes that we can facilely transcend our social context and attain an ideal perspective from which we can generate timeless conclusions. By invoking the majesty of reason itself, such conclusions evince neutrality and universality. Unfortunately, proponents of such methodologies are sorcerers without magic wands: they must resort either to a suspicious essentialism that foists unchanging natures on humans or to a radically problematic metaphysics that invokes an immanent normative world order. In fact, the moral conclusions that such methodologies generate are more likely to reflect the class and social perspectives of their proponents than the imperatives of a timeless world order.

I am not criticizing advocates of these methodologies for not doing the impossible: discovering the inexorable laws of morality embedded in the universe. Instead, I charge that their pretension that they have accomplished the impossible results in a false imperialism that obscures other perspectives, ignores social context, and fails to appreciate the historical and economic genesis of moral perceptions.

My critique of the first form of the mistake of ahistoricism must not be construed as an implicit embrace of normative relativism.

Such an interpretation would itself assume a false moral dilemma: either an objectivism that presents timeless and universal normative conclusions, or a relativism that conflates current social opinion and moral truth and degenerates into abject moral skepticism. I have elsewhere[1] examined this false moral dilemma and will summarize that analysis below.

The second form of the mistake of ahistoricism concedes the problems accompanying the search for timeless, universal moral truths. This form takes refuge in a presumed social consensus and applies the dominant normative ideology of a culture at a particular time. The error of this form is its reluctance, or refusal, to interrogate received cultural opinion. The result of such reticence is, at worst, an arid conventionalism that simply mirrors the collective judgments of the advantaged social classes. The result, at best, is a moral parochialism that marginalizes the voices of historically disadvantaged groups and fails to consider the genealogy of dominant ideologies.

My critique of the second form of the mistake of ahistoricism does not commit the "genetic fallacy": the critique does not assume that moral conclusions can be proved false by impugning their origins. But the critique does demand that such origins be examined thoroughly. Moreover, if these origins are deemed morally suspicious or deficient, such findings provide strong evidence against the truth of the correlated moral conclusions. Accordingly, a genealogical inquiry can at times soften the strident confidence of the political and social status quo.

When observing normative disputes between political centrists and leftists, one is tempted to throw up one's hands and conclude that mainstream analytic philosophers, given our predilection for coherence and disdain for contradiction, and leftist critics, given their appreciation for paradox and abhorrence of abstraction, are alien discourses that simply talk around each other. Lacking enough common ground to engage in genuine dialogue, each merely recasts the other's central aspirations as criticisms, while the other, recognizing this, sneers back, "So what!"

But perhaps things are not so bleak after all. While it is probably true that "there can be no escape from plurality—a plurality of traditions, perspectives, philosophic orientations,"[2] we—mainstream philosophers and leftist critics—share a larger situated framework that makes it most unlikely that our "conceptual schemes are so self-enclosed that there is no possibility of reciprocal translation, understanding, and argumentation."[3] Rather than approaching contrasting views as philosophic opponents to be confronted and reduced gleefully to absurdity, Richard Bernstein advises us to "begin with the assumption that the other has something to say to us and to contribute to our understanding. The initial task is to grasp the other's position in the strongest possible light . . . [U]nderstanding does not entail agreement. On the contrary, it is the way to clarify our disagreements."[4] If analytic philosophers and leftist critics have reached impasse, it is because they have shared an adversarial style of confrontation that precludes the type of "engaged fallibilistic pluralism" that Bernstein exhorts.

> [Engaged fallibilistic pluralism] means taking our own fallibility seriously—resolving that however much we are committed to our own styles of thinking, we are willing to listen to others without denying or suppressing the otherness of the other. It means being vigilant against the dual temptations of simply dismissing what others are saying by falling back on one of those standard defensive ploys where we condemn it as obscure, woolly, or trivial, or thinking we can always easily translate what is alien into our own entrenched vocabularies.[5]

In order to break dialogical impasse, leftist critics must restrain their inclinations to portray normative analysis in so cynical and one-sided a fashion; to dismiss moral conclusions as nothing more than sham and pretense; to disdain analytic philosophy as merely the conceptual henchman of capitalistic patriarchy; to ridicule the quest for consistency and coherence as either psychological error or aggressive male weaponry; and to castigate critics of their views as capitalistic oppressors or patriarchal collaborators. For if leftists deflect and disable all criticism—as flowing necessarily from malevolent despots or their sycophants—then leftists trivialize themselves. Likewise, analytic philosophers must curb our tendency to assault with deranged avidity the perceived doctrinal weaknesses of leftist critique. For such butchery blinds us to the undeniable insights constituting leftist perspectives: "morality's" complicity in the historical disenfranchisement of women and racial and religious minorities; the subtle ways in which the views of disadvantaged classes are marginalized and trivialized in social life; the dangers of a "blind" justice that further oppresses the already disadvantaged; the blatant prejudices and biases built into our language and reflected in our experience; and the inadequacy of a gender-neutral approach in a society that has historically nurtured so much gender, racial, and economic oppression.

Accordingly, the solution to the error of ahistoricism begins with an insight from the phenomenology of normative discourse: once inside the enterprise of normative debate, once we are actually arguing for and evaluating moral conclusions, we all presuppose that "some claims are better than others, that some are right and others wrong."[6] The arguments we advance to support our favored normative conclusions are not supported by *different* esoteric arguments that claim that our conclusions are objectively correct. As Ronald Dworkin points out: "But now suppose someone, having heard my arguments [that slavery is unjust], asks me whether I have any different arguments for the further view that slavery is objectively or really unjust. I know that I do not because, so far as I can tell, it is not a further claim at all but just the same claim put in a slightly more emphatic form."[7]

Unlike discussions about matters involving only subjective preferences—Which food is superior, Italian or Chinese? Which color is more attractive, red or violet?—the phenomenology of normative discourse necessarily implicates an intricate network of beliefs, attitudes, and social practices that themselves generate internal theoretical constraints on judgments. Normative discourse, unlike debates about matters of merely subjective preference, is characterized by argument in a strong sense: defending one's position with nonarbitrary reasons that at some point implicate concepts of human interests. This process, although constituted by numerous historically shaped criteria, is a structured and rule-governed enterprise. The experience of robust argument distances normative discourse from disagreements over matters of merely subjective preferences, but does not necessarily commit us to strong and implausible foundationalist assumptions.

The aim of normative discourse so conceived is not necessarily the end of disagreement and the solace of objective final answers, but rather a commitment to moral disputation in its most zestful form: the liberating recognition that more is up for grabs than habit and convention generally permit; that creativity and experimentation not only always have a place in, but are at the center of, social deliberations; that the historical forces of class oppression cannot be justified by appeals to ahistorical entities, such as inherent human nature, which themselves lack independent justification. Under such a conception, we seek a deeper understanding of disagreement and incommensurability and a profound comprehension of the connection between the people we are and the disputes in which we engage. The aim here, however, is not to denigrate but to clarify the possibility of moral assessment or moral insight.[8]

Accordingly, we do not begin with aspirations for an ideal vantage point or an abstracted universal human chooser. Rather, we start with the values we presently embody and the social world that is our context: our traditions and conventions have currency because they partly constitute who we are. This does not counsel an arid conventionalism, because social transformation is necessary, among other reasons, to close the gap between our moral expectations and our institutional outcomes. Once we self-consciously abrogate the search for certainty and fixed foundations, our normative inquiries can attend to the social contexts in which we participate in the process of acquiring understanding and knowledge.

This conception of normative discourse assumes that we cannot transcend theory-laden contexts.[9] Normative justification is thus constituted by theoretical explanation. The rationality of normative enterprises emerges from its self-correcting but nonfoundational dimensions.[10] Moreover, a different notion of objectivity, one based on practice and behavior, emerges here. For example, Hilary Putnam insists that: "If we find that we must take a certain point of view, use a certain 'conceptual system,' when we are engaged in practical activity . . . then we must not simultaneously advance the claim that it is not really 'the way things are in themselves.' "[11] This conception of objectivity, however, does not force us to relinquish the pluralism and fallibilism urged here: "One does not have to believe in a unique *best* moral version, or a unique *best* causal version, or a unique *best* mathematical version; what we have are *better and worse* versions, and that *is* objectivity."[12]

Thus, we may legitimately reject the view that facts and reasoning must be either metaphysically objective or abjectly conventional. The facts and reasoning indigenous to normative enterprises often involve both objective factors and human choices. The social decisions pertain to the classification and categorization of the objective factors. These factors and practical activity themselves constrain the range of permissible classifications, but generally do not ordain any particular classification. This, underscoring as it does the themes of pluralism, fallibilism, and experimentation, has a salutary effect on the human inclination to identify current practice as the only natural or the one correct mode of being.

Much of the paradigm for this version of normative discourse emerges from a contemporary portrayal of philosophy of science. As Ronald Dworkin notes, "None of the beliefs we have, about the world and what is in it, is forced upon us by a theory-independent recalcitrant reality. . . . There is no paradox in the proposition that facts both depend on and constrain the theories that explain them."[13] Moreover, Putnam adds that "a hypothesis or a statement may be warranted, may be reasonable to believe, in an objective sense of the words 'warrant' and 'reasonable,' even though we cannot specify an experiment (or data) such that were we to perform it (or were we to collect them) we would be able to confirm or disconfirm the hypothesis to an extent which would command the assent of all educated and unbiased people."[14]

Other elements of the paradigm for normative discourse emerge from a vigorous conception of praxis, which holds that cognitive forms emerge from historical development and immanent critique, such emergence is influenced by and reflected in the social institutions of labor and production, and particular cognitive forms and ideologies are offshoots of and may modify socially dominant practices. Still other elements of the paradigm flow from fallibilistic, pluralistic themes. The power of certain propositions and conclusions is grounded not in abstract cognition, but in societal practices and activities.[15]

Normative discourse resembles more closely these conceptions of philosophy of science and of praxis than it does discussions about matters only of subjective preferences. But we must also acknowledge that the networks of theoretical structures accepted in the scientific community converge more than those contending for dominance in the moral, political, and legal arenas. Understanding that contestability and disagreement are part of a robust conception of rationality, and that convergence of conclusions is neither guaranteed nor always desirable, we must soften the stern claims of objectivism while cleansing the self-delusion and arrogance of conventionalism.

Thus, I am privileging a type of pragmatism as a way to mediate the apparent cognitive dissonance generated by the clash of mainstream methods and their leftist critics. This program requires an antifoundationalist outlook which abrogates reliance on fixed segments of knowledge and special cognitive faculties. Moreover, despite the way institutions solidify and emit the appearance of naturalness and inevitability, we should appreciate the contingency of current arrangements and the possibilities of transformation. Rather than regretting the loss of fixed foundations and authoritative trumps of reason, we should revel in increased opportunities for freedom and collective deliberation. Further, we should not assume that convergence of opinion is the necessary goal of rational discussion. Certainly there will be many basic matters upon which otherwise divergent ideologies will converge. But where there is a hardened orthodoxy of views on virtually all normative matters, we should suspect the presence of stultifying authoritarianism. Finally, our institutions should not strive to eliminate ideological and political conflict; rather, they should rechannel controversy as a way to invigorate social life.

But what grounds support the privileging of the pragmatic mode? Here I can only use an intuitive strategy and appeal to the following considerations on behalf of the pragmatic mode: it best fuses theory and practice and is thus better suited than other modes to a practical enterprise such as ethics; it more closely tracks an engaged fallibilistic pluralism than do other modes; it can better ameliorate, although not eliminate, cognitive incommensurability; it rejects both extreme foundationalism and simple reductionism; and it offers the best possibilities for transcending the hopelessly effete objectivist-relativist polarity.

4. Isolationism

Virtually all theories of sexual ethics limit themselves by committing the mistake of isolationism: confining moral assessment to the parties engaging in sex and their spouses, if any. However, it is undoubtedly too bold to call this proclivity a "mistake," given that most theorists who focus only on the parties do so self-consciously.

The problem with isolationism is that it unnecessarily limits the scope of a theorist's moral conclusions. Isolationism brushes aside an important feature of moral reasoning: even the most decorous sex under the most pristine conditions between two heterosexuals acting from the most laudatory motivations can be, all things considered, immoral under various (unusual but conceivable) contexts. Moreover, independent of philosophers' ingenious but improbable counterexamples, isolationism wrongly ignores common, foreseeable, and morally relevant third party effects that often accompany sexual interactions and relationships.

The obvious solution to the problem of isolationism is the inclusion of foreseeable third party and general societal effects in our moral calculus. This inclusion complicates an analysis of sexual morality, but promises rich conceptual rewards for those who are industriousness enough (pedantic enough?) to accept the challenge and tackle numerous otherwise-neglected issues.

5. Rigidity

Theories of sexual ethics often press the case for bright-line rules and clear distinctions between concepts such as wrongful exploitation/praiseworthy mutual use, human needs/human wants, illegitimate threats/permissible offers. While such concepts are, indeed, distinct, the quest for vivid lines sometimes degenerates into stultifying rigidity. This rigor mortis of the spirit reveals itself at the borderlines of the various distinctions. More precisely, theorists often become obsessed with hornswoggling a hard case into one of the distinct concepts, instead of accepting the moral ambiguity indigenous to such cases.

I do not intend here to demean the necessity of making moral judgments and acting upon them. Instead, I disparage maniacal efforts to classify neatly all borderline or "penumbra" cases. Such efforts invariably involve clever (and sophistical?) conceptual appeals that slice the bologna too thin.

The antidote to obsessive rigidity is an appreciation of the continuum that constitutes the range of actions we label, for example, "seriously wrongful exploitation" through "morally praiseworthy mutual benefit." Explicit understanding of this requires that where we approach the middle of such a continuum—the borderlines of the distinction—our efforts are better spent on adducing the positive and negative aspects of the action at issue rather than obsessing over which pole of the continuum must name it.

6. Assimilation

In earlier chapters, I raised and briefly reviewed the question whether sexual exchanges are different from other contractual arrangements. On one hand, libertarians and numerous liberal contractualists evaluate sexual interactions by the same criteria and under the same assumptions by which they evaluate nonsexual exchanges of commodities and services. On the other hand, most feminists, moderate conventionalists, and conservatives claim, for somewhat different reasons, that "sex is different" and thus ought not to be viewed as a series of commodity exchanges.

My earlier inquiries into this question were tentative. Indeed, I suggested in Chapter 5 that feminist attempts to clarify the alleged differences between sex and other exchanges were inconclusive.[16] It simply was not clear whether feminists viewed the alleged differences as inherent—founded on reproductive differences between men and women or on the fact that sexual activity, unlike exchanges of mere commodities, is necessarily constitutive of human self-identity—or socially created.

But the time for decision is at hand. The theory urged here assumes that sex *is* different from exchanges of commodities and nonsexual services. To think otherwise is to commit the mistake of assimilation: conflating all human agreements under one conceptual rubric. Assimilation in the present context is a mistake because it ignores the social meaning of sex in our culture.

My firm conviction is that sex is not necessarily different: I am gravely suspicious of efforts to establish the inherent differences of sexual and nonsexual interactions. I can imagine a society where sexual activity, for better or worse, is not accompanied by the theological, patriarchal, and other historical baggage which shadows it in our culture. I can imagine a society where sexual activity, for better or worse, is not constitutive of human self-identity. I can imagine a society where citizens accept and internalize sexual activity, for better or worse, much as they do nonsexual commodity exchanges. Further, I suspect that such societies are not merely hypothetical possibilities, but that a thorough canvassing of anthropological and sociological literature would reveal historical and contemporary approximations.

However, in our culture sexual activity has a variety of social meanings that distinguish it from ordinary wage labor, exchanges of goods and nonsexual services, and other contractual arrangements. Even though the differences are neither necessary nor inherent, they are nonetheless real and thus must be taken into account by a comprehensive theory of sexual ethics. Accordingly, the solution to the mistake of assimilation is similar to the antidote for the related mistake of abstractness: attention to the particularity of the parties, the concreteness of their historical context, and the social meaning of their activity.

THE BASELINE THEORY OF SEXUAL ETHICS

Prior to explaining and justifying sexual morality in five tiers, it is fruitful to examine a position developed by Thomas Mappes, a position I call "the baseline" theory of sexual ethics.[17]

The baseline theory aspires to capture the meaning of sexual exploitation: "A immorally uses B if and only if A intentionally acts in a way that violates the requirement that B's involvement with A's ends be based on B's voluntary informed consent."[18] So conceived, sexual exploitation "can arise in at least two important ways: via *coercion*, which is antithetical to voluntary consent, and via *deception*, which undermines the informed character of voluntary consent."[19] Later, the baseline theory adds "taking advantage of another's desperate situation"[20] as a form of sexual exploitation.

So far there is nothing to distinguish the baseline theory from standard libertarian-liberal accounts of sexual morality: interacting with someone, such as a child, incapable of informed consent, the use of force, threats of harm, fraud, withholding of relevant information, and taking advantage of another person's desperate situation contaminate the moral quality of sex. However, the baseline theory recognizes that the libertarian-liberal account requires further refinement: it must define the difference between an impermissible threat and a freedom-enhancing offer, between an impermissible use of another's desperate situation and a morally salutary benefit to the disadvantaged, and between a person's desires and her needs.

The baseline theory begins to unravel these mysteries by invoking a distinction between threats and offers animated by the work of Robert Nozick and Michael Bayles.[21] A threat is such that noncompliance with its terms engenders, if the threats are carried out, undesirable results for the recalcitrant party. An offer, on the other hand, constitutes an inducement: if the offer is approved, desirable consequences ensue for the accepting party.

The difference can be understood graphically in this way. Imagine an offeree's situation prior to the proposition advanced by an offerer. This constitutes the offeree's baseline situation. Now imagine the offeree's situation directly after she has refused the proposition. The distinguishing mark of a threat is that the offeree's noncompliance will worsen her baseline—because of the proposition, the offeree's situation after her refusal will be worse than her baseline situation. The undesirable consequences accompanying noncompliance with a threat either "render the victim of coercion materially worse off than he or she has heretofore been . . . [and/or deprives someone of something] to which the person is entitled."[22] Hence threats are a form of coercion that undermines the voluntariness of consent, all of which translates into (at least attempted) sexual exploitation or immoral sexual use of one party by another.

An offer, on the other hand, is different. Here the offeree's noncompliance will not worsen her baseline—the offeree's situation after her refusal will not be rendered worse than her baseline situation. The offeree here merely refuses the inducement proposed by the offerer and thus declines to accept (what the offerer took to be) desirable consequences that would have improved the offeree's baseline situation: "An offer is fundamentally welcome to a rational person in the sense that the content of an offer necessarily widens the field of opportunity and thus provides, in principle, only potential advantage."[23] Thus, offers create opportunities and provide inducements, whereas threats jeopardize entitlements or augur harms.[24]

The surest way to explain the baseline theory of sexual exploitation is through analyses of examples. To avoid misrepresentations, the cases examined will mirror those actually illustrated by Mappes.

Case 1

Professor Harry Hott approaches student Mary Average. Hott tells Average that her final grade in his course is a C, but he will assign a D unless Average has sex with him. For the baseline theory, this is a paradigm example of a morally impermissible threat and an attempt at sexual exploitation. Although Average is entitled to a C in accordance with professionally accepted grading practices, Hott threatens to deprive her of that entitlement if she does not comply with his sexual demands.[25]

Case 2

Hott tells Average that her final grade in his course is a C, but he will assign an A if and only if Average has sex with him. If Average refuses, she will still get her C.[26] The baseline theory concludes that while here, as in Case 1, Hott abuses his "institutional authority"[27]—by irresponsibly assigning grades on irrelevant grounds—he is not guilty of sexual exploitation. If Average refuses Hott's proposition, her baseline situation will not change: she was antecedently entitled to a C, and her noncompliance with Hott's proposition will not deprive her of that entitlement. (Here we concede that Hott has enough integrity to keep his word.) The baseline theory thus construes Hott's proposition as an offer, not a threat: if Average complies, she will realize, at least in one respect, an improvement in her baseline situation as her C grade inflates into an A.

We begin now to see the inadequacy of the Nozick-Bayles distinction between threats and offers and of the use of that distinction by the baseline theory. Unless we completely submit to the mistakes of ahistoricism and abstractness, it is impossible to analyze Case 2 as a benign offer that is morally flawed only by Hott's abuse of professional grading propriety. Even if Average, upon refusal of Hott's proposition, realizes the C to which she is antecedently entitled, it hardly follows that her situation after her noncompliance is unchanged by Hott's proposition.

The proposition itself must be viewed in context. A relatively empowered male professor initiates a sexual proposition to a relatively unempowered female student under his authority. Such overtures bear the indicia of unilateral control, rather than mutuality and noninstrumentality. As a sexual overture, the proposition conjures a host of pernicious stereotypes: females can get ahead only by submitting to male sexual demands, males can legitimately assume access to females as a prerogative of male power, female sexuality is a commodity appropriate for barter, to name a few. Given the social meaning of sexuality in our culture, Hott's proposition is radically different from nonsexual propositions under the same circumstances.

Suppose all other circumstances were the same except that Hott told Average that he would assign her an A if and only if she washed and waxed his car, or toiled in his garden for a day. Such nonsexual propositions would be accompanied by their own moral deficiencies, but would be unlikely to constitute inherently a kind of harassment. Sexual propositions of this sort, however, are reasonably viewed as wrongful because of the social meaning of sexuality and the established power differentials in our culture between men and women, and teachers and students. Accordingly, the baseline theory clearly manifests several of the classic mistakes of theories of sexual ethics: it assimilates propositions of a sexual nature with all other propositions; it abstracts people such as Hott and Average from their respective sexual contexts; and it ignores history as it aspires to a clear analytical distinction between threats and offers that transcends the vicissitudes of culture.

Advocates of the baseline theory might respond by pointing out that the theory is self-consciously limited: it is not a full-blown theory of sexual ethics; instead, it aspires only to define sexual exploitation and illicit sexual use. Thus the baseline theory could agree that the sexual proposition in question is, all things considered, morally flawed, but still maintain that it is not an example of (attempted) sexual exploitation.

This is a cogent rejoinder, but its persuasiveness depends heavily on the offeree retaining her baseline situation—her entitlements just prior to the proposition—after she rejects the "offer." The instant case is not clear on this point. Even if the student rejects the offer and subsequently receives the grade (C) to which she is entitled, and even if the spurned professor makes no additional efforts to set back her interests, the student's general well-being may have been altered detrimentally. The proposition itself, independent of its specific terms, may constitute a type of sexual harassment that sets back the student's interests and her antecedent entitlement to a nonhostile work/study environment. Accordingly, it is not so clear that the student's antecedent entitlements remain at the baseline established just prior to her rejection of the professor's sexual proposition.

I am not arguing that the proposition at issue *must* have the suggested deleterious effects on all female students to whom it is advanced. Such an argument would be transparently unsound. There is much variation in the reception the professor's proposition would receive: these could range from the wildly enthusiastic—some students might well have longed to have sex with him regardless of his grading of them—to the thoroughly disgusted and debased—some students might view his actions as a paradigm of patriarchal abuse of power and male dominance of female sexuality.

The point, however, is that the baseline theory's analysis is too simple. We should not merely observe that just prior to her professor's sexual proposition the student was entitled to a C; after she rejected that proposition she still received the C; thus the professor, despite a breach of institutional and professional standards, extended a benign or even freedom-enhancing offer to the student. It may well be the case that in many, perhaps most, of these propositions there is an immediate (and lingering?) setback of the offeree's interests.

Would the conclusion be different if the offerer were a female professor and the offeree were a male student? The same analysis would hold, but a male student would be less likely to suffer an immediate setback of his interests than a female student in the Professor Hott case. In our culture, the social meanings of the propositions are different. While a female student can reasonably view Hott as an exemplar of a patriarchal sexual pariah indicative of a wider power disparity between men and women, a male student might view his female professor's proposition as a compliment, as a validation of his manliness and irresistibility. Again, these subjective interpretations admit numerous variations, and I do not intend here to reinstate social stereotypes of the two sexes. Instead, I am only speculating inductively on the actual interpretations the majority of offerees would invoke given the undeniable power differentials between men and women in our culture.

Case 3

Mappes describes another example: "Ms. Starlet, a glamorous, wealthy, highly successful model, wants nothing more than to become a movie superstar. Mr. Moviemogul, a famous producer, is very taken with Ms. Starlet's beauty. He invites her to come to his office for a screen test. After the screen test, Mr. Moviemogul tells Ms. Starlet that he is prepared to make her a star, on the condition that she agree to sexual involvement with him. Ms. Starlet finds Mr. Moviemogul personally repugnant; she is not at all sexually attracted to him. With great reluctance, she agrees to his proposal."[28]

The baseline theory finds no sexual exploitation here. As in Case 2, Moviemogul has abused his institutional authority, but has neither sexually used Starlet nor coerced her consent. Presumably, she is free to reject his offer without detriment to her baseline situation: Starlet had no prior entitlement to Moviemogul's efforts to make her a movie star, thus her noncompliance with Moviemogul's proposition would neither deprive her of an entitlement nor otherwise impair her antecedent situation. Further, Starlet's judgment is not impaired by desperate circumstances or dire needs. Starlet is a "glamorous, wealthy, and highly successful model," not a materially disadvantaged member of the underclass who must barter her sexuality for essential food, clothing, and shelter.

Mappes considers the rejoinder that critics might levy: Isn't Moviemogul's proposition an "overwhelming inducement"[29] that is literally too enticing to refuse? Mappes rejects this criticism by reiterating that Starlet merely wants to be a star, she has no basic need to be a star: "She *wants* very much to be a movie star. I might want very much to be thin. She regrets having to become sexually involved with Mr. Moviemogul as a means of achieving what she wants. I might regret very much having to go on a diet to lose weight. If we say Ms. Starlet acts against her will . . . then we must say I am acting against my will in embracing 'with great reluctance' the diet I despise."[30]

Again, the baseline theory of sexual exploitation manifests its deficiencies. First, we should not dismiss Starlet's entitlements so hastily. While she, indeed, possesses no antecedent entitlement to be a movie star or to Moviemogul's efforts to make her a star, she does have entitlement to evaluation based on her screen test and not on her willingness to have sex with Moviemogul. Thus it is not so clear that Moviemogul leaves intact Starlet's prior situation. The notion of "entitlement" is every bit as slippery and indeterminate as the notion of "sexual exploitation" it is intended to help explicate. In fact, Mappes explicitly includes moral, and not merely legal, entitlements when he explains a person's baseline situation and legitimate expectations.[31] This concession, however, threatens to unravel the baseline theory because moral entitlements are often, perhaps usually unsettled by sexual overtures of the instant kind. Critics will long for a clearer distinction between moral expectations whose defeat triggers sexual exploitation and moral expectations whose defeat does not translate to sexual exploitation.

Second, we should not place inordinate weight on the needs/ wants distinction. While Starlet does not need to be a movie star to fulfill her basic physical requirements of food, clothing, and shelter, it is unclear whether Starlet needs to be a movie star to fulfill her basic psychological requirements of intimacy, self-value, acceptance, and so on. We lack sufficient information to make a refined judgment of this matter. The fact that she is a "glamorous, wealthy, and highly successful model" does not tell us enough about her psychological state. In any event, the specific point is that the baseline theory seems to honor only basic physical needs and to ignore basic psychological needs. The general point is that the baseline theory fails to recognize that "overwhelming wants" often closely resemble "basic needs." Accordingly, the baseline theory is guilty of the mistake of rigidity. The distinction between wants and needs is less of a bright-line and more of a continuum. Hence the distinction will not bear the heavy analytic burden with which the baseline theory saddles it. Third, Moviemogul's proposition itself can be viewed reasonably as wrong for the reasons offered previously in the analysis of Case 2.

At least equally disturbing is the baseline theory's understanding of consent. In fact, the baseline theory defines sexual exploitation as deficient consent—"acting against one's will," "agreement coerced by harm or its threat," "taking advantage of another's dire situation," circumstances which render agreement suspicious. But while it may be true that in some sense Starlet's acceptance of Moviemogul's proposition is not "against her will," it does not follow that she is thereby neither sexually used nor exploited. It is plausible to contend that a person can agree to an interaction that exploits him or her. One prime example is the case of a sane adult with relatively low self-esteem whose self-image centers around victimization. Such a person, while on libertarian-liberal grounds capable of informed consent, may agree to a host of sexual and nonsexual interactions which are exploitive. The mere fact of agreement in the absence of explicit force, fraud, or dire physical need is insufficient to absolve the moral stain of an otherwise exploitive interaction. Under such circumstances, it can be plausibly argued that the offerer's moral culpability multiplies rather than vanishes. This is especially so if the offerer in this case knew and took advantage of the offeree's particular psychology. Moreover, even in the absence of such peculiar psychology, humans often agree to interactions that can reasonably be viewed as exploitive. In any case, the offeree's uncoerced agreement does not, by itself, ratify the interaction as nonexploitive; at best, it only establishes as illegitimate one possible complaint— "it was against my will"—that the exploited party might subsequently be tempted to lodge.

The striking irony of the baseline theory, which is intended to chastise sexual exploitation, is that its acceptance would eviscerate much of our understanding of sexual harassment policies. Although it recognizes abuses of "institutional authority," the baseline theory perceives hazily the ways in which sexual overtures are different from nonsexual propositions that abuse institutional authority. Indeed, in those cases where the offerer lacks institutional authority over the offeree, the offerer is free to invoke the baseline theory as actual justification for his sexual proposition. Consider the following exchange between a sexually voracious worker and his female co-worker:

Dearest Gina,
For some time now I have yearned for sexual contact with you. Sensing that you were less than enthusiastic about that prospect—from the way you vomited when I suggested sex after lunch last week—I sought a suitable inducement. At last, my entreaties have been answered! I now have two front row tickets for the Celtics–Lakers playoff game on Friday. The game is sold out and I know how much you love the Celtics. Here is the deal:

I'll give you *both* tickets if and only if you have sex with me Saturday night. I await your response with eager and sensuous anticipation. I know you will be hot!

Lustfully yours,
Horny Harry

Harry:

Not only do I refuse your "offer," I find it disgusting and demeaning. You seem to harbor the "thought" that I would trade my sexuality for a commodity. That assumption reveals the worst forms of a pernicious patriarchal mindset that contributes to the general oppression of women. Your sexual propositions, irrespective of their terms, are unwelcome, unsettling, and chilling. Take a hike!

Yours in Celtic Victory,
Gina

Dearest Gina,

On the contrary, my sexual propositions are freedom-enhancing offers of the most impeccable moral quality. Should you refuse, your baseline situation is unchanged: I neither deprive you of your entitlements nor threaten harm in any way. I will not bring about undesirable consequences in the event you reject my sexual proposition. On the contrary, I seek only to bring about mutually satisfying consequences should you comply with my offer. I do not abuse my institutional authority because I have no authority over you. I merely create for you a window of opportunity, provide a mutually fulfilling set of inducements, and seek to enhance, not lessen, your baseline context. Even if you refuse my sexual propositions you should thank me for taking such initiatives. I aim to please!

The Offer Still Stands,
Harry Still Horny

P.S. You are even sexier when you are angry!

Hard-core baseline theorists who cast their lot with Horny Harry commit the usual litany of mistakes: assimilation, abstractness, and ahistoricism. While such theorists might insist that Harry's actions are not attempts at exploitation, even if some find them otherwise morally deficient, the earlier rejoinders still pertain. In sum, even if the baseline theory is persuasive as an analysis of "sexual exploitation," it provides a feckless analytic tool for a wider theory of sexual ethics; and if, as I contend, the baseline theory is inadequate as a definition of sexual exploitation because it focuses our concern too narrowly on the notion of uncoerced agreement, then it noxiously diverts our attention from other paramount normative matters.

SEXUAL MORALITY IN FIVE TIERS

A persuasive and comprehensive framework for sexual morality must elude, to the extent possible, the six mistakes adumbrated above. Moreover, it must understand the lingering power of mainstream positions on sexual ethics while at once recognizing the intellectual currency of contemporary radical critiques. Thus, a remodeled theory of sexual ethics emerges from the attempt to mediate the seemingly irreconcilable tensions between politically centrist analysts of morality and their leftist critics. I call my preferred version of sexual ethics, reimagined and remade, "sexual morality in five tiers."

Tier 1: Libertarian Agreement

As we saw in Chapter 4, libertarians insist that the paramount values are individual freedom and autonomy. Thus it is tyranny to insist on a particular kind of sexual interaction or to prescribe a specific domain for acceptable sex. The test of morally permissible sex is simple: Have the parties, possessing the basic capacities necessary for autonomous choice, voluntarily agreed to a particular sexual interaction without force, fraud, and explicit duress? Accordingly, sex is impermissible if one or both parties lack the capacities for informed consent (e.g., underage, significantly mentally impaired, or nonhuman); or if there is explicit duress (threats or extortion), force (coercion), or fraud (one party deceives the other as to the nature of the act or the extent of his or her feelings as a way of luring the other to accepting the liaison).

The strength of libertarianism lies in its clear and uncompromising pinpointing of moral defects that adulterate sexual acts. To the extent that libertarianism affirms sound social values such as freedom and autonomous consent and celebrates the requirement of informed choice, it provides an undeniable service.

The fragility of this perception, however, manifests itself in the corollary libertarian proposition that the presence of the prescribed agreement between the parties is sufficient to establish the moral permissibility of their sexual act. The most glaring weakness of this position is that it ignores numerous moral distortions that occur in the realm of contract: radically unequal bargaining power, prominent differences in psychological vulnerability, the oppression of destitute circumstances, or the treatment of important attributes constitutive of human personality as if they were mere commodities subject to barter. Such distortions call into question whether a particular contract is truly morally permissible. Accordingly, the existence of a contract based on the presence of libertarian agreement is not morally self-validating. Once we know that a contract, arrived at through "voluntary consent," exists, there remains the further question: Are the terms of that contract morally permissible? The libertarian corollary can succeed only if voluntary contractual interaction comprises the totality of morality. But it does not.

The antidote to these deficiencies is supplied when we moderate libertarianism and accept only one of its central claims: informed agreement is a necessary condition for morally permissible sexual interaction. Thus, sexual morality in five tiers rejects the libertarian corollary that informed agreement is a sufficient condition for morally permissible sex.

Some readers, however, might recoil at even this moderate version of libertarianism. They might argue that making informed agreement a necessary condition for moral sex is still too strong. They would conjure hypothetical cases where the consequences of failing to initiate nonconsensual sex were so disastrous that truculent adherence to informed agreement as a necessary condition for moral sex seemed irrational.

For example, suppose that only by raping someone could ten other people's lives be saved. Is it morally wrong under such circumstances to rape? Would the rape be permissible even though the victim, fully aware of the operative facts, refused? If one failed to rape under such circumstances, what would be said to the ten people about to die and their families?

We could, of course, raise the stakes even higher. Suppose the rape would save one thousand people? ten thousand? ten million? the entire world population? Surely, a critic might argue, an absolutist interpretation of informed agreement as a necessary condition for moral sex is irrational if it could lead to the destruction of the entire world!

Moreover, we could alter the example even further. Suppose that only by raping someone could ten other *rapes* be prevented. Now we are no longer trading a rape for other lives, but a rape to prevent other rapes. Thus, those who take rape to be an unspeakable horror, perhaps more noxious in magnitude even than death, are effectively muted: as terrible as rape is, the critic could underscore, it is axiomatic that ten rapes are much worse than one rape of the same sort.

What response is available to these examples? One temptation is to stigmatize all such illustrations as fanciful, radically hypothetical, and unhelpful in real world moral analysis. Here we might refashion the adage "hard cases make for bad law" into "unrealistic, bizarre cases make for bad moral analysis."

This approach, however, evades confrontation by dismissing troubling counterexamples straightaway. This strategy is too easy and ultimately unsatisfying. The force of the counterexamples is not in their specificity, but in the general point they illustrate: Are there not times when the consequences of nonconsensual sex invalidate an absolutist rendering of the libertarian agreement principle? Are there not times when the ends do justify the means?

Hence, undermining the plausibility of the specific examples leaves the general point unscathed. With sufficient ingenuity and care, critics could conjure counterexamples much "closer to home"—cases that did not trade on seemingly farfetched circumstances or unbelievable contexts. Such counterexamples could not be brushed off so easily. Accordingly, sexual morality in five tiers resists the temptation to dismiss cravenly such cases by mocking their bizarre terms and invoking the need for realism.

A second approach to parrying the threat of unsettling counterexamples is a "lesser of two evils" analysis. Under this view, nonconsensual sex is still immoral, but its initiation is excused because it prevents even worse evil or facilitates an otherwise unobtainable good. Given the contexts conjured earlier, it is plausible to argue that, while libertarian agreement remains a necessary condition for moral permissibility, under the relevant circumstances an immoral sexual action may be the lesser of two evils when we confront an unappealing and inescapable moral dilemma. Engaging in the sexual act under such circumstances does not remove its stigma, but does supply the act's initiator with an excuse: "I know the act was morally wrong, but because of the circumstances, I cannot be held morally culpable."

At first blush, this approach offers an appealing compromise between those who aspire to an absolutist rendering of the libertarian agreement principle and those who yearn to prove that informed agreement cannot be a necessary condition of sexual interaction. But the compromise is unstable and unsatisfying at its core. First, those critics who would offer counterexamples such as those outlined above do so to show that the ends sometimes justify, and not merely excuse, the means needed to secure them. They want to argue that nonconsensual sex can be the morally right thing to do in certain situations, not merely that such sex is always morally wrong but sometimes excusable: "I know that nonconsensual sex is almost always wrong, but because of the circumstances in this case, such sex is not only morally permissible but perhaps morally obligatory." Thus, such critics would be unfulfilled by any lesser-of-two-evils approach that concludes that nonconsensual sex is always morally wrong but sometimes excusable.

Second, those who hold that libertarian agreement is a necessary condition of morally permissible sex would also be disturbed by the proffered compromise. They would want to hold that any sexual activity that violates the informed agreement principle renders itself morally wrong. To say in the instant cases that nonconsensual sex is wrong but excusable as the lesser of two evils holds the libertarian agreement principle hostage to the exigencies of the moment and to recurring aggregations of overall benefit. This would lead, it may be argued, to a crude instrumentalism in which there are no necessary conditions for moral interactions. This, in turn, implies that we have only constant situational calculations of right and wrong, or fragile prima facie moral principles that are themselves hostage to their ability to produce generally optimal outcomes.

The advocates of the libertarian agreement principle contend that nonconsensual sex is immoral and inexcusable. Their critics offer counterexamples that allegedly manifest how nonconsensual sex can be morally justified in certain extreme situations. The lesser-of-two-evils approach concludes that nonconsensual sex is always immoral but sometimes excusable. As such, this approach will satisfy neither the advocates of the libertarian agreement principle nor their critics. Accordingly, it should be clear that the lesser-of-two-evils approach achieves its compromise by slyly recasting the positions of the two protagonists.

In the face of all this, sexual morality in five tiers bites the bullet and affirms the libertarian agreement principle despite the critics' counterexamples. Thus, this theory subscribes to the inviolability of persons in certain important respects, one of which is sexual access. We cannot deny others their status as freely choosing, rationally valuing people with moral personality. The value of personhood is not determined by choice, but is, instead, presupposed in the very notion of informed choice. There must be some moral constraints on what can be done to individuals against their will in the name of advancing the collective good. Whether we call this limit "inviolability," "human dignity," "human rights," "taking seriously the differences between persons," or any similar slogan is less important than that we recognize at least some necessary moral constraints on using people against their will for the benefit of others. This recognition blocks a social appeal to aggregate consequences in justifying violations of these constraints. Instrumentalism, at least in its cruder forms, eviscerates the constitutive attributes of personhood by permitting their adjustment according to the dictates of the optimal calculus of the moment. As such, crude instrumentalism is anathema to sexual morality in five tiers, because the former portrays all constitutive human attributes as contingent while the latter embraces (a few) necessary, nonconsequentialist moral constraints.

As already noted, however, sexual morality in five tiers moderates libertarianism's gushing and boundless veneration of human choice. The theory urged here takes libertarian agreement to be a necessary, but not sufficient, condition of morally permissible sex.

What moral coinage, then, does Tier-1 analysis mint? At this stage of analysis we are not concerned with addressing moral subtleties such as exploitation, commodification, unequal bargaining power, and destitute circumstances. We ask only the basic libertarian question: Have the parties, possessing the basic capacities necessary for

autonomous choice, voluntarily agreed to a particular sexual interaction without force, fraud, and explicit duress? If the answer is negative then we need go no further: the sexual act is morally impermissible. If the answer is affirmative then the sexual act must meet the
requirements of the other four tiers if it is to gain the honorific title
of "morally permissible."

A critic might claim that my argument assumes that we can evaluate the consensual properties of particular sexual acts independently of their historical and cultural contexts. This may suggest
that sexual morality in five tiers falls prey at the outset to errors
identified previously: essentialism and universalism.

Such a reading is based on a misunderstanding. The perceptions of
the properties of libertarian agreement are themselves culturally and
historically shaped. That is why sexual morality in five tiers necessarily provides only a framework for analysis rather than concrete,
timeless, universal, substantive conclusions. The distinction here is
between an analysis, such as my own, that argues only that libertarian agreement must be present for morally permissible sex and an
analysis that specifies the precise properties which constitute libertarian agreement at all times and places. The latter analysis would
be fairly subject to charges of essentialism and universalism, while
the former is not. In sum, Tier-1 analysis tells us only that libertarian agreement is a necessary but not sufficient condition of morally
permissible sex; it does not claim that we can evaluate consensual
properties of particular sex acts ahistorically.

Tier 2: General Moral Considerations

Although I am presenting the theory in discrete levels of analysis,
sexual morality in five tiers is not so easily categorized. Often the
questions implicated at one level of analysis replicate themselves at
another level or require answers supplied at least partly from analyses at other levels. These facts are clearest in Tier 2.

Here we look to general considerations which are applicable when
evaluating all moral decision making. There are a number of prima
facie principles of morality acknowledged in our culture: keep promises; tell the truth; return favors; aid others in distress when doing so
involves no serious danger or sacrifice to oneself or innocent third
parties; make reparation for harm to others that is one's own fault;

oppose injustices when doing so involves no great cost or sacrifice to oneself; promote just institutions and facilitate their continuation and refinement; assume one's fair share of societal burdens and thus avoid being a "free rider"; avoid causing pain or suffering to others; avoid inexcusable killing of others; and avoid stealing or otherwise depriving others of their property.[32]

This is not an exhaustive litany of our moral duties, but it does constitute the general framework from which we derive other specific obligations. Accordingly, Tier-2 analysis encompasses all of those relevant considerations that must be consulted when assessing morally any human interaction. The principles listed above are prima facie, not absolute. Their respective imperatives often conflict, and thus it is often impossible to fulfill all of their dictates in every moral context. Moreover, appeals to consequences and the real effects of actions will often compel the overriding of a prima facie moral principle.

In Tier 2 we cannot ask simply, "Has a lie been told?" and conclude that if the answer is affirmative then the surrounding sex act is automatically immoral. Although I have claimed that libertarian agreement is a necessary condition for morally permissible sex, I also recognize the quite obvious truth that transgressions of one or more of the prima facie principles listed above are often morally justified.[33]

At this tier we must also confront the motives and intentions of the parties engaging in sex. Further, we must evaluate ancillary issues such as abuse of one's institutional role and social power and the foreseen and actual consequences of the sexual acts in question. Although the primary focus in Tier 2 is on the interacting parties themselves, full evaluation of the justifiability of transgressions of prima facie moral principles will often require an inquiry into issues described in Tiers 4 and 5. It is thus impossible to separate plausibly the five tiers into fully autonomous layers of analysis. We probably come the closest in Tier 1, but even there we must ponder questions of fraud, force, and deception which implicate and overlap issues in other tiers.

Tier 3: Sexual Exploitation

Interpersonal exploitation, in its morally pejorative sense, is characterized by the following: One party (E) takes advantage of another party's (V) attributes or situation to exact gain for E and/or E's compatriots.[34] The various types of exploitation display various degrees of coercion. Joel Feinberg points out that "exploiters are typically opportunists; they extract advantage from situations that are not of their own making. Coercers, on the other hand, are typically makers rather than mere discoverers and users of opportunities."[35]

At times, exploitation is explicitly coercive, which destroys the possibility of mutually informed consent and libertarian agreement. At other times, exploitation is subtly coercive: E may capitalize on V's relatively inferior bargaining power or special vulnerabilities. At still other times, exploitation may not seem coercive at all: V may render fully informed libertarian agreement to V's misuse by E.

In noncoercive exploitation, V's consent is relevant to, but not dispositive of, moral assessment. That Jones renders fully informed consent to Smith's mutilation of Jones's body, for example, does not entail that Smith's act is morally permissible. Thus, V's consent may prevent V from lodging a credible claim that V has been personally wronged by E's opportunism, but it does not by itself exonerate E from charges of wrongful exploitation: "What we must mean by (unfair) exploitation is 'profitable utilization of another person that is either on balance unfair to him, or which in virtue of its other unfairness-producing characteristics would be unfair on balance to him but for his voluntary consent to it.' "[36]

At the heart of exploitation is the profit extracted by E from E's use of V: "We must employ an admittedly extended sense of 'gain' including both gain in the strict sense and fulfillment of one's aims, purposes, or desires, including altruistic and conscientious ones. The 'gain' in question, moreover, need not be a *net* gain if there should happen also to be attendant losses."[37] E's profit is procured at V's expense: V either suffers an overall setback to V's interests, or no gain, or a disproportionately meager gain. All this yields the flavor of exploitation as one person "using another as a mere means" for her own ends. The images here are those of V being regarded as less than V is: not as an equal subject of experience, but as a mere instrument for the advance of E's purposes and profits.

Explicitly coercive exploitation is of little interest to Tier-3 analysis because such actions necessarily vitiate the possibility of libertarian agreement. Thus, Tier 1 would dismiss such cases straightaway. Instead, subtly coercive exploitation and consensual exploitation are of greater interest here.

Unsurprisingly, it is much easier to provide a general framework for exploitation than to detail a mechanical method of identifying specific cases. Tier-3 analysis, however, assumes the following: as a result of socially created and other historical conditions, sexual contracts are different from nonsexual exchanges of goods and services; the relative situation of men and women, taken as classes, differ historically, as does the relative situation of heterosexuals vis à vis homosexuals; and when evaluating the presence of exploitation, attention must be given to the particular circumstances, vulnerabilities, prior entitlements, relative bargaining power and social status, and wants/needs of the parties.

In this vein, the paradigm of subtly coercive exploitation consists of an E with relatively strong socioeconomic bargaining power; a V with special vulnerabilities, needs, or deep wants; and a proposition, initiated by E and formulated for E's advantage and at V's loss or disproportionately small gain, that has the effect of narrowing or closing V's overall opportunities.[38] Such exploitation is "subtly coercive" because the force used to secure "consent" is not so obvious as to trigger a violation of libertarian agreement, yet not so benign as to translate clearly to fully informed, mutual consent.

However, we cannot be mystified by our paradigms of exploitation into thinking dogmatically that only men are sexual exploiters and only women are the victims of exploitation. Academics, under the spell of the prodigious amount of contemporary literature sympathetic to feminist concerns, sometimes stumble into believing that our paradigms—for example, a socially powerful, lecherous male misusing his advantages to coerce overtly or subtly a relatively less powerful woman to engage in sexual acts she otherwise detests—constitute the whole of sexual exploitation. While it is undeniable that our society has an inglorious historical record with regard to women's full enfranchisement in the public sphere and that our society, indeed, embodies numerous patriarchal vices, it is also true that in the sexual microcontexts that men and women create, either party can be exploited. Virginia Held, a feminist philosopher, captures this well:

> In their dealings with one another, man and woman discover not only that man can overpower woman . . . and woman can over-

power man—that is, at the level of *sexual* power, as opposed to muscular and other power, they really *are* equal. What human beings also discover is that in this relation, mutual respect is only possible when neither overpowers the other, and coercion of any kind, including the use of sexual power in coercive ways, is transcended.[39]

That brings us to the special problems raised by the third type of exploitation, consensual exploitation. Here V renders fully informed consent to V's misuse by E. One might be tempted to argue that so long as V consented, it is presumptuous of others to deem the interaction a "misuse." For who is a better judge of V's interests and preferences than V?

But as I argued in Chapter 4, a person's perceptions of her best interests and what would advance them are not incorrigibly correct. Moreover, there are moral limits to what we may do to others even with their consent. Feinberg tells us:

> exploitation of another's rashness or foolishness is *wrong*, even when because of prior voluntary consent it does not violate the other's right. . . . It is wrong because the actor believes on good evidence that it will probably set back [the victim's] interest, and deliberately choosing to be an instrument of another's "harm" (setback to interest) for one's own gain is often something we ought not to do, even though the other can have no [personal] grievance against us when we do.[40]

The key here is to distinguish different sorts of risks that others are willing to take, but that we would refuse. When is consent to an uncommon action "rash and foolish" and thus likely to "set back" V's interests? When is it mere risk taking that reveals nothing more than V's adventuresome and unrepressed nature? The answers are found when we assess the prospects of V's gain relative to E: Will E realize significant "profit," as defined earlier, while V suffers loss, no gain, or disproportionately paltry gain? Does V's consent betray V's vulnerabilities, negative self-image, misfortune and destitute circumstances, or human weaknesses? Has E manipulated V by appealing to such vulnerabilities, circumstances, and weaknesses? Has E thus pandered to the worst aspects of V? It becomes clearer that to establish "exploitation," we must attend not merely to the foreseeable effects on V's interests but also to E's motives, intentions, and expected gain.

Accordingly, the totality of circumstances surrounding V's consent is paramount. Who initiated the proposition which formed the basis of possible exploitation is especially relevant. For example, E may have won V's consent through subtle manipulation which traded on V's known weaknesses through "seductive luring, beguiling, tempting, bribing, coaxing, imploring, whimpering, flattering, and the like, short of deceptive innuendo, threats, or coercive offers."[41] Such manipulation is more probative of exploitation then straightforward offers and explicit propositions. There are, of course, numerous other ways E might initiate the proposition:

> Less likely to be unfair are fishing expeditions in which [E] merely hangs his lure within range of vulnerable [V], attracting his voluntary agreement to a scheme that is in fact likely to promote [E's] gain at [V's] expense. [E] may initiate the process by making a proposal to [V] which [V] after due contemplation, but no manipulative persuasion, readily accepts. Least likely of all to be unfair to [V] are those agreements which [V] himself initially proposes and to which [E] reluctantly responds.[42]

I must underscore, however, that the circumstances surrounding the initiation of the proposition are one, but only one, source of evidence where we evaluate the possibility of wrongful exploitation. The reason that V's initiation of the proposition makes exploitation less likely is that it manifests V's antecedent willingness to participate in the acts constituting the proposition and precludes the possibility that V complied because of overt threats. But, although V's initiation of a proposition is less likely to trigger exploitation than is E's coercive, manipulative, and straightforward offerings, it is still possible for V to initiate a proposition that results in V's wrongful exploitation by E. Once again, the keys are V's special vulnerabilities, circumstances, and relative bargaining power, the fashion in which these were used in the acts constituting the proposition, and the distribution of gains and setbacks to interests as between E and V.

Tier 4: Third Party Effects

Sexual acts can be immoral despite the presence of libertarian agreement, the absence of exploitation, and compliance with general moral considerations vis à vis the consenting parties.

For example, we can imagine a married couple who mutually agree to have sexual relations with other parties. Suppose further that within the confines of the acts performed by these other parties and the married couple all general moral considerations are honored, no exploitation occurs, and full libertarian agreement is present. However, the children of the married couple suffer greatly as a result of their parents' sexual profligacy. Without detailing the precise nature of that suffering, we can hypothesize that it is caused directly by the parents' sexual experimentation and is serious enough to constitute clear harm. (We must concede that harm to children because of their parents' sexual excesses does not necessarily imply a failure of parental moral duty—we can summon cases where we would be more sympathetic, from a moral perspective, to the parents than to their suffering children—but stipulate here that the instant case is no such aberration.)

In such a situation it is reasonable to declare the married couple's actions morally impermissible. Invoking the presence of libertarian agreement among the sexually involved parties, the absence of exploitation, and the parties' mutual fulfillment of prima facie moral requirements via à vis one another would be insufficient to redeem morally the sexual acts in question.

Accordingly, third party effects become an important tier of analysis for sexual ethics. We are concerned here mainly with the reasonably foreseeable and actual consequences of the sexual acts in question on the immediate circle of people affected by the acts. The wider social effects of the sexual acts are more appropriately analyzed in Tier 5.

I must underscore, however, that the mere presence of harmful or offensive effects to others by a sexual act is insufficient to establish that the act in question is morally flawed when judged by Tier 4. Consider the following example: Jones and Smith are a racially mixed couple who enjoy taking walks on the main street of a small town. Biggs and Boggs are deeply offended by these walks because the two men are vehemently opposed to miscegenation. The reader can use his or her imagination and summon the details, but stipulate that Biggs and Boggs suffer gravely as a result of the racially mixed couple's strolls. Obviously, Jones and Smith are not guilty of immoral actions simply because the two bystanders are deeply offended.

Consider another example: Jackson and Johnson have dated for three years. After a period of discontent, Jackson informs Johnson that she wishes to stop dating him. Shortly thereafter, Jackson begins dating Russo. Johnson, who still pines for Jackson, perceives Russo as an intruder. He accuses Russo of "cutting my grass." Are Jackson and/or Russo immoral simply because Johnson suffers as a result of their liaisons? Certainly not under the illustration as it is sketched here.

In both of the examples above, and in innumerable others we might construct, the "victims" have not been wronged by the facts that lead to their suffering: their rights have not been violated nor have their interests been transgressed unjustifiably. In that important sense, they have not been harmed. Instead, their suffering is the result of the offense they take at the actions of others. This observation does not lessen the extent of that suffering, but it does tend to exonerate morally the people whose fully permissible actions led to that suffering. Negative third party effects are most compelling, from a moral perspective, where they result from unjustified harming. They are much less commanding where they result from offense taken by bystanders.

The fact that people are offended by certain actions is relevant in moral assessment, but only some cases of rendering offense are morally culpable. To determine whether offensive conduct translates into moral culpability, Joel Feinberg recommends that we balance the seriousness of the offense caused by an act against the reasonableness of the act.[43] The seriousness of the offense caused by the act is calculated by the following: (1) the magnitude of the offense as measured by its intensity, duration, and extent; (2) the extent to which the offense was reasonably avoidable; (3) whether the offended party voluntarily assumed the risk of experiencing the offensive act; and (4) whether the offended party had an abnormal susceptibility to offense. The reasonableness of the act is calculated by the following: (1) the importance of the offending conduct to the actors; (2) the social value of the act; (3) whether the act is a case of free expression; (4) the availability of alternative opportunities for the actors to engage in the act; (5) whether the animating motive of the act was malicious or spiteful; and (6) whether the act was performed in locales where it is common and expected, or in locales where it is rare and unexpected.[44]

In sum, Tier 4 focuses on the way sexual activity affects the interests of the immediate circle of third parties. Specifically, it asks the following questions: Have these third parties been unjustifiably harmed? Has the sexual conduct at issue rendered wrongful offense?

Tier 5: Wider Social Context

There are times when sexual activity accompanied by libertarian agreement nevertheless has detrimental social effects. Such acts might reflect and reinforce oppressive social roles, contribute to continued social inequality, gestate new forms of gender oppression, or otherwise add to the contamination of the wider social and political context surrounding sexual activity.

Although liberal-centrists venerate personal choice and private morality, doing so often marginalizes the wider social background and effects attending sex and illustrates a subtle form of the error of isolationism. Marxists and feminists are most diligent in pressing this point: sex acts are not always merely discrete interactions between consenting parties.

In this vein, the self-described "Lesbian-Feminist" Colleta Reid argues that "[Sex] is not private; it is a political matter of oppression, domination, and power."[45] Moreover, "In a world devoid of male power and, therefore, sex roles, who you lived with, loved, slept with and were committed to would be irrelevant. All of us would be equal and have equal determination over the society and how it met our needs. Until this happens, how [women] use our sexuality and our bodies is just as relevant to our liberation as how we use our minds and our time."[46]

For example, numerous feminists insist that the depiction of women in books and movies as sexual playthings and sexually submissive entertainers of men demeans women generally. Regardless of the fully informed consent of those women who participate in such ventures, feminists claim that all women share the attributes at issue and thus women generally are degraded by the demeaning portrayals of the consenting models.[47] Such observations lead numerous Feminists to conclude that "the personal is *always* political" and that heterosexual acts *must* reinforce a social structure that is antecedently and irredeemably flawed. Marxists could make a parallel claim that particular occasions of bourgeois heterosexuality necessarily reflect and reinforce the socially incapacitating imperatives of capitalism. As such, both perspectives could argue that conventionally accepted sex within a corrupt social setting is necessarily wrong because of its subsidizing effects.

Sexual morality in five tiers, subscribing as it does to the possibility of heterosexual couples creating salutary microcontexts even within an otherwise unhealthy social structure, cannot endorse this leftist prescription in its unregenerative form. However, sexual morality in five tiers does not thereby reinstate the liberal-centrist axiom that sex is securely within the domain of personal choice and private morality. The challenge, then, is to avoid the Scylla of leftist necessitarianism and the Charybdis of liberal-centrist isolationism.

This challenge, however, is more easily raised than fulfilled. In their respective ways, leftist necessitarianism and liberal-centrist isolationism both embody the virtue of easy applicability: each generates moral conclusions quickly and clearly. On the other hand, perspectives such as sexual morality in five tiers, which aspire to chart courses less traveled, require careful attention to specific cases and resist inflexible characterizations. Moreover, this fifth tier raises issues of widespread social effects that invite speculation and evaluation that are unsusceptible to easy verification.

Accordingly, users of sexual morality in five tiers must attend carefully to the specifics of each case and answer questions such as the following: Does this sex act contribute in a specific and articulable way to the general oppression of women (or any other disadvantaged class) by men (or any other advantaged class)? Does this act facilitate intermediate institutions (such as prostitution) which reflect and reinforce social oppression? Does this act hinder in a specific way the establishment of intermediate institutions which might rectify social oppression? Is this act public enough to affect directly the social roles of disadvantaged and advantaged classes?

QUANTIFYING THE FIVE TIERS

Moral analysis evades mathematical precision. But, often, we can roughly quantify a theory to illustrate more clearly its underlying commitments and aspirations. In this vein, we can take the five tiers—libertarian agreement (LA), general moral considerations (MC), sexual exploitation (SE), third party effects (TP), and wider social context (SC)—and sketch a formula or test for sexual morality:

$$\text{Sexual Morality Quotient} = LA \times (MC + SE + TP + 1/2 \, SC)$$

We could use this formula in the following way when evaluating a sexual interaction: Libertarian agreement is assigned a score of either 1, if it is present, or 0, if it is absent. Libertarian agreement is a necessary condition of morally permissible sex. Thus if it is lacking in the instant case then the action is morally wrong. By assigning "LA" as 0 in such cases we ensure that the act's morality quotient is 0 (as 0 times any number is 0).

The other four elements—general moral considerations (MC), sexual exploitation (SE), third party effects (TP), and wider social context (SC)—are assigned scores of 0 to 100. These scores represent the range from the thoroughly depraved and morally irredeemable (0) to the morally permissible but mundane (80) to the morally supererogatory and ideal (100). The score that is assigned the fifth tier, wider social context, is multiplied by 0.5 to reflect the difficulty and speculation necessarily involved in evaluating the issues raised by this tier. These problems militate that fifth tier analysis should count less than the analyses of the other tiers.

A perfect cumulative score is 350. This represents morally ideal sex, whatever that may be. We cannot fully describe this type of sex, but we can say generally that it goes above and beyond the call of moral duty. It is sex that is not merely morally permissible, but morally exemplary. It would involve some extraordinary moral benefits to others not attainable in merely morally permissible sex. I am hesitant to describe it further because such an exercise requires extensive delineation of our moral duties and how we might exceed them. My more pressing concern is adumbrating morally permissible, not morally ideal, sex. Hence this work is pitched to the morally conscientious, not the saintly.

A cumulative score of 280 represents morally permissible sex. Such sex does not violate our moral duties, but it is not so praiseworthy as to rise to the level of a supererogatory act. A cumulative score below 280 represents morally impermissible sex. Such sex violates our moral duties. But, of course, not all such acts are equally wrong. The formula permits users to conclude not simply that a sex act is wrong, but also the degree of its moral deficiencies, ranging from the utterly depraved (0–50) to the thoroughly defiled (51–100) to the clearly contemptible (101–240) to the somewhat contaminated (241–265) to the mere peccadillo (266–279).

Moreover, for those sex acts that violate the requirement of libertarian agreement and automatically earn a 0, users can still complete the rest of the formula to determine which of two such impermissible acts is morally worse: the act that scores higher on assessment of the remaining four tiers is less wrong to that degree than the other act. Finally, we have the case of two morally impermissible acts of the following sort: the first fails the test of libertarian consent but, should we continue the analysis, scores reasonably well on the tests of other four tiers; the second passes the test of libertarian consent but scores woefully on the tests of the other four tiers. The former might be represented by $[0 \times (80 + 80 + 80 + 40)]$, while the latter might be represented by $[1 \times (40 + 60 + 60 + 30)]$. Given its scores, the former would have been judged morally permissible if and only if it had passed the test of libertarian agreement, while the latter is clearly contemptible despite the fact that it did pass the test of libertarian agreement. Which of the two is, all things considered, morally worse? I am inclined to view the first act as morally worse than the second act. While there may be extraordinary cases where we would want to conclude otherwise, in most such comparisons my inclination would remain, due to the primacy I place on libertarian agreement as a necessary condition of morally permissible sex.

Some readers will recoil at this entire effort at quantification. They may wonder whether I have fallen prey to one of the very analytic traps I have already disparaged: rigidity. Has the apostle of flexibility and the shameless shill of continuums suddenly been exposed as just another anal-retentive bean counter? Perhaps—but I must resist such harsh characterization. The horizontal line joining the two poles of the thoroughly depraved and morally irredeemable (0) and the morally supererogatory and ideal (350) remains a continuum. But in moral theory we must draw at least one other vertical line to distinguish the morally permissible from the morally impermissible. There comes a time, at the end of moral analysis, when inquiring minds demand to know: Is the act morally right or wrong?

Readers may also scoff at assigning scores to each tier of the analysis. How does one quantify a lie, a broken promise, or a laudatory third party effect? How does an 80 represent anything? The answer here is that we make comparative judgments of this sort all the time. We judge of two morally impermissible acts that one is worse than the other. We declare actions morally right and morally wrong. We decide that certain morally permissible actions are of higher moral quality than other morally permissible actions. And so on. Perhaps we do not literally assign exact scores to such judgments, but we surely make relative comparisons in a figurative fashion. Such comparisons may not require a slide rule or computer, but they do demand, among other things, relative weighing of moral principles, careful consideration of context, and aggregation of numerous, often competing, factors. Although moral reasoning is not susceptible to mathematical precision, it necessarily requires quantification in some form to some extent.

Accordingly, the sexual morality quotient urged here is neither self-executing nor rigid. Instead, it merely provides a theoretical framework into which substance must be supplied by general moral theory. The explanation and justification of a full-blown moral theory is necessarily beyond the scope of this work, but I can provide many of the commitments and presuppositions that animate the conclusions to specific cases that will follow.

A PARTIAL LIST OF ANIMATING ASSUMPTIONS

Although I call the following "assumptions," it will be clear to the assiduous reader that I have argued for most of them earlier in this work. Other animating assumptions are delineated clearly in my explanation of sexual morality in five tiers and will not be repeated now.

1. Sex cannot legitimately be reduced to only one of its numerous aspects. Human sexuality does not have one particular natural function. Instead, there are a variety of morally permissible purposes for which sex may be undertaken (for example, procreation, pleasure,

expression of love, fulfillment of needs for intimacy, and so on). The legitimacy of such purposes in specific contexts must be examined by general moral theory.

2. Thus, neither desire to procreate nor antecedent love and intimacy is a necessary condition of morally permissible sex.

3. Sex is different from ordinary contractual exchanges of commodities and services. Sex in our culture has a socially charged meaning that in most cases implicates more of our constitutive attributes and thus puts more of our self-identity in jeopardy than do other mundane voluntary exchanges.

4. The fact that sex is different from ordinary contractual exchanges of commodities and services does not imply that sex must be different. It is more likely that sex is different because of contingent historical and cultural reasons than because of underlying, immutable features of human nature.

5. The voluntariness of sex is often, but not always, impaired by economic reality and the imperatives of particular economic structures.

6. The sexual domination of women by men is a particularly widespread and pernicious form of oppression, but it is not clearly the "fundamental" or "basic" or "underlying cause of" (all) oppression.

7. In a generally patriarchal context, it is still possible for a woman to exploit sexually a man. Specific women may have power advantages over specific men based on culturally defined physical attractiveness and seductiveness, as well as economic and political leverage.

8. In a generally patriarchal context, it is still possible for women and men to create a microcontexts that sufficiently expunge gender conflict to facilitate morally permissible sex.

9. To the extent possible, we must avoid the six major flaws of numerous popular analyses of sexual ethics: reductionism, abstractness, isolationism, ahistoricism, rigidity, and assimilation.

10. Homosexuality is not inherently immoral or "unnatural" or "perverted." Instead, it is susceptible to analysis by sexual morality in five tiers. We must, however, pay careful attention to moral issues and problems that often accompany homosexuality more commonly than they accompany heterosexuality, and vice versa.

SPECIFIC ILLUSTRATIONS

The following examples are each intended to illustrate one or two aspects of sexual morality in five tiers. I will not fully analyze these examples or assign them an aggregate quantitative score because to do so requires much more circumstantial detail than I provide here. Moreover, it should be clear that sexual morality in five tiers does not mechanically generate moral conclusions. Instead, it serves as a conceptual framework which highlights certain questions and outlines the issue relevant to sexual ethics. The content of the analysis of sexual morality in five tiers—the animating assumptions and specific arguments leading to general answers to moral questions and conclusions to concrete cases—can only be supplied by descriptive and prescriptive world views. Thus, ideology, in its benign sense of general social and political vision, is required to generate the moral conclusions that follow.

The ideology to which I subscribe is fueled by my ambition to mediate the tensions between mainstream Western morality and its leftist and feminist critics. If these efforts are judged successful, readers will perceive the ideology of sexual morality in five tiers as a sensible synthesis of several traditions, each of which captures an important dimension of sexual morality, but none of which adequately explains and justifies our sexual theory and practice. If these efforts are judged unsuccessful, readers will perceive the ideology of sexual morality in five tiers as the flaccid eclecticism of a hopelessly conflicted academic.

Case 1

Jones is a woman who has tested positive for HIV. Smith is a man who wants to have sex with Jones. Jones would like to have sex with Smith but does not wish to transmit HIV to Smith. At the time the couple is contemplating their sex act, condoms and other methods of preventing the transmission of HIV are unavailable to them. Smith tells Jones he still desires sex with her despite the risks of transmission. Jones reasons that Smith has issued fully informed consent and thus Smith has voluntarily assumed the risks. The couple engages in sexual intercourse.

We could fill in the details further if necessary to convince skeptics that libertarian agreement is in place. Jones, after all, does not try to convince Smith to have sex, she tries to dissuade him. Hence, Jones cannot reasonably be charged with playing on Smith's vulnerabilities, deep yearnings, desperate circumstances, or the like. Also, from the meager facts given there are no adverse third party effects or wider societal implications. There is, however, a problem with Tier 2: Smith's fully informed consent and assumption of risk are not sufficient to satisfy the relevant general moral considerations. Such factors may well be sufficient to block a subsequent moral claim or legal complaint by Smith that he was personally wronged by nonconsensual sex, but they are insufficient to satisfy our general moral duty to refrain from needlessly or unjustifiably harming others.

Although Smith's decision is probably not rash or hasty in view of the deliberations he undertook, his action was clearly more than imprudent: it was reckless and perhaps self-destructive. All of this should be apparent enough to Jones. Moreover, given that Smith and Jones could engage in much safer sex if they waited until suitable prophylactics were available and that the value of their particular sex act pales in comparison to the risks of HIV transmission, Smith's fully informed consent does not exonerate Jones from moral culpability.

Case 2

Russo and Rossi are a young married couple with strong sexual urges. They decide to capitalize on their proclivity for and lack of self-consciousness about sex. They seek and gain employment as sexual exhibitionists in Times Square in New York City. They perform their act before those who pay for the privilege of viewing it. The act consists of Russo, the husband, sadistically brutalizing Rossi, the wife, and forcing her to submit to his sexual will. The act trades on many prevalent stereotypes: a dominant male whose submissive female initially says "no" but really means "yes"; a sexual interaction in which the fulfillment of male desires is paramount; a female of generally subordinate status who deserves the treatment meted out by the dominant male; and so on. Russo and Rossi consider the act great fun. They truly love each other and would never engage in such actions away from their jobs. They are, indeed, acting. In sum, they consider their act a bit silly, but they enjoy it and consider their salary to be more than enough compensation.

This case triggers the suspicions of at least two tiers. First, we must wonder about third party effects: Does the act encourage and legitimate male sadism in its viewers? Is there a cause and effect (or contributing factor) relationship between viewing the act and increasing sexual brutality? On the other hand, does the act decrease sexual brutality because viewers experience cathartic effects and become less likely to engage in the viewed acts? The answers to specific empirical questions are beyond the scope of this work, but sexual morality in five tiers recognizes the need to consider and resolve the probabilities of such third party effects.

Second, we must look to the wider societal context: Do these sex acts contribute in a specific and articulable way to the general oppression of women by men? Do the acts facilitate intermediate institutions (such as sadomasochism) that reflect and reinforce social oppression? Do the acts hinder in a specific way the establishment of intermediate institutions that might rectify social oppression? Is this act public enough to affect directly the social roles of disadvantaged and advantaged classes? In the instant case, a solid case can be advanced that women are degraded generally by the Russo-Rossi sexual dramas, which contribute to a widespread atmosphere of patriarchal domination. Thus, regardless of the specific effects on the paying clientele with regard to sadomasochistic behavior, the sexual dramas in question may well contribute, intentionally or not, to a demeaning conceptualization of woman's role in society. Such a conceptualization itself echoes and legitimates a host of pernicious social injustices. Accordingly, although we would need more specifics to make a confident determination, it appears that sexual morality in five tiers would judge the Russo–Rossi sexual dramas to be morally flawed despite the lack of direct harm to the parties themselves.

Case 3

Ace Zerblonski is a degenerate gambler. For a long time, Wanda Stringer has yearned to have sex with Ace, but Ace has made it clear that he finds Wands sexually unattractive. One day Wanda hatches a scheme. She knows that Ace loves to wager on horse races and she asks Harry Handicapper, who owes Wanda a favor and who is an excellent evaluator of racing probabilities, for his "best bet" at the racetrack that night. Armed with that knowledge, Wanda approaches Ace and makes an explicit proposition: Wanda will supply Ace with Harry's selection if and only if Ace has sex with her that afternoon. Wanda and Ace both know that Harry cannot guarantee that his selection will win, but they also know that Harry wages profitably on horses and that his best bets are particularly successful. Ace has no other way of discovering which horse is Harry's best bet that night. After some deliberation, Ace decides he must find out Harry's selection, and he accepts Wanda's proposition despite the deep revulsion he experiences at the thought of having sex with her. Ace and Wanda engage in afternoon delight. Wanda is thrilled by the experience. Ace, unsurprisingly, is disgusted by the sex but eager to go to the track that night and bet Harry's tip.

Sexual morality in five tiers judges this act morally impermissible. First, there is the element of libertarian agreement. Depending on the extent to which Ace can resist his gambling urges, a case can be made that he was incapable of fully informed consent. By labeling Ace a "degenerate gambler" we have suggested the presence of the sort of irresistible impulses that characterize addictions. As such, it may be argued plausibly that the resulting sex act was inherently flawed because of a lack of libertarian agreement. All this, however, is a bit speculative and we would need more detail on Ace's psychological condition before we could make a confident determination that he was incapable of fully informed consent.

Second, even if we stipulate that Ace was capable of fully informed consent and that the condition of libertarian agreement was satisfied fully in the instant case, a problem remains. Wanda appears to have exploited Ace by preying upon his known vulnerability to gambling information. Even if Ace cannot be clinically described as a gambling "addict," Wanda has opportunistically profited at Ace's expense: she has achieved the sexual gratification she had for so long sought unsuccessfully, while Ace experiences deep disgust and wins only the chance to wager on Harry's preferred selection. Bear in mind that even if Ace wins that wager, it is extremely doubtful that his long-range interests will be thereby served. Cashing his winning tickets may place some extra cash in his pocket over the short haul, but over the long haul it may only reinforce Ace's self-destructive gambling impulses and perhaps strengthen Wanda's newfound leverage over him. Accordingly, many elements of our paradigm for exploitation are present: Wanda initiated a proposition that traded on Ace's known vulnerability; the distribution of gains disproportionately favors Wanda, while the distribution of setbacks to interests hinders Ace; Ace's consent may well betray not only his weakness for gambling but his more general negative self-image and self-destructive inclinations; Wanda single-mindedly pursues her gratification with little or no regard for the probable negative effects on Ace's interests; thus, Wanda seems to be regarding Ace as a mere instrument to advance her purposes.

It may be objected to my analysis that Wanda's deeper motive was establishing a loving relationship with Ace, a relationship that could allow Ace to transcend his vulnerability to self-destructive gambling. Under this view, my characterization of Wanda's motives and intentions is overly harsh and clearly uncharitable.

My rejoinder is that from the facts given, it is overly charitable to sanctify Wanda's actions with such a pristine aura. Putting that aside, however, a number of questions remain: How realistic was Wanda's evaluation of the situation? How intelligent was her method of achieving her alleged aspirations? How probable were her chances for success? How likely was her strategy to worsen Ace's situation? Thus, the critic's immaculate depiction of Wanda's alleged deeper aspirations does not necessarily exonerate her from charges of exploitation, even though it may mitigate her culpability.

It may also be objected to my analysis that, if taken seriously, it would label pejoratively most commercial transactions. After all, business people are often (usually?) striving to gain disproportionately from their trades and to take advantage of the desires and vulnerabilities of their counterparts. Surely we do not wish to throw in league with Marxists and declare all such transactions "exploitative" just because the long-term interests of one of the parties are set back or only enhanced meagerly.

My rejoinder to this claim is that we must attend carefully to the circumstances surrounding exchanges. In a capitalistic business context there are a variety of well-established and well-known standard operating procedures: assumption of risks, puffery, adversarial strategems of negotiations, language that cannot be taken literally, the single-minded advance of self-interest, and so on. Commodification is not merely the accepted, but the defining characteristic, of commercial exchange. Sexual relations, however, become especially morally suspicious as they begin to resemble more closely the transactions of business. For better or worse, our social theory and practice portray capitalistic business exchanges as closely resembling a libertarian model, while they depict sexual agreements as more closely resembling other ideological models. Although I reject the Marxist tenet that capitalistic business transactions are inherently exploitative, it is indeed possible for such exchanges to exhibit exploitation. As ever, to make these determinations, we must evaluate carefully the totality of circumstances surrounding the exchanges.

Finally, it may be objected to my analysis that its content is fueled by a series of contestable value judgments: What if Ace had consented to have sex with Wanda because she offered him a candy bar he desired but could not otherwise obtain? Would the resulting sex act be exploitative? Could not consuming a special candy bar be every bit as valuable to someone as obtaining a wagering tip was for Ace? Doesn't the example trade on the disinclination most self-styled intellectuals have for gambling? As such, isn't the analysis patronizing and paternalistic to Ace's desires? Who are we to say that he is the victim of exploitation given that he judges the trade to be to his advantage?

The answer here is that once we abrogate the libertarian credo that insists individuals are always the incorrigibly correct judge of what is valuable to them and that asserts the domain of morality is constituted only by voluntary exchanges that do not violate negative rights, contestable value judgments are inevitable. We have seen in Chapter 4 the emotional and moral poverty implied by the libertarian credo, a bankruptcy that militated our rejection of the credo's crude formulation. Once we are committed against crude libertarianism, we find ourselves on less certain philosophical terrain. Invoking a totality-of-circumstances approach or a balancing-of-factors-in-context method necessarily requires an appeal to a host of descriptive and prescriptive assumptions. In this fashion, ideology supplies the ballast for sexual morality in five tiers.

In the present example, Ace was described as a "degenerate gambler," not merely as an adventurer who enjoys the excitement of an occasional night at the track or trip to Las Vegas. By definition, Ace's proclivities are a special vulnerability, not merely another of his mundane desires. This determination, along with the others discussed previously, facilitated the conclusion that Wanda's actions exploited Ace. It is more difficult, although not impossible, to conceive of a desire for a candy bar as a special vulnerability. In those cases where the offer of a candy bar was accepted, we would be likely to conclude that the offeree could not have had a deep antecedent aversion to sex with the offerer: in such cases the value of a candy bar seems meager compensation for performance of an intimate act the offeree was otherwise loathe to do. In those cases where the desire for a candy bar did seem to be a special vulnerability, perhaps an indication of a desperate, immediate need for food, we could reasonably argue along the same lines as in the Wanda–Ace illustration that the offerer exploited the offeree.

Accordingly, I agree enthusiastically that contestable value judgments emanating from ideological assumptions inundate the analysis of sexual morality in five tiers. But there is no plausible alternative. We are all condemned to our freedom: moral assessment is neither mechanical nor indisputable. Instead of constituting a sheepish concession, however, this observation is a methodological presupposition that forges a theoretical advantage.

Case 4

We can now return to an illustration considered previously in this chapter: Professor Harry Hott informs a female student that she has earned a grade of C in his class, but he will award her an A if and only if she has sex with him. If she refuses, then she will receive the C she deserves. The student is repulsed by Hott, but agrees reluctantly to his proposition because she desires high grades.

Sexual morality in five tiers judges this act morally impermissible even if we stipulate that the condition of libertarian agreement is satisfied; that is, even if we construe the proposition as an offer rather than a threat and eliminate the possibility that the student has pathological impairments that call into question her capability to render informed consent. First, the proposition itself can be viewed as a type of harm, a form of sexual harassment that wrongly assumes that sexual commodification is appropriate and that conjures a host of gender stereotypes that partly constitute wrongful social inequalities. The student may also be intimidated by the proposition because she wants to refuse its terms but she fears the consequences of doing so. This may be the case despite Hott's repeated assurances that she is free to refuse without future prejudice. Also, the student may suffer a subsequent loss of self-respect, which in turn may diminish her capacity to perceive sex as an important part of her own self-development.[48] Moreover, Hott abuses his institutional authority and both he and the student engage in a type of cheating: they unfairly conspire to award grades on a nonpublic criterion that remains unavailable to other students (at least unavailable to those Hott finds sexually unattractive). Second, Hott can reasonably be viewed as having exploited the student: he has used his power advantage, and her relative vulnerability, to fulfill his desires, while her gains seem meager by comparison.[49] As Linda LeMoncheck argues:

Sex is a less effective vehicle for dehumanizing men than it is for women. Men typically have no rape mentality; sex does not threaten them or harm them in the way it can women. And in general, men typically have no submissive mentality in sex; indeed, they live in a society that fosters independence and dominance and in which conventionally valued social, economic, and political status all but require such traits.[50]

I must note, however, that despite the entrenched image of the lecherous male professor preying unrepentantly on innocent, vulnerable female students, by changing a few factors in our example we can easily visualize the student exploiting the professor. Imagine a female student to whom sex is an activity no more intimate than walking and a rather timid male professor who has experienced sex only with his wife. The student is flunking his course and she proposes that they have sex and he then award her an A in the course. He refuses, citing a host of moral and prudential considerations. She then appears in his office every day for the next two weeks, flirtatiously reiterating her proposal. He eventually relents and accepts her terms. It is plausible to view this as a case where the student has employed her relative sexual advantage, a type of power differential, to exploit the professor's vulnerability. Her gains here are not merely the tiny increase in her cumulative grade point average, but also the empowerment she experiences as she dominates her professor's will:

she is using him, she knows it, and she relishes it. The professor in this case experiences a loss of integrity and deep humiliation as, for the first time, he compromises his professional standards.

The point here is that we must be careful not to rely on entrenched images when evaluating specific cases. In each case, we must attend carefully to the myriad of factors relevant to assessment by sexual morality in five tiers.

Case 5

Bonnie Hughes is a widow with three small children. Stud Wallace is a well-known playboy who has wished for a long time to add Bonnie to his extensive list of sexual conquests. Stud has often made his desires known to Bonnie, but Bonnie has always spurned Stud's entreaties as the "evil conjurings of a loathsome man." Upon hearing this phrase, Stud has always sneered, laughed, and insisted that one day Bonnie would relent. Stud has often added that her constant refusals only make Bonnie more desirable to him. Bonnie's disgust with Stud has intensified over time.

But events soon conspire in Stud's behalf. Bonnie and her family suffer horrible financial setbacks. They are forced to sell most of their personal possessions and, eventually, find it exceedingly difficult to honor their mortgage payments. The holder of the mortgage threatens to foreclose. Bonnie can find no alternative to losing her family's home.

Stud Wallace, a consummate opportunist, offers to make Bonnie's mortgage payments on a continuing basis if and only if Bonnie agrees to accompany Stud for two weeks of sex and sun at Stud's favorite resort in Perkinsville, New Mexico. Bonnie, although horrified by this exchange, grudgingly accepts Stud's proposal.

This is, of course, a classic case of exploitation, an illustration chronicled in numerous movies and cartoons from the days of silent pictures to the present. Stud Wallace has taken advantage of Bonnie's desperate situation, overwhelming need, lack of bargaining power, and absence of viable alternatives to secure what he could not otherwise win. Accordingly, Stud's actions clearly violate Tier 3 analysis, and, depending on fuller details, may well transgress other tiers as well.

One sidebar is appropriate here. It must be clear that when we conclude a sexual act is "morally wrong," we do not thereby necessarily hold each of the participants morally culpable. For example, in the instant case we would hold the exploiter, Stud Wallace, morally culpable, but many of us would fully excuse the participation of his victim. Here we recognize a well-known distinction between the morality of an action and the morality of the agent who performs or participates in it: an action can be morally right, but if the agent who performs it does so from ersatz motives and intentions, we would hold her culpable to some degree; an action can be morally wrong, but if its agent is guided by proper motives and intentions, we could excuse or even justify her conduct in at least some cases; an action can be morally wrong, yet we may hold one party fully culpable, while excusing or justifying the conduct of the other party; an action can be morally wrong and we may hold all parties jointly and severally culpable, and so on.

Case 6

The Fracks are a happily married couple with generous but compatible sexual appetites. They enjoy sex whenever and wherever they both feel the urge to indulge. They often copulate in the backyard of their home and are unconcerned about the spectating habits of their neighbors. Their neighbors the Fricks, however, are religious fundamentalists who are gravely disturbed by the Fracks' libertine proclivities. While this disturbance does not necessarily rise to the level of a personal wrong against the Fricks, it does constitute serious offense. For a variety of reasons having to do with the location of the respective homes of the Fracks and Fricks and the time of day that the Fracks have sex, it is virtually impossible for the Fricks to avoid the erotic spectacle.

This example illustrates the problem of nonharmful but offensive third party effects. Under sexual morality in five tiers, the Fracks' sexual actions are immoral if and only if the balance of relevant factors favor the Fricks. The relevant questions to ask here are: How intensive, extensive, and enduring is the offense to the Fricks? Was the offense reasonably avoidable? Did the Fricks voluntarily assume the risk of experiencing the acts? (For example, if the Fricks moved into the neighborhood although forewarned of the Fracks' sexual propensities, then they may well be morally estopped from their subsequent complaints.) Are the Fricks abnormally susceptible to taking offense at viewing sex? Or is their reaction one commonly shared by others? How important to the Fracks is this particular act in this particular place? What social value, if any, does the act embody? Is such sexual activity an important case of free expression? Do the Fracks have adequate alternative opportunities to engage in their activity? Do the Fracks act maliciously or spitefully? Do they copulate mainly in order to give offense rather than from sexual desire? Is the Fracks' behavior common and expected in the backyards of their neighborhood? Or is it rare and unexpected?

Again, the details of this illustration are sketchy, but the likely conclusion is that the Fracks are morally wrong. In this case, one would suppose that adequate alternate outlets are available for the satisfaction of the Fracks' sexual urges; that the Fricks' reactions to the Fracks' public displays are common and understandable; that the Fracks' behavior is uncommon and unexpected in the location in which it occurs; that the act in that locale has limited social value; that the Fricks have neither assumed the risks of viewing nor can avoid easily the Fracks' spectacle. It is morally wrong to needlessly or to unjustifiably offend others, and once the Fracks are aware of the Fricks' reactions, their continued sexual activity suggests gratuitous infliction of distress. In this case one of the paramount but unusual stipulations is that the Fricks could not avoid easily the spectacle. Hence, the Fricks were not merely offended by the mere knowledge that the Fracks were sexual libertines, but by specific observations of the Fracks in action.

One must be cautious, however, in sanctimoniously declaring sexual activity immoral merely because it offends third parties. Offenses are not personal harms. Thus, offenses are less likely than harms to trigger a negative assessment by sexual morality in five tiers. In fact, in the overwhelming number of cases, the balance of factors will weigh in favor of the actors and not the offended parties.

Case 7

Although the various tiers of my analysis often overlap and mutually support one another, there are other times when various tiers may conflict and thereby suggest an ambivalent aggregate moral assessment. Consider a case in which one party violates a general moral duty owed the other party: a lie is told (triggering the suspicions of Tier 2) but tremendous gains are realized by third parties (pleasing Tier 4) or salutary effects are produced for the wider social context (results sanctioned by Tier 5). Is the sexual act in question moral or immoral?

Sexual morality in five tiers cannot provide what general moral theory lacks: a rigorous, sharply defined, mechanical method to adjudicate normative disputes. We can, however, adumbrate the relevant questions to address: What is the magnitude of the lie as measured by its extent and surrounding context? What is the magnitude of the adverse consequences suffered by the victim? What is the importance of the moral principles violated? What is the magnitude of the positive effects enjoyed by third parties and the salutary reforms to the wider social context? Could the advantageous effects produced by the act have been realized in a less morally obtrusive fashion? Did the moral principle violated constitute an indispensable constraint on the social use of individuals?

The ends do not always justify the means required to secure them: as argued previously, a persuasive view of morality requires that we acknowledge some constraints (e.g., the prohibition on rape) that cannot legitimately be relaxed in deference to the greater social good. But when assessing the morality of an act, we cannot ignore the results produced by it or the numerous (often conflicting) duties at issue. Only a pernicious fanatic contends that morality is comprised entirely of absolutist rules. In sum, there will be numerous occasions when actions that typically transgress morality (e.g., lies) will be justified by the tremendous benefits they produce in certain contexts or by the weightier duties or purposes they serve. Again we see that the five tiers are not fully autonomous layers of analysis.

The point here is that sexual morality in five tiers is in the same position as any nonabsolutist rendering of moral evaluation: when assessment in one tier seems to diverge from assessment in another tier, we can only raise and answer as best we can the questions which permit us to arrive at an overall judgment in the totality of circumstances. Competing conclusions here echo and legitimate divergent descriptive and prescriptive world visions—rival ideologies—choosing between which is as much a matter of sensibility as of logical argument.

The seven cases adumbrated above illustrate the configuration, animating assumptions, and general direction of sexual morality in five tiers. Obviously, those who harbor conflicting ideologies can use my theory to arrive at different substantive conclusions. At that point, we must argue more about our general moral and political theories than about our competing views of human sexuality.

The seven cases may suggest a normative puritanism which scorns most sex as morally wrong. On the contrary, sexual morality in five tiers assumes there are few sex acts that are *inherently* morally wrong: nonconsensual sex, thoroughly sadomasochistic sex, and any other sex that by its very nature must violate the directives of one or more of the five tiers. It should be clear that this is a modest imperative that permits a wide range of sexual passion, adventurism, and experimentation.

What makes sexual activity morally wrong in certain contexts is what makes other human activity wrong: the unjustified violation of moral principles, duties, and purposes. What makes proper sexual conduct of special concern is the socially created role it plays in our self-development, self-image, and physical and psychological well-being.

Thus, any critic who claimed that sexual morality in five tiers is inherently puritanical or antisex would be in error. The analysis itself takes no sex acts to be intrinsically immoral except those lacking libertarian agreement. All other sex acts must be evaluated contextually and historically by the other tiers of analysis with the (rebuttable) presumption that they are permissible: sex is inherently a human good that is important for our flourishing, but it can be rendered morally impermissible by certain transgressions and conditions. Unless a critic holds that libertarian agreement is not a necessary condition of moral permissibility—opening the way for the permissibility of rape—or that appeals to the other four tiers of analysis necessarily and inappropriately stigmatize sex as impermissible, he cannot successfully claim that sexual morality in five tiers is animated by an antisex outlook.

In fact, the opposite is the case. My analysis is animated by the following concerns: to mediate the tensions between mainstream thought and its leftist critique; to neither accept nor reject either tradition in its totality; to embrace an engaged fallibilistic pluralism; to recognize the social meaning of sexuality in our culture as the starting point of analysis, but to subject that starting point to critical interrogation; and to evolve a sexual ethic that is both realistic yet aspirational. In any case, my interests lie less in converting others to my ideological preferences and more in exposing the proper questions to ask and in heightening the level of public discourse on the topic.

There remains, however, one other cause for concern: Does sexual morality in five tiers embody an insidious conservative (in the sense of "status quo preserving") bias? Notice how prevailing judgments, received opinions, third party reactions, and dominant social contexts seem to play such paramount roles in the theory's analysis. Can it not be argued powerfully that evaluation of sexual activity by this method will inevitably reinforce precisely those prevailing ideas that resist hygienic social transformation? Is sexual morality in five tiers thereby an unwitting stooge in the perpetuation of social injustice?

It is clear that sexual morality in five tiers necessarily exhibits indeterminate form. Substantive conclusions can be drawn only after that form is animated by ideology. Thus, it is possible that one could use this form to reinforce patriarchal excesses or fanatical puritanism or self-defeating romanticism or virtually any other normative malady. In sum, the framework of sexual morality in five tiers cannot guarantee the ideological agenda to which it may be harnessed. Accordingly, sexual morality in five tiers is neither inherently conservative nor inherently transformative. As with any normative framework, sexual morality in five tiers cannot freeze the terms of ideological disputation.

8

A WALK ON THE WILD SIDE
Bestiality, Necrophilia,
Incest, and Prostitution

Sexual morality in five tiers assumes there are few sex acts that are inherently morally wrong: nonconsensual sex, which transgresses libertarian agreement, thoroughly sadomasochistic sex, which inevitably involves significant harm, and any other sex that by its very nature must violate the directives of one or more of the five tiers. In this chapter, I conclude the book by canvassing several uncommon sex acts which often arouse societal condemnation.

Acts of bestiality, necrophilia, incest, and prostitution raise special questions about the moral status of certain entities, the source of moral taboos, and the relationship between men and women in our society. Further, these questions afford extraordinarily rich opportunities to connect sexual ethics to sociopolitical theory and core philosophical issues: the moral status, if any, of animals and corpses; codes of appropriate sexual behavior for persons who are closely related; and the politics and economics of female prostitution. It is to such issues that we now turn.

BESTIALITY

Bestiality refers to sexual relations between a human and an animal. For our purposes we will confine the discussion to acts between humans and animals that are relatively high on the evolutionary scale (e.g., canines, horses, sheep). The act, although repugnant and unthinkable to most people in our society, raises a host of interesting philosophical issues: Does bestiality necessarily entail the rape of an animal? Or is rape, with its heavy psychological connotations, a term properly reserved for human nonconsensual sex? Can animals

228

be legitimately used for any ends or purposes individual humans declare valuable? Do humans who desire sex with an animal by that fact alone reveal a psychological disorder? Does sex with an animal necessarily lead to a psychological disorder regardless of the human's antecedent mental condition? Or can humans and animals actually build an intimate relationship of sorts?

We can unravel such questions only by addressing the moral status of nonhuman animals. It should be clear that a human who uses an inanimate object in his sexual activity does not necessarily commit moral wrong, at least not any wrong to the object. Inanimate objects lack feelings and consciousness and thus lack interests.

> To say X has an interest in Y may mean (i) that Y, on balance, improves X's well-being (or opportunity for well-being) or (ii) that X desires, wants, or seeks Y. It seems possible for X to be interested in (to desire) something that is not truly in his interests; and it is also possible for something to be in X's interests regardless of the fact that X is not presently interested in (does not presently desire) it . . . regardless of whether interests are analyzed in terms of some objective criterion or whether they are simply the class of an individual's wants and desires, it seems clear that one important claim we make when we talk about human interests is that desires, wants, needs, and aims are crucial to that concept.[1]

Animals, unlike inanimate objects, possess the capacity for suffering and enjoyment and thus embody the prerequisites for having interests. Jeremy Bentham, in an often quoted passage, advanced the case for the moral status of animals:

> The day *may* come when the rest of the animal creation may acquire those rights which never could have been witholden from them but by the hand of tyranny. The French have already discovered that the blackness of the skin is no reason why a human being should be abandoned without redress to the caprice of a tormentor. It may one day come to be recognized that the number of the legs, the villosity of the skin, or the termination of the *os sacrum* are reasons equally insufficient for abandoning a sensitive being to the same fate. What else is it that should trace

the insuperable line? Is it faculty of reason, or perhaps the faculty of discourse? But a full-grown horse or dog is beyond comparison a more rational, as well as a more conversable animal, than an infant of a day or a week or even a month, old. But suppose they were otherwise, what would it avail? The question is not, Can they *reason*? nor Can they *talk*? but, *Can they suffer*?[2]

Joel Feinberg defines "interests" in this way: "all those things in which one has a stake . . . a person has a stake in X . . . when he stands to gain or lose depending on the nature or condition of X . . . interests . . . are distinguishable components of a person's well-being: he flourishes or languishes as they flourish or languish. What promotes them is to his advantage or *in his interest*; what thwarts them is to his detriment or *against his interest*."[3]

Their possession of interests accords animals moral stature. Although animals are not themselves moral agents—we cannot persuasively predicate moral responsibility to them—they possess interests that can be ignored, harmed, or facilitated by humans who are moral agents. Thus, animals can be morally wronged where their interests are unjustifiably impaired by human action.

It does not, however, follow logically that animals must be accorded moral status equal to humans. I claim only that animals, unlike inanimate objects, have some moral status based on their possession of interests. A full examination of that moral status—Is vegetarianism morally required? Under what conditions, if any, is medical and scientific experimentation morally permissible? Is the use of animal skins for clothing inherently immoral?—is well beyond the scope of this work. Instead, I will address the interests of animals only in the context of bestiality.

While bestiality is inherently nonconsensual, to talk of the rape of an animal is too strong. The horror of rape transcends involuntary penetration of a sex organ. Rather, it includes the lingering psychological experience of violation, subjugation, and victimization. To be raped is to suffer a special sort of mental, as well as physical, torment. Animals can be physically violated, but I have seen no evidence that as a result of bestiality they endure any of the psychological horrors of rape. Accordingly, it is better to view bestiality as nonconsensual sex, but not rape in its fullest meaning.

Sexual morality in five tiers depicts nonconsensual sex as necessarily in violation of libertarian agreement. But our analysis is complicated in the case of animals because they do not suffer the full horrors of rape, they typically have a lower moral status than humans, and, unlike humans, they are incapable of rendering consent to the act in question: no nonhuman animal is capable of entering into a valid sexual contract with a human. Moreover, although it is reasonable to suppose that the interests of animals are not typically advanced by sex with humans, is it so clear that their interests are necessarily significantly impaired by bestiality? Thus, the absence of an animal's consent seems insufficient to establish the inherent wrongfulness of bestiality.

Perhaps we can peer at the problem from the vantage point of the lascivious human who initiates acts of bestiality. Do humans who desire sex with an animal by that fact alone reveal a psychological disorder? Does sex with an animal necessarily lead to a psychological disorder regardless of the human's antecedent mental condition? Certainly we would be suspicious of any person who preferred bestiality to sex with another human. We would take such a preference as indicative of a deeper psychological problem. But does this bare fact manifest the immorality of bestiality? Undoubtedly not. There are men who prefer sex (masturbation?) with inflated dolls or inanimate mannequins to sexual intercourse with actual women. This preference might well suggest excessive shyness, lack of basic social skills, deep insecurities, or worse. We would think that such men could spend their time better in counseling sessions to remedy the underlying psychological problems. But none of this, without more qualification, establishes the immorality of the acts adumbrated. (In fact, one could argue that any sex that does not harm the other "party" is better than no sex at all.) Moreover, it is not clear that such sex must violate some duty to self. Finally, we have been assuming that a person who engages in bestiality must do so frequently, habitually, and to the exclusion of more common forms of sexuality. Obviously, this need not be the case.

There is yet another approach to this problem. It may be argued that bestiality implies the use of an animal as a mere means for the ends of a human; animals are sentient beings that embody interests; thus they ought not to be treated as if they were mere instruments for human purposes; therefore, bestiality is inherently immoral because it necessarily treats a sentient creature as less worthy than that creature is in fact.

I find this argument quite appealing and persuasive. Its tone is appropriately high and refined, and it sounds as if it echoes and sustains an unavoidable deontological insight. But, upon closer scrutiny, it also exudes an unhealthy dose of question begging. The reason that it is generally considered morally wrong to use a being with moral status as a mere means for another's ends is that such action invariably wrongs the used party by setting back his or her interests. In the instant case, it is unclear whether an animal's interests are necessarily set back by bestiality. There may well be cases where the animal's interests are simply unaffected to any significant extent. Furthermore, bestiality does not necessarily treat animals as less worthy than they are in fact. It is easy to imagine instances where an amorous human treats his animal partner as more worthy than the animal is in fact: he fantasizes a "relationship" with his beloved sheep or his sexually loyal collie that, in deluded fashion, anthropomorphizes the animal.

Accordingly, it is unclear whether sexual morality in five tiers can declare bestiality inherently immoral. Although the act is necessarily nonconsensual, it does not necessarily set back the interests of either the human or animal party. Because it is not inherently immoral, discrete acts of bestiality, although nonconsensual, can be morally redeemed by their concomitant third party benefits (Tier 4) or salutary social effects (Tier 5). It is difficult to imagine such cases, but not impossible.

It is, however, fair to say that bestiality is typically immoral: it typically uses an animal as a mere instrument for human purposes; it typically involves the exploitation of the animal (we note the coercive elements of the act, the narrowing of the animal's sexual opportunities, and the distributions of gains from the act); if it is habitual and ongoing, it can prevent the animal from engaging in its more natural and satisfying sexual experiences with others of its species; it often reflects and reinforces the unhealthy psychological conditions of the human initiator; if it is habitual and ongoing, it can prevent the human from engaging in fuller sexual experiences with other humans; given society's revulsion, bestiality can ultimately preclude the human from a healthy self-image and self-development; it can lead to rampant spread of venereal diseases; and so on.

Surely, given such circumstances, the burden of persuasion should always be placed on the person who claims that a particular act of bestiality is morally permissible.

Moreover, acts such as bestiality, necrophilia, incest, and, perhaps to a lesser extent, prostitution fall piteously short of generally held moral ideals. Even where such acts do not strictly violate general moral obligations, they generate a revulsion based on how far they stray from our most deeply felt images of the beauty of sexual experience. When humans gather to construct salutary paradigms of ego-enhancing, spiritually elevating, life-sustaining sex, few seriously invoke visions of a passionate shepherd with his flock, a salacious ghoul with an uprooted corpse, or a lascivious father caressing erotically his daughter.

Although there is no universal moral obligation for humans to adopt one particular vision of ideal sex, acts such as bestiality, necrophilia, and incest stand diametrically opposed to the various ideals of sex held by the overwhelming majority of rational people. To the extent a person engages in such acts, he or she is correctly perceived as having ersatz, opprobrious, woeful sex. While none of this proves such sex acts must be personally debilitating or, strictly speaking, immoral, it does account for the disdain these acts engender and does underscore the prudential arguments for recognized prohibitions against them.

NECROPHILIA

Necrophilia is an erotic attraction to dead bodies. For our purposes, we will confine the discussion to acts between living humans and human corpses. Necrophilia is more repugnant to many of us than even bestiality. Like bestiality, however, the act raises a host of interesting philosophical issues: Does necrophilia necessarily entail the rape of a corpse? Or is rape, with its heavy psychological connotations, a term only reserved for nonconsensual sex between living humans? Can corpses legitimately be used for any ends or purposes living humans declare valuable? Do humans who desire sex with a corpse by that fact alone reveal a psychological disorder? Does sex with a corpse necessarily lead to a psychological disorder regardless of the human's antecedent mental condition?

One component of our analysis must be the moral status, if any, of corpses. On one hand, it does not seem that a corpse has interests: a corpse is not a sentient being, it does not appear to have a stake in whether it is used sexually or not, and it lacks all capacity for suffering and enjoyment. In short, a corpse seems more like an inanimate object that lacks moral status than a being with interests who embodies moral status. But on the other hand, a corpse is different from an inanimate object: it was once part of a sentient being who possessed not only desires and wants about the present, but also about the future. I have now desires about numerous events that can only occur after my death: the disposition of my estate, the care and handling of my corpse, my reputation after death, among others. Such desires can only be fulfilled or transgressed after my death.[4] I have a stake in such matters, but my interests in them cannot be affected while I am living. My biographical life seems to transcend my biological life.[5] Moreover, the revulsion we experience at necrophilia goes well beyond our negative reaction to sex with an inanimate object. Thus, we confront a paradox: a human corpse lacks the prerequisites for possessing interests, yet cannot be deprived of moral status as easily as inanimate objects.

One way out of this paradox is to account for our revulsion to necrophilia on grounds other than the harming of corpses and to outline more clearly the reasons why corpses cannot have interests and thus cannot be morally wronged.[6] I will now examine four such arguments: the argument from cognitive awareness, the transference argument, the argument from offense, and the argument from sentiment.

The argument from cognitive awareness states that suffering negative sensations is a necessary condition for having one's interests harmed; the dead lack the capacity for experiencing sensations; therefore, the dead cannot be harmed. If successful, this argument would show that the wrongness, if any, of necrophilia cannot be derived from the moral status of corpses. The argument, however, is not successful. It confuses being wronged with knowing that one has been wronged. A person's interests can be violated, yet she may be unaware that her interests have been violated and thus suffer no negative sensations. Should she discover the violation, the negative sensations, the hurt, she would then experience do not constitute the harm; instead they result from the victim's recognition that she has been harmed. Even if the victim had never learned of her transgressor's acts, her interests would have been harmed by those acts: neither suffering pain because of another's act nor becoming aware of that act is a necessary condition of having one's interests harmed by that act. Accordingly, the argument from cognitive awareness fails, for it cannot be claimed legitimately that dead humans cannot be harmed because they cannot know that others have acted against their previously expressed desires or because dead humans do not experience negative sensations in response to the noxious acts of others.

The transference argument states that the interests and rights of a person are transferred to relatives and survivors upon that person's death; any transgression of those interests and rights, such as necrophilia, is a violation against the interests of those relatives and survivors; therefore, the dead cannot be harmed because they have no interests. If successful, this argument locates the wrongness, if any, of necrophilia in the way that act violates the interests of the living. The claim that it is wrong to perform sex acts on a corpse, or to slander the dead, or to violate wills because harm results to the dead person's surviving relatives, does have an intuitive appeal. A will typically benefits a dead person's relatives or designated survivors, and transgressions of the terms of that will often directly harm the interests of the living. Moreover, these living humans typically do take umbrage if the dead person is maligned, slandered, or used sexually.

The transference argument, however, is not successful. What if a dead person has no surviving relatives? What if the surviving relatives do not care if the dead person is maligned or his corpse mutilated? What if the surviving relatives, themselves, are the ones who do the maligning or mutilating? Would we truly conclude that no wrong has taken place? All this suggests that it is not merely our aversion to insulting the heirs and relatives of the dead that accounts for our thinking that certain acts performed by the living against the dead are morally wrong. At best, the transference argument provides only a partial explanation of the wrongness of acts such as necrophilia.

The argument from offense states that acts are wrong (at least sometimes) because people are offended by them; the dead cannot be offended; but certain acts toward the dead are wrong; therefore, these acts are wrong because they offend the living. If successful, this argument pinpoints the wrongness of acts such as necrophilia in the offense taken by wide segments of the living, and not narrowly in the offense taken by or interests harmed of the dead person's heirs and survivors. It is true that necrophilia and the needless degradation of corpses offend most of us. Stories about the shameless manner in which morbid medical students treat corpses or of the erotic preferences of certain sexual deviates are clearly likely to be offensive to those of us with a more refined sense of the appropriate. Thus, there is a kernel of truth in the argument from offense.

But are such actions wrong because we are offended, or are we offended because the actions are wrong? The offense we take at learning about such acts may partially constitute our collective recognition that the acts are independently wrong. Part of the explanation for our response may involve our firm conviction that necrophiliacs and those who mistreat corpses perform actions that violate what the person would have desired (or did desire) to happen to her body after her death. Would you want your corpse used by necrophiliacs? Would you want your corpse ridiculed by disrespectful, sophomoric medical students? Would you want your reputation unjustifiably demeaned after your death? At best, the argument from offense captures one of the reasons why necrophilia is typically morally wrong: the unjustified offense it brings to the living. Surely, the analysis of offense given earlier in my explanation of Tier 4 would conclude that necrophilia typically results in unjustified offense. But this need not always be the case, especially where a necrophiliac's actions remain hidden from the public. It is more likely that the argument from offense points us in another direction, on a quest to unmask the deeper reasons why necrophilia is wrong and why the act offends the living so thoroughly.

Those who insist that it makes sense to talk about affecting the interests of those now dead can point to the granting of posthumous awards. Does not the issuing of such honors suggest that the living do assume that the dead can be rewarded? Critics, however, advance the argument from sentiment which states that the living have deep emotional attachments to the dead; the living often present posthumous citations to the dead; the dead cannot be aware of such awards; if the dead cannot be aware of the awards, then they cannot benefit from them; therefore, posthumous citations are awarded because of sentiment only. If successful, this argument would block another avenue sometimes taken by those who claim moral status for the dead.

Again, this argument embodies an element of truth. Many gestures toward the dead are merely sentimental. Those who try to converse with their dead spouse, or who communicate with famous dead people by means of spiritualists, or who burn sacrificial offerings, may well be labeled sentimental or superstitious. But not all actions toward the dead fall so easily into these categories.

Suppose that various rules and conditions that specify who shall receive certain prizes or honors are set forth. A person who satisfies these qualifying conditions earns an entitlement to the award at issue unless an overriding consideration invalidates the claim in some legitimate fashion. Assume, upon fulfilling the qualifying conditions for the award, the person, overwhelmed by her achievement, suffers a massive heart attack and dies. Does this mean that no award should be issued? Does this mean that if an award is issued, it is merely a sentimental gesture? I think not. If an award is not issued under such circumstances, in the absence of overriding considerations, an injustice takes place—a denial of the entitled person's due. That person would be wronged by failing to receive the award to which she is entitled.

One need not claim personally an award, or even be able to claim it, to be in fact entitled to it. In the absence of other overriding considerations, only the person's explicit denial of her claim to it can justify the withholding of the award. In this case, the dead person has issued no such denial.

Of course, if a couple were entitled to a trip to Paris because they won this prize in a sanctioned lottery, but they died prior to embarking on the journey, we need not place them in caskets and carry them around Paris. Corpses do not have the ability to benefit from such treatment, and this is the sort of overriding consideration that justifies us to withhold the prize. The dead, however, do have the ability to benefit from not being slandered and from receiving numerous posthumous awards: humans have an interest in a good reputation *simpliciter*. Regardless of whether our heirs and survivors appreciate what we did, we want to be remembered in light of what we accomplished and the kind of person we were. Indeed, we deserve such recognition based on our past performances and works.

Our desire, while living, to be remembered fondly is not necessarily an irrational fancy built on a desperate hope for personal immortality. Instead, this desire can be viewed as a demand that the imperatives of justice be acknowledged in dealing with us even after we are dead. Under this view, many things done to the dead are immoral because they violate the demands of justice.

Accordingly, not all posthumous awards are merely sentimental gestures. They are often requirements of justice: to withhold such an award would often be a denial of what is owed, or due, another as a matter of entitlement. The mere failure to be sentimental is not an injustice; but the denial of what is owed another, even if she cannot personally claim her due, is often an injustice. It is not obvious that we can transgress morality by being unsentimental. It is clear that we violate morality when we are unjust. Even after we die certain things can happen to our corpses, our reputations, and our estate. Some of these things are morally wrong not because they are offensive or a discomfort to our surviving heirs, but because they violate two constitutive principles of justice: desert and entitlement.

What does all this have to do with necrophilia? We have examined four arguments that try to locate the moral intuitions we share about treatment of the dead in areas other than the interests of the dead. Thus, these arguments intend to make coherent our considered judgments that certain actions involving the dead are wrong with the proposition that the dead lack moral status. But the four arguments, at best, capture only partial truths. I have tried to show that they cannot account fully, either jointly or severally, for our considered moral judgments about the treatment of the dead. Thus, the possibility that the dead have moral status retains vitality.

We have already seen that possessing interests is a necessary condition for embodying moral status and that necrophilia is morally wrong because it harms the dead only if the dead have moral status. My dissection of the four arguments, however, has at least one troubling, perhaps question-begging, feature: my analysis often assumes, rather than establishes, that the dead have interests that can be fulfilled or thwarted.

There is a grave metaphysical problem here: interests cannot be free floating; they must attach to an interest-bearing entity. To what interest-bearing entity do the alleged interests of the dead attach? Moreover, there is a serious temporal problem: that I *now* have certain desires and interests regarding matters such as the disposition of my will, my surviving reputation, and the treatment of my corpse does not establish that after I am dead I retain those interests. After all, there is presumably no "I" that persists after death; there is only my soon-to-be-rotting corpse. Thus, we return to our original questions: How can a mere corpse, which apparently lacks all the prerequisites for interests, have interests predicated of it? How can the dead have moral status if they are not interest-bearing entities? Even if necrophilia is morally wrong, how can that be based on harm inflicted on an inanimate corpse?

Joel Feinberg and George Pitcher[7] have provided far the best and most innovative answers to such questions, and I will borrow freely from their insights. We must first concede that one's biographical life, the narrative that constitutes one's entire story, is lengthier than one's biological life, the chronology of events between one's birth and death. There is a distinction between those interests that expire with a person, interests that can no longer be affected by posthumous acts, and those interests that survive a person's death because they can be, and in some cases can only be, fulfilled or blocked after the person's death. It is clear that humans typically have objects of interest that transcend the subjective experiences that constitute their biological lives.

> We can think of some of a person's interests as surviving his death, just as some of the debts and claims of his estate do, and that in virtue of the defeat of these interests, either by death or by subsequent events, we can think of the person who was, as harmed. . . . He is of course at this moment dead, but that does not prevent us from referring now, in the present tense, to his interests, if they are still capable of being blocked or fulfilled . . . The final tally book on a person's life is not closed until some time after his death.[8]

That certain of our interests survive our deaths has a seductive appeal, but there remains a paramount issue: How do such interests survive and to what interest-bearing entity do they attach? Feinberg, following Pitcher, says the following:

> Interests harmed by events that occur at or after the moment a person's nonexistence commences are interests of the living person who no longer is with us, not the interests of the decaying body he left behind. . . . All antemortem persons [persons as

they were at some stage of their lives] are subject not only to being described, but also to being wronged after their deaths, by
betrayals, broken promises, defamatory lies, and the like, but no
"postmortem person" [a person as he is in death] can be
wronged at all.[9]

Thus, it is not a corpse, a postmortem person that is harmed by
necrophilia, but the antemortem person which that corpse once partially constituted. But when is the antemortem person harmed? If
not postmortem, how can an act occurring then cause harm at an
earlier time when the person was living? How can an act at $T + 1$
(some postmortem moment) cause harm to the antemortem person
at T (some moment of the person's biological life)?

> The antemortem person was harmed in being the subject of in-
> terests that were going to be defeated whether he knew it or not
> [at T and before]. It does not become "retroactively true" that as
> the subject of doomed interests he is in a harmed state; rather it
> was true all along. . . . Exactly when did the harmed state of the
> antemortem person, for which the posthumous event is "re-
> sponsible," begin? . . . "at the point, well before his death,"
> when the person had invested so much in some postdated out-
> come that it became one of his interests.[10]

Hence the antemortem person is in a harmed state prior to death.
It is not at $T + 1$, the postmortem moment at which the act affecting
the person's interests occurs, that the antemortem person is harmed.
Instead, $T + 1$ marks the moment when "it becomes apparent to us
for the first time that it was true all along—that from the time [the
antemortem person] invested enough in his cause to make it one of
his interests, he was playing a losing game."[11]

The Feinberg-Pitcher account is refreshing and seductive. Lingering doubts may accompany its seeming fatalism and clever (but
questionable) finesse of the temporal sequence problem, but it explains powerfully our numerous moral intuitions about posthumous
awards, deathbed promises, postmortem defamations, and the like.
Moreover, it clarifies how death itself harms human interests.[12]

Under this account, necrophilia does not harm a corpse; instead,
it can harm the relevant antemortem person. As such, while necro-

philia is almost always nonconsensual, to talk of the rape of an ante-mortem person is too strong. As with bestiality, the lingering psychological experience of violation, subjugation, and victimization are absent. The antemortem person may be harmed by necrophilia, but cannot be hurt by it: the antemortem person cannot suffer the special sort of mental and physical torment that typically constitutes rape.

This invites a question about the weight of the antemortem person's interest, upon death, in not being a sexual object for necrophiliacs. Although this interest would vary somewhat in proportion to the antemortem person's regard for her corpse, it could not weigh as heavily as the antemortem person's interest in avoiding rape or as heavily as other important interests the person embodies. Thus, human corpses can, under certain circumstances, justifiably be used for purposes other than those which would please their relevant antemortem person: facilitating paramount interests of the living can often morally trump fulfilling an antemortem person's interests with regard to her corpse.[13] Of course, in the instant case it is virtually impossible to make a persuasive case that the necrophiliac's interest in sex is a requisite "paramount interest of the living" which could outweigh the antemortem person's interest in proper disposition of her corpse.

What about the status of the necrophiliac? Do humans who desire sex with a corpse by that fact alone reveal a psychological disorder? Does sex with a corpse necessarily lead to a psychological disorder regardless of the human's antecedent mental condition? We are even more suspicious of a necrophiliac than we are of a person who prefers bestiality to sex with another human. We would take such a preference as indicative of a deeper psychological problem. Given the social meaning of necrophilia and the nearly universal cross-cultural concern about proper disposition of the dead, necrophilia exhibits special horrors and maladies.

But do such observations manifest the inherent immorality of necrophilia? Although I swallow hard as I write this, the answer is no. It is possible that the antemortem person could waive her presumed interest against the sexual use of her corpse. Consider the case of antemortem consent: an antemortem person stipulates sincerely in her will that "anyone wishing to use my corpse for sexual purposes may do so between the hours of 10–11 PM on Fridays at St.

Patrick's Cemetery." Those few necrophiliacs among us who would avail themselves of this opportunity on the appointed day and time would not thereby violate any of the antemortem person's interests. Unlike instances of consensual exploitation, it is difficult in this case to ascribe persuasively harms or hurts to the antemortem person once she renders consent. The sex acts would thus pass Tier I scrutiny. They would be morally permissible if and only if they met the criteria of the remaining four tiers.

Such sex acts, however, would typically fail the criteria of some of the remaining tiers. There are numerous relevant questions here: Does necrophilia psychologically harm the initiator of the act himself? Will the act be public enough—bare knowledge of the act is often sufficient—to offend seriously and unjustifiably third parties, including surviving relatives and friends? Do wider social dangers accompany the honoring of testamentary provisions that consent to sexual use of corpses? For example, would the general symbolic value of corpses be unjustifiably diminished by necrophilia?

Actual cases of necrophilia fail the criteria of sexual morality in five tiers; and it is virtually impossible to summon realistic instances where nonconsensual necrophilia could be morally redeemed by concomitant third party benefits or salutary social effects. But philosophers, being who we are, can imagine a completely private case of consensual necrophilia which neither manifests nor facilitates psychological harm nor engenders offense nor demeans the symbolic value of corpses nor violates our analysis of sexual ethics in other ways.

INCEST

Incest is a sexual union between persons who are closely related. Jerome Neu claims that incest consists of "prohibited sexual relations where it is the identity of the persons involved rather than the nature of their acts that is essential; and where the relevant features of the parties are defined in terms of social roles or positions."[14] In a world that embodies major cross-cultural differences, conflicting global visions, and starkly disparate stages of economic development, social condemnation of incest is nevertheless universal.[15]

This widespread disparagement provides strong evidence, although it does not logically imply, that incest is inherently immoral.

There are numerous specific objections that can be raised against incest: wholesale inbreeding will facilitate genetic disasters that will weaken the survival capacities of the entire species (the "genetic claim"); incest confuses well-established family roles and engenders additional family conflicts (the "family breakdown" claim); the universal prohibition of incest suggests that the act is unnatural and instinctively repulses humans (the "natural law" claim); incest unleashes a familial sexuality that prevents the proper self-development of children (the "self-development" claim); and incest prevents proper socialization because it promotes an unhealthy isolation of the family from wider social interactions (the "tribalism" claim).

The genetic claim is less persuasive than it may first seem. By using proper contraceptive methods or by engaging in acts other than intercourse, a related couple can eliminate, or at least minimize, the dangers feared by the genetic claim. Moreover, for such dangers to culminate in a significant threat to the human species, incest would have to emerge over a period of decades as the much preferred mode of sex. Thus, while the genetic claim expresses real social problems, it falls far short of establishing the inherent immorality of incest.

The family breakdown claim suggests that the family structure would be radically and deleteriously altered by incest. Images of irate mothers in competition with their daughters for the husband-father's sexual attention, of adversarial fathers vying with their sons for the wife-mother's favors, and general blurring of tribal roles emerge concurrently with incestuous relations. However, what if, for example, the family in question has no live-in mother, or the mother does not resent her daughter's sexual relations with the husband-father, or the mother affirmatively encourages those sexual relations? This shows the danger in locating the wrongness of incest in the adverse reactions of the nonparticipating family members: there may be no such reactions. Moreover, depending on the extent and type of incest engaged in, it is not clear that family roles must be radically transformed or that if they are transformed, it is necessarily for the worse.

The natural law claim cites the unnaturalness of incest and the revulsion we experience at the bare knowledge that it exists: we need not personally observe an act of incest to be thoroughly disgusted. However, we have seen in other contexts the radical indeterminacy of claims of "unnaturalness." Moreover, if the act is inherently unnatural, many of the fears of the other arguments against incest must evaporate: it is unlikely that an act so instinctively repulsive will realize widespread acceptance and practice. Finally, the natural law claim does not explore *why* most of us are repelled so thoroughly by incest: Do we have an incest taboo because we are instinctively repelled by incest? Or are we "instinctively" repelled by incest because we have internalized the preexisting incest taboo? Can clearer reasons be given for our revulsion?

Neu explains the self-development claim:

> Each generation must win its identity, partly through struggle with the older generation and partly through something like mourning for its loss. The "something like mourning" amounts to identification. But the identification makes sense only through difference, as a culmination of the effort to overcome infantile dependence and achieve autonomy. Incest destroys difference; categories collapse, people cease to have clear and distinct sexual and social places . . . with the destruction of difference people cease to have the possibility of shifting from one place to another as they develop. . . . While destroying difference and confusing roles and perhaps undermining authority, [incest] would not overcome dependence—which . . . is a biological and social necessity. Violation of incest taboos or their abolition would not . . . allow the establishment of a stable, mature, independent identity.[16]

This is a powerful claim, but it trades on only one image of incest: a relatively powerful guardian abusing his or her institutional role by exploiting the vulnerability of a relatively unpowerful child. Such abuse will, indeed, retard, perhaps even prevent, the child's full self-development. But, once again, ersatz self-development may not be the underlying reason why incest is wrong. That reason, instead, may account for why the victim's self-development is harmed. Moreover, what about incest that occurs outside the prevalent image described above? Suppose a 50-year-old father and his 32-year-old daughter voluntarily agree to sex of a type in which no child could be conceived. Presumably, both parties have the "self-development" of adults, and most, if not all, of the dangers feared by the self-development claim are muted. If the imagined act is still morally wrong, then it must be for reasons other than those embodied by the self-development claim. And if the act is morally permissible, then the self-development claim must restrict its domain to certain kinds of incest and not condemn incest *simpliciter*.

The tribalism claim has a Freudian flavor:

> It is tough enough to break out of the family as it is, with the addition of sexual relations and dependence it becomes virtually impossible. Incest is (literally) anti-social. Dependence comes with the relations. Sexual urges (in the context of incest prohibitions) are among the leading forces for breaking out of the family and forming complex social structures and relationships; necessary conditions for civilization. . . . The parties [who engage in incest] may become sufficient unto themselves . . . society is more likely to break up into little divided family enclaves, perhaps cooperating where they must but never forming a community.[17]

Again, much is persuasive here. But the dire consequences that are feared—a radical tribalism which precludes true community and sociability—depend on incest becoming the favored sexual outlet for the overwhelming majority of people. Certainly the assumptions of the tribal claim are at odds with those of the natural law claim. Moreover, in a society as complex and interdependent as our own, it seems impossible for a significant number of people to merely cooperate "where they must but never form a community." Community and socialization depends on much more than the mutual search for sexual partners. Thus, the tribal claim exaggerates its insights.

Most of the traditional objections against incest trade on the allegedly noxious effects that would accompany its widespread acceptance and practice. But all such objections are secondary and speculative: If these harmful societal effects did not occur, would that morally redeem incest? If incest were accepted and practiced by only a small segment of the population, would that minimize the feared harmful societal effects and thereby attenuate the immorality of the incestuous acts that do occur?

Sexual morality in five tiers has a simpler way of accounting for the immorality of incest: the act typically constitutes rape. Incest involves all the physical and psychological horrors accompanying rape. Incest often adds to such horrors because it typically includes abuse of the parental/custodial role and betrayal by adults who hold themselves out as trustworthy; but at the core of incest's immorality is nonconsensuality. Incest typically involves a special sort of abuse: the rape of a child under the adult rapist's custodial care. Thus it is true that incest will invariably harm the child-victim's general self-development and her capacity to view sex as one aspect her self-development. Moreover, the "confusion of roles" so feared by the family breakdown claim is recast better as the special psychological trauma a child experiences when betrayed and sexually abused by the adult, usually a biological parent, who poses generally as her most concerned caretaker.

The immorality of incest is mitigated neither by its infrequency nor by the child-victim's "agreement" to the incestuous sexual act. Many countries and regions have statutory rape laws which prohibit sex between adults and children. Such laws recognize that those below a certain age are from the outset incapable of making informed judgments regarding sexual behavior, or, alternatively, those below a certain age are too easily swayed, fooled, or cajoled by adults of superior bargaining power and experience.

Viewed as an especially venomous form of rape, incest typically fails the first tier of moral assessment: it lacks libertarian agreement. Moreover, incest typically constitutes other harms as well: it retards gravely the child-victim's self-development, it unjustifiably produces deleterious third party effects, and so on. Accordingly, our "natural revulsion" against incest is well founded.

But what about incest that occurs outside the prevalent image described above? Suppose a 50-year-old father and his 32-year-old daughter voluntarily agree to sex of a type in which no child could be conceived. Is this act, which is by definition incestuous, necessarily immoral? I suspect not. We would need more details to arrive at a complete evaluation by sexual morality in five tiers, but the act in question could exhibit libertarian agreement and pass the assessment of the other four tiers. Such acts would be rare but conceivable.

PROSTITUTION

Prostitution is the solicitation and acceptance of payment for participation in sexual acts. While it is begrudgingly acknowledged as the "world's oldest profession," it is also widely condemned by both the political right and left for vastly disparate reasons: as inherently illicit sex; as a threat to family and societal structures; as socially and economically exploitative; as wrongful commodification of constitutive human attributes; as mirroring and reinforcing harmful patriarchal prerogatives; and as inevitably leading to other sexual and nonsexual social ills. I will concentrate on the most common form of prostitution: female vendor and male client.

What, then, can be said in favor of prostitution? We can start with the fundamental libertarian value, freedom of contract. Libertarians, and numerous liberals, depict prostitution as "an ordinary business transaction, the sale of a service; in this case, of a sexual service. Because the prostitute engages in it out of economic motivation, liberals view prostitution as quite different from a sexual act committed by physical force . . . they see it as a contract like other contracts, entered into by each individual for her or his own benefit, each striking the best bargain that she or he is able."[18] Prostitution, it is argued, involves the selling of sexual services, not the selling of the prostitute. Thus, a contract for prostitution is different from more typical purchase contracts only in the type of services at issue and the fact that the former contracts are not legally enforceable.

One of the better philosophical defenses of prostitution is provided by Lars Ericsson.[19] Ericsson insists that there is nothing inherently illicit, harmful, or wrongful about prostitution; instead, it is society's response to prostitution that engenders the harm that often accompanies sex for sale: "The major culprit is the hostile and punitive attitudes which the surrounding hypocritical society adopts toward promiscuous sexual relations in general and prostitution in particular. . . . If public opinion accorded prostitutes the same status as say, social workers, most of the hazards connected with hustling would probably disappear. And those that would remain would not be thought to make hustling undesirable."[20]

Ericsson rejects the rationales commonly advanced against prostitution. Regarding prostitution as a threat to family and societal structures, he contends "that prostitution neither is nor ever was a threat to reproduction within the nuclear family is too obvious to be worth arguing for. Nor has it ever been a threat to the family itself. People marry and visit whores for quite different reasons. In point of fact, the greatest threat to the family is also the greatest threat to prostitution, namely, complete sexual liberty for both sexes."[21]

Regarding prostitution as wrongful commodification of constitutive human attributes, Ericsson concedes that "certain areas of life should be as exempt from commercialism as possible,"[22] but takes this to be an ideal state of affairs currently beyond our reach. Noting that sex is no less basic than food, clothing, and shelter, Ericsson underscores the reality that food vendors, haberdashers, and contractors are not regarded with contempt merely because they profit economically from providing basic human needs. In an ideal world, all such basic needs would transcend commercialization, but in our imperfect world "that we have to pay for the satisfaction of our most basic appetites is no reason for socially stigmatizing those individuals whose profession it is to cater to those appetites . . . it seems to me inconsistent to hold that prostitution is undesirable on the ground that it involves the selling of something that, ideally, should not be sold but freely given away."[23]

Ericsson addresses the Marxist charge that prostitution is socially and economically exploitive and points out that the link between capitalism and the commercialization of sex is unconvincing: "The truth is that prostitution has proved to be highly insensitive to variety in economic organization. In one form or another whoredom has existed in primitive, feudal, and capitalist as well as socialist societies."[24] Moreover, the familiar Marxist picture of prostitution—a voracious bourgeois male patronizing an impoverished proletarian female—fails to capture the reality of commercial sex: "what empirical data seem to show is that prostitution reflects class society in the following sense. Middle- and upper-class men tend to visit "high-class" whores (call girls, and the like), while working-class men tend to visit "low-class" whores (streetwalkers, bar and dancehall prostitutes, fleabags, etc.). And "high-class" prostitutes more often than not come from a background that is not working class."[25]

Finally, Ericsson confronts the feminist charge that prostitution mirrors and reinforces harmful patriarchal prerogatives and gender oppression: "That the customer treats the harlot as a means to his ends is only partly true. The other part of the truth is that the prostitute treats her customer as a means to *her* ends. Thus, the complete truth . . . is that prostitute and customer treat *one another* as means rather than as ends."[26] Although he concedes that prostitutes suffer oppression, Ericsson denies that this oppression is gender based:

> [Prostitutes] would not have chosen to become hustlers if some better alternative had been open to them. They are very much aware of the fact that to be a prostitute is to be socially devalued: to be at the bottom of society. To become a hooker is to make just the reverse of a career . . . none of this warrants the charge that prostitution means the oppression of the female by the male sex. The oppression just described is not an oppression on the basis of sex, as male franchise would be. The "oppressor" is rather those social conditions—present in practically all known social systems—which offer some individuals (both men and women) no better alternative than hustling.[27]

Although Ericsson highlights numerous insights, the case against prostitution remains overwhelming. We may begin by interrogating the notion of freedom of contract. The allegedly "voluntary consent" of the prostitute must be examined more closely. For example, feminists sometimes argue that women become prostitutes not simply because of economic coercion, but also because of psychological pressures and unconscious self-hatred facilitated by patriarchal ideology.[28] This argument has several parts: patriarchal society does not reward adequately those intellectual and creative labors of women that are applicable to the public sphere; instead, patriarchal society sends women the incessant and unrelenting message that their main value resides in their sexuality, reproductive activity, and nurturing functions; in this fashion, prostitution is one of the talents of women that patriarchal society encourages in various ways; thus it is reasonable to depict prostitution as a piece of a wider puzzle that reflects and sustains such indefensible gender inequalities. Prostitution, then, may be an example of how a subclass of women assimilate ideological conceptions from a dominant group to explain and justify their lives.[29]

Accordingly, feminists charge that libertarian apologists for prostitution wrongly identify submission with consent. In the absence of free commitment and agreement by equals, Carole Pateman argues that "consent as ideology cannot be distinguished from habitual acquiescence, assent, silent dissent, submission, or even enforced submission."[30] Thus, one's consent must be taken in societal context.[31] Although such feminist charges are contestable and perhaps unprovable in a strict sense, they embody significant vitality when combined with our earlier conclusion that libertarian agreement is not self-validating and is thus insufficient to establish moral permissibility.

Ericsson's observation that many of the alleged maladies of prostitution result from society's puritanical attitudes about sex is true, but fails to support prostitution. He is correct in thinking that prostitution is not inherently wrong. He is correct in thinking that prostitution need not be accompanied by the types of harms with which it is typically associated: physical assaults, robberies, spread of disease, rampant drug abuse, forced sexual slavery, and so on. He is correct in thinking that society's reactions often compound whatever undesirable aspects surround prostitution. But he is incorrect in so cavalierly dismissing the contingent social meaning of prostitution. There are a host of human interactions that are not inherently wrong but that are contingently wrong because of the collective values and meanings projected on them by various cultures. We can imagine a society in which the selling of sex is treated much like any other service profession. We can imagine a society in which sexuality is bartered and commercialized without any loss to personal integrity. We can imagine a society in which the selling of sex is extremely rare or even nonexistent. We can imagine a society in which sellers of sex are accorded special social status and political prestige.

But none of these societies would exemplify "prostitution" as we know it: by their portrayals of the selling of sex such societies would transcend the social meaning of prostitution as it exists for us. Recall that in our society "prostitution" has a derivative social meaning that goes beyond sex: the selling of oneself for an unworthy cause. Thus, in our society the sobriquet "prostitute" is always pejorative, while in our imagined societies those who sell sex either are typical vendors or have honorific status.

Ericsson might respond that I have underscored precisely his point: society molds perceptions of prostitution through its reactions; change those perceptions and a society can morally redeem the selling of sex. To the extent that such a response presupposes that there is nothing inherently or necessarily immoral about the selling of sex, I concur. I do not insist that selling one's sexual services must alienate constitutive attributes or must dehumanize the vendor. But we need to address the institution of prostitution not abstractly, but in its present context.[32]

Given its current (and long-standing) social meaning in our culture, the institution of prostitution is immoral. Moreover, the wide-ranging social transformations that might unsettle the social meaning of prostitution and herald a reincarnation for the selling of sex are radical conversions. No mere series of marginal adjustments or incremental changes can remedy the maladies that contingently accompany the institution of prostitution in our culture. The hitherto imagined societies where the selling of sex is viewed much like any other service profession, or where sexuality is bartered and commercialized without any loss to personal integrity, or where the selling of sex is extremely rare or even nonexistent, or where sellers of sex are accorded special social status and political prestige, would be radically different in numerous respects from our society.

It is clear that both the general and specific social meanings of prostitution in our culture are pejorative. This is especially true when the act of prostitution is the selling of sex and the vendor is a woman.[33] The apparent core of the feminist critique of prostitution is that female sellers of sex are collaborating in their own domination by men and in their own wrongful commodification.[34] But the deeper objection concerns how prostitution echoes and sustains general societal ideology which is pernicious. Laurie Shrage states that prostitution

epitomizes [certain] cultural assumptions—beliefs which . . . serve to legitimate women's social subordination . . . rather than subvert patriarchal ideology, the prostitute's actions, and the industry as a whole, serve to perpetuate this system of values . . . female prostitution oppresses women, not because some women who participate in it ''suffer in the eyes of society'' but because its organized practice testifies to and perpetuates socially hegemonic beliefs which oppress all women in many domains of their lives.[35]

Thus, numerous feminists perceive prostitution as yet another area of life where men exert their relative power advantage to dominate women.[36] Moreover, the institution of prostitution reinforces the stereotype of women as mere sex objects and thus sustains the myth of female inferiority.[37] All this harm is allegedly compounded by the fact that in our culture women, unlike men, are identified significantly by their sexual activity.[38]

This analysis resurrects the question of whether we can distinguish contracts involving the selling of sex from ordinary wage labor agreements: Is sex truly different such that it must implicate the wrongful commodification of constitutive personal attributes? The libertarian-liberal view exemplified by Ericsson invokes freedom of contract that places sexual activity in the same category as ordinary wage labor. In fact, he claims that sex is a basic need, all nonsexual basic needs are already subject to market exchange, and there is no reason to exclude sex from market forces, at least once we reform the current institution.[39]

But the libertarian-liberal argument misses the mark because it obscures the social meaning of sex in our culture: the way sex is used to define certain groups such as homosexuals and women; the fashion in which sexuality is partly constitutive of our identities; the manner in which sexual activity is connected to other forms of social oppression; and the central role sex plays in our individual lives and social institutions.[40]

Sex is especially different from mundane agreements for groups such as women and homosexuals. Linda LeMoncheck notes that

> sex provides a unique vehicle for demeaning women as less morally virtuous or socially esteemed when connected to certain kinds of sexual activity . . . women can lose a kind of self-respect for their own sexual needs which, among other things, diminishes their capacity to use sex as a vehicle for their own self-development . . . because sex and sexual relations seem to have a special kind of significance in our lives . . . dehumanization in one's sexual relations will have a significance in our lives that it will not have in other areas.[41]

Again, I do not claim that sexual contracts are necessarily different from other wage labor agreements, only that in our culture they are contingently different. Moreover, unlike Ericsson, I am firmly convinced that only radical and far-reaching societal transformations, not mere marginal adjustments to the status quo, can morally redeem the institution of prostitution.

It is often said that prostitution involves sexual objectification. LeMoncheck puts it this way: "The sex objectifier treats the sex object as less than a moral equal . . . she is treated as if she lacked one or more of the distinctive human capacities upon which her rights to a certain level of well-being and freedom are based."[42] Such sexual objectification has at least two dimensions: derivative and direct. The sex objectification is often derivative in the fashion described earlier: prostitution generally facilitates an oppressive stereotype of women as sexual and moral subordinates of men. This stereotype stigmatizes women as the moral inferiors of men and nurtures "certain intimidating kinds of sexual role expectations for women that make it difficult for them to live self-determined lives."[43] The direct encounter between prostitute and customer is typically characterized by the prostitute's focus on the customer only as a source of money,[44] while the customer regards the prostitute as an instrument of satisfaction.[45] As such, the typical act of prostitution involves mutual objectification.[46]

I have addressed derivative objectification earlier. As for direct objectification, the power of its critique depends on whether sex acts are different from ordinary wage-labor contracts. After all, we often are morally permitted to fail to attend to numerous constitutive properties of those with whom we transact business. Our society evinces few moral qualms about subjecting human labor power and its products to the allegedly impersonal forces of market exchange, and such exchanges often include mutual objectification of the sort described above. It is only if sex is an area where such failures bear moral culpability that the direct objectification critique would exude vitality. As we have seen, the contingent social meaning of sex in our society does imply that more is at stake in prostitution than mutual satisfaction of the parties' narrowly conceived ends—sex for the customer, money for the seller—and thus direct wrongful objectification does typically (and contingently) occur. Moreover, the buyer's treatment of the prostitute as a mere means to his ends is not morally redeemed by the prostitute's similar treatment of the buyer. The fact that the objectification may be mutual rather than one-sided does not erase prostitution's moral taint, it multiplies it.

We should also repeat the specific Marxist critique of prostitution, which indicts capitalism and describes prostitution as yet another instance of alienated labor where money substitutes for specific human characteristics.[47] The basic Marxist attack on capitalism ignores the widespread historical presence of prostitution in virtually all societal contexts and underscores the wrongful commodification of labor.[48]

Thus, the Marxist perspective discerns all the classic indicia of alienation when analyzing prostitution in a capitalist setting: a class-based genesis; labor performed not as free, creative expression, but as satisfaction of another for payment required for economic survival; and labor, in this case sexuality, commodified such that the laborer is dehumanized as her value as a person is reduced to its market value. As we noted earlier, the solution to the social ills of prostitution requires the inexorable dismantling of capitalism. Then historical necessity occurs, and after several stages of state socialism have conspired to set the stage for the "final form of society," the economic and class functions for prostitution supposedly wither away. As ever, Marxists hypothesize that prostitution will disappear under communism because its sustaining economic and class functions have evaporated: people will choose neither to be nor to frequent prostitutes because their underlying general alienation and economic exploitation, the animating forces of prostitution under capitalism, will have vanished.

It should be clear that the Marxist critique cannot be accepted fully. First, it is not obvious that prostitution, given its cross-cultural and cross-temporal popularity, will ever disappear. Second, the adequacy of any analysis of capitalism that assimilates sexual and reproductive labor to ordinary wage labor is questionable. Third, the Marxist analysis, at best, accounts for only a small part of the phenomenon of prostitution: bourgeois customers frequenting proletarian vendors. Fourth, the emphasis on class and economics as the genesis of prostitution obscures the importance of gender, racial, and religious oppressions.

The remaining power of the Marxist critique rests on its often subtle understanding of alienation, commodification, and dehumanization. These notions and others have been coopted and transformed by feminists, who have a clearer vision of the influence of gender oppression on the flourishing of prostitution.

In any event, the number and gravity of all these objections cut to the heart of the freedom of contract defense of prostitution and Ericsson's general libertarian-liberal apology for the selling of sex. Furthermore, I have not even begun to unravel the most obvious abuses that often accompany prostitution as we know it: the prevalence of physical assaults, the harmful actions of the subclass of male pimps, the widespread presence of drug abuse, the tragic dispersion of venereal and other diseases, and so on.

Accordingly, I conclude the following: (1) the selling of sex is not inherently immoral; (2) but the institution of prostitution as we know it is immoral; (3) the most powerful reasons why prostitution as we know it is immoral emerge from feminist and leftist critiques and from analyses of the limitations of libertarian agreement; (4) thus, we can adjudicate the immorality of prostitution in our culture independently of numerous obvious abuses that often accompany it; and (5) the transfigurations that might morally redeem prostitution in our culture would be radical and much more far-reaching than merely a change of societal attitudes and few marginal reforms of the way prostitution is currently conducted. (I have no definitive conclusion on whether the selling of sex would occur in an ideal society of near perfect social and economic equality.)

At least one issue remains: Are some acts of prostitution within our culture morally permissible despite all that has been said here? Placed under the rubric of sexual morality in five tiers, certain feminists argue that acts of prostitution as we know it necessarily fail Tier 5 analysis: their general societal effects of reinforcing patriarchal prerogatives transcend the possible presence of libertarian agreement. Although I am impressed strongly by the feminist critique of prostitution, I remain unconvinced that acts of prostitution in our culture necessarily bear such harmful general societal effects. Even in our otherwise flawed social context, there may be acts of selling sex that translate into neither tangible reinforcement of the sociopolitical status quo nor wrongful commodification of (part of) a woman's constitutive attributes. Again, it is possible, although most difficult, to nurture salutary microcontexts within a generally flawed society.

What would characterize such a microcontext with regard to prostitution? One type of morally permissible sex selling would exhibit these characteristics: the female vendor of sex would neither assume a sexually subordinate role nor ply her trade out of economic necessity. Instead, she would moderate her working conditions, select and monitor her clients, and experience her work as an unalienating expression of creativity; she would suffer no social disapprobation for her career choice; and both she and her customers would exhibit reciprocal care and thus not view each other as embodying merely instrumental value.[49]

This microcontext, however, appears less like prostitution and more like a certain kind of sexual therapy. As such, it is not clear that I have described prostitution or even the selling of sex; instead, the vendor in question would be a sex therapist whose main goal is the alleviation of a sexual problem rather than the selling of sex *simpliciter*. Moreover, the customer would appear more as a seeker of the proper form of counseling and treatment for a perceived malady than as a purchaser of sexual gratification as such.

A second type of morally permissible sex selling would exhibit many of the characteristics of the first type but would abrogate all pretense to therapy. Here the female vendor would be neither sexually subordinate nor economically coerced: she might be a well-educated, economically advantaged woman who chooses selling sex from among a myriad of attractive career options; again, she would moderate her working conditions, select and monitor her clients, and experience her work as an unalienating expression of creativity; she would suffer no social disapprobation for her career choice (perhaps because her vending of sex is unknown to all except her clients and a few nonjudgmental friends and family members); the sex acts in which she engaged would be seen by both parties as primarily aimed at pleasure for pay, but both she and her customers would exhibit reciprocal care and thus not view each other as embodying merely instrumental value. This might describe roughly certain high-priced "call girls."

There are, however, at least two remaining problems with this characterization. First, some feminists would argue that the woman in question does not freely choose her occupation because in our culture she has been socialized to fulfill male sexual expectations and desires. She, as all women, may appear to herself to be making a free choice, but in fact her choice reflects her internalization of dominant and pernicious patriarchal ideology. Further, the prostitute, willingly or not, reinforces that ideology by the very act of submitting to male sexual expectations and desires. Second, the vendor in question would still be engaging in an illegal occupation.

These problems are real but not insurmountable. The power and pervasiveness of dominant ideology is hardly universal in our culture. Those feminists who insist that all female vendors of sex must be under the mystifying spell of patriarchal ideology unconsciously and ironically attribute more power to a certain class of males than is warranted. Recall that the illustration stipulated a well-educated woman who had and understood a variety of career options. It is possible that such a woman, contrary to the feminist objection, could choose to be a seller of sex yet not be an abject victim of patriarchal brainwashing. In a similar vein, numerous self-employed women currently produce what they take to be feminist pornography.[50]

Only if feminists assume that such a woman's choice is itself nonrebuttable proof of her internalization of patriarchal ideology can they assert dogmatically that she has necessarily been subtly coerced. This assumption, however, rests on at least three dubious propositions: that patriarchal ideology related to sex is omnipotent and pervasive; that even socially and economically advantaged women are necessarily and thoroughly victimized by such ideology and are immune from the effects of counterideology; and that it is impossible for any woman to choose freely to sell sex, regardless of the circumstances and terms under which she labors. While the feminist objection may well be strong and true for the majority of women, it may not be so convincing as to rule out even the possibility of a woman choosing to sell sex for reasons other than those emanating from patriarchal ideology. To think otherwise may be to exhibit ironically an essentialist view of women or of sexuality itself. While the instant case of the eager prostitute requires much more detail to be fully convincing, it still points to the possibility of a microcontext of morally permissible sex selling in our otherwise flawed cultural setting.

Likewise, I reject the view that *every* act of sex selling must contribute to a reinforcement of the social and political status quo. Such a view embodies the mistake of abstractness, an error I disparaged earlier. While "the personal is political" is a generally sound slogan, not every imaginable act has tangible social ramifications. To think

otherwise is to conflate totally the private and public realms, a con-
flation that is as erroneous as the rigid separation of the two realms
by the minions of centrist politics.

Finally, the illegality of the sex acts in question does not establish
their immorality: there may be sound reasons for declaring prostitution illegal that do not imply that every individual case of sex selling
is immoral. Further, we should not assume that the fact of illegality
itself must cause the sex vendor social disapprobation or alienation.
In the instant case, the prostitute presumably recognizes such distinctions and concludes that while most prostitution is contingently wrong, her interactions are permissible for the reasons cited
previously.

9
MORAL REASONING
Science or Sham?

Our intellectual excursion through some of the issues of sexual ethics has ended. But more needs to be said about the nature of moral reasoning itself. It should be clear that sexual morality in five tiers provides only a framework for analysis: the substantive content of normative vision must contribute the ballast necessary to derive moral conclusions. As such, our normative reasoning cannot transcend ideological disputation.

Some thinkers will recoil at such a conclusion and demand that we adopt a more "scientific" outlook when analyzing sexual ethics. In that vein, a recent book by Richard Posner[1] deserves attention here.

Posner hopes to advance a theory of sexuality that is both descriptive and normative: one that explains current social practice yet prescribes some reforms of the regulations governing sex. He identifies procreation, hedonism, and sociability as the primary ends or benefits of sexual activity. He claims that although sexual passion is irrational in the sense that it is not fully volitional, sexual behavior is nevertheless regulable by market forces[2] because it is rational in the sense of "well adapted to the actor's ends."[3] "Normal" sex, then, for Posner is sexual behavior that conforms to an accurate assessment of the costs and benefits to the actor. Thus, the organizing perspective of his theory is economic analysis.[4] By understanding and implementing social scientific knowledge of sexuality and by altering social incentives and constraints, Posner argues that we can conjure reforms in law and public policy.

Posner is firmly convinced that moral and legal reasoning are feckless analytic tools for analyzing sexual ethics: "The economic approach differs from the familiar . . . approaches in assigning less weight to power, exploitation, malice, ignorance, accident, and ideology as causes of human behavior and more to incentives, opportunities, constraints, and social function."[5]

Posner unabashedly endorses sociobiology. For example, he accepts the following: sexual reproduction increases the likelihood that a species will survive;[6] sexual differentiation simplifies the development of a fertilized human cell and eases specialization in essential human tasks;[7] differentiation of sex organs commands "different, although complementary, optimal sexual strategies for the two sexes";[8] the inclination of males toward promiscuity is a function of their "vast potential reproductive capacity,"[9] while a female "who wants to maximize her reproductive success must be charier of her sexual favors";[10] thus females have a weaker sex drive than men because "a powerful sex drive would probably stimulate a taste for sexual variety, or at least make it more difficult to adhere to a strategy of being choosy about one's sexual partners";[11] men, competing for women of maximum reproductive fitness, "find healthy-looking women of childbearing years more attractive sexually than women who are either younger or older, or who appear unhealthy";[12] women, putting less emphasis on physical attractiveness and youth, "screen suitors for those who have the willingness and the ability to ensure the survival of [their] children";[13] and men "have an incentive to try to curb woman's promiscuity in order to establish secure paternity."[14]

Although he argues that our basic sexual impulses and preferences are derived from our genes and from early childhood development, Posner explains that the way such impulses and preferences manifest themselves in actual behavior is a function of social opportunities, resources, and constraints.[15] Hence, two cultures can differ significantly in sexual practices even though the genetic and early developmental features of their respective populations are similar.

> Much of the variance in sexual behavior and customs across cultures and eras is explained by a handful of factors, such as the sex ratio [proportion of males to females], the extent of urbanization, and, above all, the changing occupational role of women. That changing role is, in turn, a function of infant mortality, the value of children, the technology of contraception,

the existence of labor-saving devices in household production . . . and the degree in which well-remunerated work not requiring great physical strength or stamina is available in the economy.[16]

Posner discerns three stages in the evolution of sexual morality. In the first stage, the women's role is one of "simple breeder."[17] Here "companionate marriage is unlikely, and without it such 'immoral' practices as prostitution, adultery, and homosexuality are likely to flourish."[18] In the second stage, where the women's role is "enlarged to include that of child rearer and husband's companion, as well as breeder, companionate marriage is possible, and leads in turn to the condemnation of the 'immoral' practices."[19] What causes the movement from the first to the second stage? Posner calls the causal connection "obscure,"[20] but he speculates that the decline of slavery may have been paramount. The third stage of sexual morality further enlarges women's role to include market employment. Here, "while such marriages as there are will be companionate, there will be fewer marriages; other forms of sexual relationship will no longer seem quite so abnormal; and the policies designed to foster premarital virginity and marital chastity for the sake of companionate marriage will lose much of their point."[21] What causes the transition from the second to the third stage? Posner cites four factors: "the decline in infant mortality, the decline in women's mortality in childbirth, the improvement in methods of contraception, and the growth of light employment."[22] These factors reduce the benefits and increase the costs of women remaining at home.

Using his economic model and available social science research, Posner is able to generate a host of conclusions on the reasons why sexual morality changes, on practical legal reforms, and on how best to manipulate public policies on sex to accomplish professed social goals. To chronicle these conclusions is well beyond the scope of this work. But I will briefly illustrate Posner's reasoning by reference to homosexuality.

He argues that the best available evidence supports the view that homosexuality is biologically determined, rather than chosen: "Homosexual preference, especially male homosexual preference, appears to be widespread; perhaps to be innate . . . to exist in most, perhaps all, societies, whether they are tolerant of homosexuality or repressive of it; to be almost completely—perhaps completely—resistant to treatment; and to be no more common in tolerant than in repressive societies."[23]

As always, he underscores the distinction between preference and behavior. By shifting the benefit-costs ratio radically enough, society can impel a number of homosexuals to substitute heterosexual behavior, but doing so does not change their sexual preferences. Likewise, those of strong heterosexual preference can be impelled to engage in (opportunistic) homosexual behavior under certain circumstances—for example, in prisons where a heterosexual partner is unavailable—but their heterosexual preferences remain stable.[24] As a result of this analysis, Posner concludes that many of the proposed restrictions on the employment of homosexuals, which are designed to protect children from being converted to homosexuality, are misplaced. Such restrictions assume, apparently incorrectly, that homosexual preference is chosen. Moreover, the removal of many current restrictions is recommended on the basis that doing so alleviates "gratuitous suffering."[25]

It would be a mistake, however, to conclude that Posner celebrates homosexual life-styles. On the contrary, he argues that "it is unlikely that when every legal disability of homosexuality has been dismantled and every heterosexual has been thoroughly schooled in tolerance, the homosexual life-style will cease to be a distinctive and, to a significant degree, an unhappy one."[26] He bases this conclusion on two fundamental observations. First, there is a universal distinctiveness to homosexual subcultures: cross-gender behavior predisposes some boys to homosexuality; effeminate homosexuals are most likely to exhibit such behavior and to be drawn to creative and artistic occupations. Thus, homosexuals "will cluster in the artistic and decorative occupations even after tolerance for homosexuality becomes general."[27] Therefore, the typical homosexual will be more neurotic than the typical heterosexual because "neurosis is the occupational hazard of artistic people."[28] Second, homosexuality typically precludes a satisfying family life. A homosexual will be unhappy in a companionate marriage with a woman. Moreover, a pair of homosexuals is unlikely to form a companionate union for the following reasons: sexual fidelity is unlikely because the inherent male proclivity for sexual variety does not have the domesticating influences in homosexual unions (viz., a woman) that accompany heterosexual couplings; and homosexual unions, even if permitted to adopt, will have fewer children than the typical heterosexual marriage because "the demand for one's own children exceeds that for adopted children."[29] Thus, he argues that homosexual unions are inherently unstable because "children are the strongest cement of marriage and the emotional, if no longer the financial, support of old age."[30] Posner does not, however, draw the clearly erroneous conclusion that homosexuality is immoral because it is inherently a less happy and stable life-style than heterosexuality.

The economic aspects of Posner's theory revolve around rational choice under conditions of risk and uncertainty, where the goal is sexual satisfaction: individuals strive to maximize their sexual satisfaction by prudently calculating costs and benefits. The sociobiological aspects of his theory attend to the genetic strategy of humans: persistent patterns of behavior are explained as ways the species has maximized its evolutionary aptitude. The sociobiological aspect allegedly supports the economic component of Posner's theory because the former describes the basic sexual preferences that rational people try to satisfy by choosing from among the more or less costly possibilities. It is unclear, however, whether sociobiology, which addresses only the evolutionary strategy of human genes, can truly support an economic component that necessarily invokes individual sexual desire and rational choice: the strategy of each person may not be identical with the evolutionary instincts of human genes.

This tension is exacerbated when Posner observes that sexual norms are largely constructed by various societies and cultural traditions. This social construction strain coalesces uneasily with the sociobiological and economic aspects of Posner's theory because it mystifies further the relationship between human intentionality and instinct. How do our biological instincts for sex relate to the intentional aspects of our sexual desire? In fact, if sexual norms are socially constructed and if they greatly influence sexual desire, then Posner's sociobiological component fades because we cannot consider sexual preferences as genetic in any profound sense. Thus, we could not explain and justify extant sexual practices as the result of rational choice based on cost-benefit analyses of various possibilities for satisfying fixed sexual preferences. Instead, we would concede that these extant social practices greatly influenced our sexual preferences. This concession, however, undercuts the sociobiological foundation of Posner's fixed sexual preferences. Accordingly, the economic, sociobiological, and social construction components of Posner's theory form a disorderly trio.

Posner's method is purportedly scientific: take the best available evidence of the social sciences; draw conclusions about the causes and genesis of various sexual behavior; assess the effects of altering the social incentives and costs of that behavior; and extract implications for possible changes in public policy. This is a functional theory, in the sense that sexual phenomena are viewed as instruments to personal or social goals. Posner unsurprisingly considers the moral theories that inform good sex to be "the uncompromising, the truly unassimilable rival of the economic theory."[31] The animating drive and fundamental error of all such moral theories is "regarding moral and religious beliefs that are irreducible to genuine social interests or practical incentives as the key to both understanding and judging sexual practices and norms."[32] Posner insists that moral reasoning obscures the clear vision available through economic theory: "Clear thinking about sexuality is obstructed by layers of ignorance, ideology, superstition, and prejudice that the acid bath of economics can help us peel away."[33]

Among the numerous claims that Posner lodges about moral theories, two are especially noteworthy. First, he tells us that moral theories can be evaluated by their factual assumptions and implications: "We can ransack [moral theories] for their factual implications and then assess the accuracy of those implications, and by that means determine whether these theories provide an adequate positive and normative analysis."[34] Second, liberal theories fail to appreciate how moral feelings are the proper data for reliable moral judgments. Posner thus both rejects the view that only beliefs for which reasons can be given are worthy of being held and insists that our most firmly grounded beliefs are those anchored in deep feelings.

> Disgust and other strong emotions in fact supply the sturdiest foundations for moral feelings. You cannot convince a person by *argument* that infanticide is a bad thing. If he demands an argument—seriously, and not just when playing philosophy—this merely shows that he inhabits a different moral universe from you and there is no arguing between universes. The revulsion that modern Americans feel against infanticide is deeper than

any reason they could give for the revulsion. An even clearer case is sexual intercourse between men and animals. Most people in our society find this a disgusting practice, yet it is hard to give reasons why.[35]

Viewed in its most charitable light, Posner's economic analysis has much to recommend it. First, the sheer audacity of striving to put normative reasoning on a scientific basis can be inspiring. Most moral theorists have experienced the extreme frustration often accompanying debates that resist resolution and seem merely to restate continually the respective normative preferences of their participants. Second, Posner offers important counsel when he instructs moral theorists to examine empirical effects more closely and to be more assiduous about recognizing the role incentives and constraints play in sexual behavior. Clearly, attention to factual matters is paramount for successful implementation of sexual morality in five tiers, particularly at the fourth and fifth levels: assessments of third party effects and wider social context. Third, his account of how and why sexual behavior changes over time bears much explanatory power. Few moral theories can explain persuasively how and why changes in moral outlooks occur. Accordingly, economic analysis can help provide indispensable empirical insight that can furnish a useful supplement to moral theory.

Posner's tendency to discuss the objects of human sexual desire as subject to comparative cost-benefit analyses reduces humans to fungible instruments of pleasure for one another. Thus, his analysis often obscures our uniqueness and inherent worth. Moreover, he misunderstands the relative autonomy of moral codes and consequently falsely depicts them as abjectly dependent on the vicissitudes of social practice and cost-benefit analysis.

In fact, economic analysis can never replace moral theory, because no strictly empirical analysis bears necessary normative conclusions. At its best, empirical analysis can tell us how to achieve our goals—what combination of incentives and constraints are most likely to facilitate desired social ends—and it can help in understanding some of the reasons why social behavior changes over time. But it cannot tell us what our social goals ought to be: no mere account of "rational actors" can by itself prescribe our proper collective ends. Moral reasoning is an independent enterprise which embodies its own internal standards of proof, discovery, and justification. One of its paramount functions is collective deliberation about appropriate human ends, purposes, and goals. While economic analysis can inform such deliberation, it cannot substitute adequately for moral reasoning. Although moral reasoning has its own limitations, it is nevertheless necessary for a full analysis of sexual behavior. To sharpen this point: no series of facts, economic or otherwise, issues moral imperatives or furnishes reasons for action or rationally compels us to embrace a particular set of values. "Scientific" investigations are necessarily insufficient for normative enterprises. At best they can explain much about our moral behavior, but they can never justify that behavior.

Moreover, human sexuality is rarely experienced as morally neutral: the phenomenology of sex mocks the pretension to purely scientific analysis. Thus, Posner's stance of moral neutrality—viewing sex as morally indifferent—embodies at least two of the errors I caution against in this book: reductionism and assimilation. The "acid bath of economics" drips calamitously with unwarranted and self-defeating cynicism about the efficacy of moral theory.

In this vein, Posner unabashedly embraces sociobiology. At its most virulent, sociobiology claims that human and animal conduct is ordered by our genetic inheritance. The most extreme version of this thesis contends that certain social arrangements and institutions, such as the dominance of men over women and fixed social roles, are inevitable features of life. Here it seems that facts, by themselves, do issue conclusive reasons for action: if, for example, male dominance is inescapable, that "fact" gives us overwhelming evidence in favor of certain actions (those which efficiently and effectively promote the inevitable) and against other actions (those which inefficiently and ineffectively tilt at windmills by trying to defeat the inevitable).

But first impressions, like veterans' life insurance policies and weeping televangelists, are often deceiving. The strong version of sociobiology is fatally flawed for at least two reasons. First, the scientific evidence supports only the conclusion that our genetic legacy fixes the range within which human behavior must conform.[36] That range is wide enough to embrace numerous possible social schemes. Second, even if sociobiology could prove that our genes make a specific social arrangement inevitable, it does not follow logically that this arrangement is morally good or that humans ought to facilitate its arrival.[37] The fact that an action is inevitable does not entail a moral duty to nurture that action, unless there is a moral imperative to facilitate the inevitable that can be derived from an independent source: this source could not itself be derived merely from other alleged facts of sociobiology. Thus, sociobiology, at least in its extreme form, cannot sustain its desired link between facts and normative social action: explanations are not equivalent to justifications.

Posner does not, however, embrace the strong version of sociobiology. The distinctions he constantly underscores between preference and behavior, and between influences and determinants of behavior, and his recurring recognition that human behavior is manipulable through effective combinations of incentives and constraints, belie a firm commitment to an extreme view of sociobiology.

But Posner does endorse a moderate version of sociobiology. He affirms, for example, that men and women historically pursue different sexual strategies, that different sexual strategies are connected to the different reproductive functions of the two sexes, and that what the two sexes find attractive in each other is linked to reproductive fitness.[38] Moreover, he accepts the respective genetic make-ups of the sexes as the source of these differences. He insists, however, that ''the reader need not accept sociobiology to find the main arguments of [*Sex and Reason*] persuasive.[39]

Posner's adherence to a moderate version of sociobiology springs from his central aspiration to place sexual behavior on a scientific foundation. Although he (wisely) refuses to embrace a strong version of sociobiology, his acceptance of a moderate version is not irrelevant to the rest of his analysis. Especially in his general accounts of heterosexuality and homosexuality, we see his reliance on assumed natural propensities. It should be made clear, however, that despite Posner's protestations to the contrary, his prescriptions for reform of the laws and social policies surrounding sex are not merely morally neutral implications of natural human propensities combined prudentially with the external factors constituting reward and constraints. Again, we must understand that alleged facts, even when added to other alleged facts, do not translate into moral or political prescriptions. For example, if a person affirms the allegedly different (natural) sexual propensities of men and women, she is not thereby committed to a particular scheme of sexual behavior or to a specific legal regime to govern it. As Posner knows well, the alleged facts of difference are compatible with a range of possible social schemes and legal regimes. Normative prescriptions materialize only after moral and political ideology animates the facts we have aggregated.

Accordingly, Posner's economic analysis smuggles in moral judgments under the protective cloak of science. Although he is, as a matter of logic, correct in claiming that a reader could accept his main arguments without a commitment to sociobiology, it is that commitment that facilitates his ability to mask the moral judgments he must make to generate substantive normative conclusions and policy recommendations. Thus, his essentialism and pretensions to a purely scientific method notwithstanding, Posner must wallow in the "muck" of ideological disputation with the rest of us.

Consider his analysis of homosexuality. He cites three basic reasons why even in a tolerant society homosexuals will typically be less happy than heterosexuals: the neurosis often accompanying artistic and decorative occupations, careers to which homosexuals are disproportionately drawn; the inherent instability of homosexual unions due to the lack of a moderating (female) influence on the male propensity for sexual variety; and the lack of a fully satisfying family life for homosexuals because of the relative lack of children, even if adoption is permitted, in homosexual unions.

First, even if we stipulate that neurosis is an obstacle to happiness, the alleged causal connection between neurosis and creative occupations is still unclear. Do the artistic and decorative occupations cause more neurosis than other occupations? Or are those who are more neurotic than normal drawn to the artistic and decorative occupations? Is there a general causal link between artistic creativity and neurosis? The point is that it may not be the homosexual qua homosexual that encounters an additional obstacle to happiness, but the homosexual qua neurotic. Thus, it may be misleading to claim that the connection between neurosis and creative occupations shows how homosexuality is typically a less happy lifestyle.

Second, the alleged inherent instability of homosexual unions rests on a series of sociobiological assumptions about male and female sexual strategies, the different roles that the two sexes assume in reproduction, and the importance of children in companionate marriage. For sake or argument, I will concede Posner's assumptions that homosexuals are less sexually faithful than heterosexuals and that the former typically will have less children than the latter. But the conclusion that the lack of enduring companionate unions between homosexuals typically leads to unhappiness presupposes a host of value-laden assumptions about the desirability of companionate marriage as the primary form of family relation. Under Posner's own central thesis, society could lower or raise the happiness-inducing prospects of various liaisons by altering their respective incentives and constraints. While the facts and causal connections between homosexual life-styles and less enduring companionate unions with fewer children may remain constant, their alleged link to happiness is contingent. Happiness is a value-laden normative concept, not a strictly scientific fact. Thus the happiness-inducing capacity of companionate marriages could be lowered, and the happiness-inducing capacity of fleeting sexual encounters could be raised by the appropriate changes in incentives, constraints, and social outlooks.

The social determination not to make such transformations, or to regard the connection between homosexual lifestyles and unhappiness inevitable, rests, at least in part, on several value judgments. It would seem that unless Posner is tacitly relying on a strong version of sociobiology here, which would imply the impossibility of the posited transformations, he can derive his conclusions about homosexuals' inevitably ersatz prospects for happiness only if he complements his economic analysis by sneaking in his own value judgments: he assumes the desirability of the continuation of, or mere marginal adjustments to, the present balance of the relevant incentives and constraints. My point here is not that Posner's value judgments are necessarily unpersuasive, but that his conclusions are not derived solely through scientific analysis and that his sociobiology tends to obscure his value judgments.

My repeated theme—that scientific analysis is insufficient to generate normative conclusions—compels attention to the place of moral theory in normative decision making. When addressing issues of moral theory, Posner reveals an almost endearing naiveté. Take, for example, his spirited approval of widespread social revulsion as a self-validating foundation for morality. First, he extends this approval quite selectively: lavishly praising society's deep revulsion as revealing its proper condemnation of infanticide and bestiality,[40] yet dismissing the comparable revulsion our society bears toward baby selling and commodification of constitutive human attributes.[41] Second, he confuses the enterprises of justification and discovery. Theorists involved in epistemological justification must draw distinctions between (a) those beliefs we hold most deeply and (b) those beliefs that can be firmly grounded in the requisite reasons and causal connections. Such theorists, however, recognize that the arguments revealing that a belief is unjustified may not persuade the holder of that belief to change her mind. After all, there may be a host of quicker and more effective ways than philosophical disputation to convince a person to change her mind, or a person may be so intractable that she is beyond conversion regardless of the means used.

We discover and can often explain our beliefs by consulting our deepest feelings, and such convictions merit considerable respect and attention; but we cannot take them to be the incorrigible foundations of our considered moral judgments. We cannot do so because history has revealed that practices that once reflected a society's deepest feelings (e.g., slavery, prohibitions against miscegenation) are now disparaged as unjustified and clearly immoral; and practices (e.g., full employment of women in the public sphere) that were once greeted by thorough revulsion are now viewed as socially progressive. More strikingly, many such changes of view result from gaining a better understanding of factual matters (e.g. there are no races that are slaves by nature, women are not domestics by nature). To take deep revulsion as morally self-validating ironically hinders the relentless search for the facts that Posner otherwise valorizes. Our deepest feelings are often permeated with unbecoming, unwarranted prejudices and fears. Humans are not equipped with a special infallible faculty for divining moral judgments. Our deepest feelings are not raw, uncontaminated glimpses of a necessary normative order; instead, they incorporate the effects of our socialization and training. Thus, our deepest feelings and sense of revulsion cannot be taken as morally self-validating: they are not incorrigibly credible for reasons independent of their coherence with other sets of beliefs held most firmly, and, accordingly, they lack special epistemological and moral status.

Posner's complaints to the contrary notwithstanding, liberal moral theory does acknowledge the importance of, although it refuses to confer infallibility on, deep feelings and moral intuitions. The process of Wide Reflective Equilibrium[42] serves as an example. This process of moral reasoning contemplates a set of considered moral judgments (which include the immediate, noninferential feelings and revulsions Posner prizes) and a set of moral principles, in addition to independent fundamental theories of the person, of procedural justice, and of the role of morality in society. First, these fundamental theories generate arguments that test competing sets of moral principles or provide a device for selecting principles. Second, we must perform tests for coherence on the sets of moral principles surviving the earlier stage and on our considered moral judgments about specific cases. The coherence test will demand mutual adjustments between our moral principles (and reasons) and our considered moral judgments to fit both sets into a consistent whole. The test or device generated by the first stage is independent of the coherence test of the second stage, because the beliefs implicated at the first stage differ from those used at the second stage.[43] This process will provide several moral codes that must pass additional tests that are independent of the considered moral judgments involved in the coherence test of the second stage: a viable moral code must be teachable, psychologically tenable, socially feasible, able to be complied with, able to resolve most conflict situations, and compatible with nonmoral facts.[44]

Under this method, intuitions and considered moral judgments do not form the sole standard for isolating acceptable moral codes. These visceral reactions to specific cases are used as data, but are not viewed as the incorrigible foundation of moral theory. Sets of independent moral principles and reasons are first tested by the arguments generated by fundamental theories mentioned above or emerge from the selection device which these theories produce. They are tested further for coherent fit with prevalent considered moral judgments, a stage which entails mutual adjustments. Finally, the resulting moral codes must meet the additional independent tests adumbrated above. Presumably, persistent disagreements will typically have their roots in a disagreement of fact or a disparity about some aspect of a fundamental theory. Such disagreements may be more manageable than those arising at the level of considered moral judgments or moral principles themselves. Moreover, we must recognize that disagreement itself is part of a robust notion of rationality and moral reasoning. We should expect to find many complex moral issues contested strongly in societies that are heterogeneous, relatively free, and not subject to rigid social roles.

I am not an abject apologist for Wide Reflective Equilibrium.[45] But, clearly, this process does more than merely arrange our common prejudices and biases into a consistent scheme. The process, for example, advocates extensive mutual revisions of considered moral judgments and moral principles to ensure their fit into a coherent whole. No particular set of intuitions or considered judgments is held as absolutely fixed or self-validating. Because theory-based revisions pervade attempts to evolve acceptable moral codes, thus precluding the absolute fixation of any set of moral intuitions, more than a merely conventionalist account of morality emerges.

Accordingly, contra Posner, liberal moral theory can certainly take moral intuitions and deep feelings seriously yet refuse to idolize them as the incorrigible foundations of moral judgments. Moreover, liberal moral theory recognizes the importance of empirical analysis, including the role of economic theory, in helping to develop more sophisticated fundamental theories of the person, of procedural justice, and of the role of morality in society, as well as in resolving numerous nonmoral factual disputes. However, the process urged here abrogates foundationalist and scientific pretensions: competing ideological prisms are inevitable; moral reasoning is neither science nor sham.

Ideology, in its most general and nonpejorative form, is merely one's descriptive and prescriptive world view. It includes, among other things, subtheories of human nature, political association, socioeconomic organization, and moral principles.

The term "ideology," however, has historically received a decidedly bad press. It has borne numerous pejorative epithets: a biased perception of particular societies and the world; the mystifying product of social conditioning by the ruling classes of a particular socioeconomic system; that which presents itself as objective and transcendent, but which is in fact propaganda serving certain political purposes. It is no wonder that we hear recurrent cries for the "end of ideology."

But ideological disputation will end only if one of the following is realized: the realization of pure, objective, normative truth; the attainment of intercultural (universal) or intracultural (limited) consensus; or the consummation of a utopian political system where we would go beyond ideology as the functions of ideology disappear. But these devices seem either theoretically impossible or practically undesirable.

Pure, objective, normative truth presupposes the possibility of an "Archimedean point" from which we might neutrally adjudicate conflicting normative claims. But such a neutral view is unavailable to historically situated humans constituted deeply by their divergent socioeconomic contexts. Further, even if such a vantage point is in some sense available, it is unclear whether and how we would know we had captured it.

Appeals to intercultural and intracultural consensus are too often attempts to mask the presence of genuine dispute. Where we find an unchallenged moral consensus, we should be suspicious: authoritarianism and repression of diversity are usually the genesis of such widespread cultural "agreement." In societies and a world where clear socioeconomic, racial, ethnic, gender, and religious differences are present, the pious entreaty for consensus may be one of the first refuges of the relatively advantaged.

The eternal aspiration for the consummation of a utopian vision reveals part of the human condition. But how could such a state facilitate the death of ideology? How could utopia imply the end of ideology in its nonpejorative sense: descriptive and prescriptive world visions? Only if one insists dogmatically that all ideology necessarily serves insidious purposes could one consistently herald the end of ideology in utopia. Only if there is no nonpejorative portrayal of ideology could the end of ideology in utopia be possible. But once we relinquish the hope for pure, objective, normative truth flowing down from the neutral perspective of an intellectual Archimedean point, we also admit the possibility that ideological prisms are not only inevitable but desirable.

We are, then, confronted by an exciting and liberating possibility: to reimagine and remake our society in accordance with our collective ideological disputations. We must recognize our collective ability to transcend our present context—but not all contexts. We must not flee from the freedom and anxiety such recognition bears.[46] The paradox here is that while our sense of adventure is heightened by our refusal to supplicate ourselves before the illusion of an Archimedean point, our yearning for security is simultaneously threatened.

Thus, our excitement is tempered by our experience of humility as we contemplate our own finiteness and the daunting normative task we confront.

As for the experience of humility that suffuses the enterprise of moral reasoning, I am reminded of a story. One of my law professors, who bore a modest physical presence, was nevertheless a stimulating and powerful orator. Each of his classes was an old-time lecture *simpliciter*: not only were questions from students not encouraged, they were affirmatively discouraged. Given that the political content of these lectures was often painfully unsettling and radically controversial, numerous students were chomping at the bit for an opportunity to confront the professor. Finally, on the morning of the penultimate class session, the professor announced that he would accept questions from the crowd of over 150 students. A multitude of hands arose immediately. The first student who was recognized presented a strident and often ad hominem critique of several of the professor's main theses. The professor absorbed the student's stentorian bravado for five minutes that seemed like an hour. Finally, the student concluded. The rest of us experienced the unbearable tension in the room, a collective anxiety to which we had all contributed. The professor turned slowly to the student and stared intensely and portentously. Suddenly, for the first time in the semester, he smiled broadly. Then he shrugged his shoulders and declared amicably, ''I came from dust and to dust shall I return!''

NOTES

PREFACE

1. The name has been changed, not to protect the innocent, but because of my faulty recollection.
2. Raymond A. Belliotti, "A Philosophical Analysis of Sexual Ethics," *Journal of Social Philosophy* 10 (1979): 8–11.
3. See, for example, *Philosophy for a Changing Society*, ed. Creighton Pedan (Reynoldsburg, Ohio: Advocate Press, 1983); *Ethics: Theory and Practice*, ed. M. Velasquez and C. Rostankowski (Englewood Cliffs, N.J.: Prentice-Hall, 1985); *Social Ethics*, ed. Thomas Mappes and Jane Zembaty (New York: McGraw-Hill, 1982); and *Moral Choices: Ethical Theories and Problems*, ed. Joseph Grcic (St. Paul, Minn.: West Publishing Company, 1989).
4. *A Companion to Ethics*, ed. Peter Singer (Oxford: Basil Blackwell, 1991).
5. Raymond A. Belliotti, "Sex," in Singer, *Companion to Ethics*, 315–326.

INTRODUCTION: SEX AND MORAL THEORY

1. See, e.g., Michael Levin, "Why Homosexuality Is Abnormal," in *The Moral Life*, ed. Steven Luper-Foy and Curtis Brown (Fort Worth: Harcourt Brace Jovanovich, 1992), 202–208, and Michael Novak, "Men without Women," *American Spectator* (October 1978): 14–16.
2. Levin, "Why Homosexuality Is Abnormal," 206–207.
3. Novak, "Men without Women," 16.
4. Ibid.
5. Ibid.
6. Ibid.
7. Roger Scruton, *Sexual Desire* (New York: Free Press, 1986), 307.
8. Much of the disparagement of homosexuality may arise from "homophobia"—a deeply irrational fear and hatred of homosexuals and their actions. Such fear and hatred may stem, in part, from a deep recognition that human sexuality is more ambivalent than most of us want to admit. The sexuality of heterosexuals is called into question, and rendered less secure, to the extent that we understand the range of human sexual behavior. For heterosexuals who are already a bit insecure about their sexuality, this

fact may trigger disproportionately strong reactions against homosexuals. The tragedy of homophobic reactions is that the value of homosexuals as people is wrongly reduced to judgments about their sexual orientation.

I must note, however, that homophobia, in the strictest sense of the term, is a term properly limited to those people who have a *pathological* fear or hatred of homosexuals. It is thus a mistake to apply the term too lavishly and assume that all critics of homosexual behavior must suffer from the psychological illness of homophobia. Such a mistake would be especially and cruelly ironic given the fashion in which all homosexuals were once tarred by charges of psychological illness.

CHAPTER 1. TRANSCENDING THE FLESH

1. W. K. C. Guthrie, "Pythagoras and Pythagoreanism," in *The Encyclopedia of Philosophy*, ed. Paul Edwards (New York: Macmillan Publishing Company and Free Press, 1967), 7:36–39.

2. W. K. C. Guthrie, *The Greek Philosophers* (1950; reprint New York: Harper and Row, 1975), 36.

3. Frederick Copleston, S. J., *A History of Philosophy*, vol. #1, pt. 1 (1946; reprint Garden City, N.Y.: Image Books, 1962), 153.

4. Plato contended that whenever numerous particular entities have a common name, they also have a corresponding idea. This idea, or form, or universal, consists of the essential qualities partly constituting the particulars, by virtue of which the various particulars can be classified accurately by a common name. For example, various particular things share the common name "chair." Plato believed that although particular chairs could be quite diverse in size, color, composition, and so on, they still share some constitutive characteristics so that we may call them by the same name. Universals thus conceived are not merely subjective concepts or conventional names; rather, as objective essences they have independent existence. Particulars depend for their being on their corresponding universals; if there were no universal "chair", there could be no particulars participating in it, that is, being chairs. However, if all particular chairs somehow passed out of existence, the universal would be unaffected. For Plato, thought grasps reality, and the objects of thought, which are in the purest sense universals, must have independent reality (ibid., 189).

But where exactly can such objective essences reside? Frederick Copleston sums up the conventional presentation of Plato's position in this way: "In Plato's view the objects which we apprehend in universal concepts, the objects with which science deals, the objects corresponding to universal terms of predication, are objective ideas or subsistent Universals, existing in a transcendental world of their own—somewhere 'out there'—apart from sensible things, understanding by 'apart from' practically spatial separation. Sensible things are copies or participations in these universal realities, but the latter abide in an unchanging heaven of their own, while sensible things are subject to change, in fact are always becoming and can never truly be said to *be*. The Ideas exist in their heaven in a state of isolation one from another, and apart from the mind of any Thinker" (ibid., 191).

5. Plato *Republic* 9.571c2–571d3.

6. Plato *Phaedo* 81b1–82a3: "If [a soul] be defiled and impure when she

leaves the body, from being ever with it, and serving it and loving it, and from being besotted by it and by its desires and pleasures . . . such a soul is weighed down and dragged back to the visible world . . . and they are imprisoned, probably in the bodies of animals with habits similar to the habits which were theirs in their lifetime . . . men who have practiced unbridled gluttony and wantonness and drunkenness probably enter the bodies of asses and suchlike animals . . . and those who have chosen injustice, and tyranny, and robbery enter the bodies of wolves, and hawks, and kites.''

Plato, however, recognizes that some souls, although not exhibiting philosophical insight, still practiced moderation and social cooperation: "It is quite plain . . . wither each soul goes: each enters an animal with habits like its own . . . the happiest, who go to the best place, are those who have practiced the popular and social virtues which are called temperance and justice, and which come from habit and practice, without philosophy or reason . . . they return into a mild and social nature like their own, such as that of bees, or wasps, or ants; or, it may be, into the bodies of men, and that from them are made worthy citizens" (ibid., 82a6–82b6).

7. "I will tell you what happens to a soul which is pure at her departure, and which in her life has had no intercourse that she could avoid with the body, and so draws after her, when she dies, no taint of the body, but has shunned it. . . . Does not the soul, then, which is in that state, go away to the invisible that is like herself, and to the divine, and the immortal, and the wise, where she is released from error, and folly, and fear, and fierce passions, and all the other evils that fall to the lot of men, and is happy, and for the rest of time lives in very truth with the gods" (ibid., 80e1–81a8)?

8. Commenting on Plato's doctrine of the immortality of the soul, Frederick Copleston cautions that: "The soul persists after death and . . . the soul's life hereafter will be in accordance with its conduct on earth. How far Plato seriously intended the doctrine of successive reincarnations, which is put forward in the Myths, is uncertain: in any case it would appear that there is hope for the philosophic soul of escaping from the wheel of reincarnation, while it would also appear that there may be incurable sinners who are flung forever into Tartarus" (Copleston, *History of Philosophy*, 240).

9. Plato *Phaedo* 82b8–82c3.

10. Plato *Laws* 841d2–841e3, 838e7–839b2.

11. "To conceive a person . . . as a dual complex of two wholly disparate things, body and mind, is nonetheless an impossible conception, on the simplest metaphysical grounds. For on this view, the body and the mind are wholly disparate things, so that any bodily change, wrought by the mind or some nonphysical occurrence transpiring therein, is a change that lies quite outside the realm of physical law. This means that human behavior is veritably miraculous . . . when we come to some precise instance of the alleged interaction of body and mind, as conceived by [dualism], we find that we are dealing with something that is not merely mysterious but wholly unintelligible" (Richard Taylor, *Metaphysics* [Englewood Cliffs: Prentice-Hall, 1963], 17).

12. "The mind or soul, it turns out in [dualist] descriptions, is just whatever it is that thinks, reasons, deliberates, chooses, feels, and so on. But the fact with which we began was that *men* think, reason, deliberate, choose, feel, and so on. And we do in fact have some fairly clear notion of what we mean by a man . . . we seek some understanding of what this mind or soul

is, we find it simply described as a thing that thinks, deliberates, feels, and so on" (ibid., 26).

13. "But philosophically, it is just exactly as good to reason that, since men think, feel, desire, choose, etc., and since men are bodies . . . then *some* bodies think, feel desire, choose, etc. This argument is just as good as the dualist's argument and does not lead us into a morass of problems concerning the connection between soul and body" (ibid.).

14. "What [dualists] need to do is state just what positive properties this [mind or soul] must possess, in order to elevate an animal body to the status of a person, and no positive properties suggest themselves at all. We cannot give it psychological properties—by saying, for example, that this soul thinks, desires, deliberates, wills, believes, repents, and so on; for if the thing we are adding has *those* properties then it is *already* a person in its own right, and there is no question of *adding* it to something in order to *get* a person" (ibid., 30).

15. Stoicism, despite common misperception, was not a philosophy of inactivity or lethargy. Rather, in an admirable attempt to reduce human suffering and misery, it aspired to combine virtuous activity with an indifferent attitude toward events outside one's control. As such, Stoicism can reasonably be perceived as a philosophy of strength, consolation, and fortitude in the face of an often cruel, heartless world exhibiting a frightening scarcity of necessary social goods (Copleston, *History of Philosophy*, 142).

16. Epictetus *Encheiridion* I. Thus, Stoics maintain that we are accomplices in the discontent, anxiety, and frustration we too often experience. Invariably such negative reactions and emotions are the result of failing to heed the counsel to accept without rebellion events that are not solely within our control. At bottom, my reactions themselves are presumably under my control, and, although the actions of others or simple bad luck may be the cause of seeming disaster and evil, the subsequent suffering I experience is the result of my own lack of discipline and understanding. In the words of Marcus Aurelius: "No one can fix on me what is ugly, nor can I be angry with my kinsman, nor hate him. For we are made for cooperation, like feet, like hands, like eyelids, like the rows of the upper and lower teeth. To act against one another then is contrary to nature; and it is acting against one another to be vexed and to turn away" (*Meditations* II, 1).

17. Epictetus describes the paradigm of the Stoic philosopher in this way: "He censures no man, he praises no man, he blames no man, he accuses no man, he says nothing about himself as if he were somebody or knew something; when he is impeded . . . he blames himself: if a man praises him, he ridicules the praiser to himself: if a man censures him, he makes no defense . . . he removes all desire from himself, and he transfers aversion to those things only of the things within our power which are contrary to nature: he employs a moderate movement toward everything: whether he is considered foolish or ignorant, he cares not: and in a word he watches himself as if he were an enemy and lying in ambush" (*Encheiridion* 48).

18. Thus, he argued that "death is nothing to us, for good and evil imply sentience, and death is the privation of all sentience; therefore a right understanding that death is nothing to us makes the mortality of life enjoyable, not by adding to life an illimitable time, but by taking away the yearning after immortality . . . when we are, death is not come, and, when death is come, we are not. It is nothing, then, either to the living or to the dead, for

with the living it is not and the dead exist no longer" (Epicurus *Fragments* para. 3).

The gods, indeed, exist, because for Epicurus the nearly universal belief in them can only be explained by their objective existence. But the gods are the embodiment of the ideal of calm and tranquility; they exist with no thoughts about or plans for humans. Therefore, there is no rational reason for humans to fear either death or the reactions of the gods. "For verily there are gods, and the knowledge of them is manifest; but they are not such as the multitude believe, seeing that men do not steadfastly maintain the notions they form respecting them. Not the man who denies the gods worshipped by the multitude, but he who affirms of the gods what the multitude believes about them is truly impious. For the utterances of the multitude about the gods are not true preconceptions but false assumptions; superstitions such that the greatest evils happen to the wicked and the greatest blessings happen to the good from the hand of the gods" (ibid., para. 2).

19. Epicurus *Fragments* para. 6.

20. Cited by Michael D. Bayles, "Marriage, Love, and Procreation," in *Philosophy & Sex*, ed. Robert Baker and Frederick Elliston (Buffalo, N.Y.: Prometheus Books, 1975), 204.

21. The admiration and esteem that Epicurus generated among his followers is best described by the following passage from Lucretius: "When human life lay groveling in all men's sight, crushed to the earth under the dead weight of superstition whose grim features loured menacingly upon mortals from the four quarters of the sky, [Epicurus] was first to raise mortal eyes in defiance, first to stand erect and brave the challenge. Fables of the gods did not crush him, nor the lightning flash and the growling menace of the sky. Rather, they quickened his manhood, so that he, first of all men, longed to smash the constraining locks of nature's doors. The vital vigor of his mind prevailed. He ventured far out beyond the flaming ramparts of the world and voyaged in mind throughout infinity . . . superstition in its turn lies crushed beneath his feet, and we by his triumph are lifted level with the skies" (*On the Nature of the Universe*, trans. Robert Latham [Harmondsworth: Penguin, 1951], 3).

CHAPTER 2. THE NATURAL LAW

1. "The Old Testament . . . portrays God as commanding his creatures to be fruitful and multiply. Nowhere in its pages is there a counsel of celibacy or an exaltation of virginity. Jephthah's daughter mourns her virginal estate; the patriarchs and kings of Israel practice polygamy; the newlywed male is exempted by the Law from military service for one year so that he and his bride may enjoy the pleasures of wedded sexual life. The assumption throughout is that a man will marry and produce offspring, even taking concubines if necessary" (W. G. Cole, *Sex in Christianity and Psychoanalysis* [New York: Oxford University Press, 1955], 11).

2. Ibid.

3. "The Hebrew Scriptures begin with the account of creation, a poetic description which is punctuated by the . . . refrain . . . 'God saw everything that he had made, and behold, it was very good.' The physical, material

world is created by God, and as his handiwork it is to be accepted and enjoyed with thanksgiving. 'The earth is the Lord's and the fullness thereof, the world and those who dwell therein' " (ibid., 9).

4. Ibid., 10.

5. Raymond J. Lawrence, *The Poisoning of Eros* (New York: Augustine Moore Press, 1989), 17.

6. Cole, *Sex in Christianity*, 12–31.

7. Ibid., 12–13, 15.

8. "Jesus is saying in this word about adultery that there is no special virtue in abstinence when one is a seething mass of lustful desire, mentally ravaging every woman he meets. He is not saying anything at all about the sexual desire of persons who sincerely love one another, of married couples" (ibid., 17).

9. "[God] created man as male and female, intending that the two should become one flesh in a lifelong bond. Divorce was no part of the divine plan. 'What God has joined together let no man put asunder' . . . Matthew puts the words, 'except for unchastity' in Jesus' mouth, but he alone does so. Both Mark and Luke leave the prohibition as an absolute" (ibid., 17–18).

10. "Jesus was not suggesting that money or sex or the family were evil in and of themselves, to be avoided and forsworn. He regarded them as roadblocks to salvation only where they represented the source of a man's ultimate security, where they assumed the role of idols. 'Seek ye *first* the Kingdom of God, and all these things shall be added to you' " (ibid., 20).

11. Ibid., 36.

12. Ibid.

13. For alternate views of St. Paul, see Lawrence, *Poisoning of Eros*, 31–53.

14. Augustine, *Confessions* bk. 2, chap. 1. Prior to his conversion to Christianity, Augustine subscribed to the religious mysticism of the Manichaeans: the world is portrayed as an arena in which the primordial forces of good and evil wage their unremitting struggle for human acceptance. Permeated by stark dualisms, Manichaeanism identified the body with evil and the soul with good. The purest Manichaeans, those who had fully accepted the light of the good, practiced an uncompromising asceticism which included chastity and vegetarianism. Augustine, however, could not be classified among these triumphant few. He was plagued by intense erotic passions which found systematic fulfillment in a variety of lovers. Haunted by the pleasures of the flesh, yet rationally committed to the proposition that the pure and holy man must seek consolation only in the contentments of the contemplative life, Augustine experienced deep internal conflict.

Eventually, after around nine years, Augustine became disillusioned with the Manichaean teachings about astronomy and with the limited intellectual powers of the Manichaean cognoscenti. Thus, he renounced his Manichaean affiliation. About four years later, Augustine converted to Christianity.

15. Augustine, *Soliloquies*, trans. Charles C. Starbuck, *Nicene and Post-Nicene Fathers*, ed. Philip Schaff (Grand Rapids, Mich.: W. M. B. Eerdman's Publishing Company, 1956), vol. 7, bk. 1, 17.

16. Augustine, *On the Good of Marriage*, trans. C. L. Cornish, *Nicene and Post-Nicene Fathers*, ed. Philip Schaff (Grand Rapids, Mich.: W. M. B. Eerdman's Publishing Company, 1956), 3:18.

17. Augustine, "Serman on the Mount," trans. William Findlay, *Nicene*

and Post-Nicene Fathers, ed. Philip Schaff (Grand Rapids, Mich.: W. M. B. Eerdman's Publishing Company, 1956), vol. 6, bk. 1, 41.

Perhaps embarrassed by the polygamy practiced in the Old Testament, Augustine rationalized that such practices were sanctioned by God in order to facilitate the production of sufficient offspring to populate a then underpopulated world. Augustine contended that the rulers of Israel did not practice polygamy because of excessive erotic inclinations, but out of a sense of patriarchal duty. In that vein, they invariably engaged in sex aimed only at reproduction. Once the need for additional children of God was satisfied, the divine sanction of polygamy ceased. Unsurprisingly, Augustine added that polyandry, a woman's having more than one husband at a single time, could never be permitted by God because the practice could serve no procreative function that was not otherwise fulfilled.

18. Augustine, *On the Morals of the Catholic Church*, trans. Richard Stothert, *Nicene and Post-Nicene Fathers*, ed. Philip Schaff (Grand Rapids, Mich.: W. M. B. Eerdman's Publishing Company, 1956), vol. 4, chap. 20.

19. Augustine, *Good of Marriage*, 3.

20. Lust arose by the decision of the will . . . both [sexual] desire and activity were controlled by the reason. No repression occurred [*sic*] because no desire arose without the will. In Augustine's terms, the male erection occurred without concupiscence, or at least without excessive concupiscence." William M. Alexander, "Sex and Philosophy in Augustine," *Augustinian Studies* 5 (1974): 203.

21. "Sexual activity took place without desire (lust). The sexual organs operated by decision of the will but without sexual excitation" (ibid).

22. Augustine, *Against Two Letters of the Pelagians*, trans. Peter Holmes and Robert Ernest Wallis, *Nicene and Post-Nicene Fathers*, ed. Philip Schaff (Grand Rapids, Mich.: W. M. B. Eerdman's Publishing Company, 1956), vol. 5, bk. 1, 32.

23. Ibid., bk. 2, 14.

24. Augustine, *Good of Marriage*, 6.

25. Ibid., 3.

26. "Is it not [the Manichaeans] who used to counsel us to observe as much as possible the time when a woman, after her purification, is most likely to conceive, and to obtain from cohabitation at that time, lest the soul should be entangled in the flesh? This proves that you approve of having a wife, not for the procreation of children, but for gratification of passion. . . . Where there is a wife there must be marriage, but there is no marriage where motherhood is not in view; therefore neither is there a wife" (Augustine, *On the Morals of the Manichaeans*, chap. 65).

It must be noted, however, that not all of Augustine's Christian contemporaries shared his fundamentally negative view of sex: "Augustine was shocked to read in Julian of Eclanum the opinion that pleasure has been attached by God to copulation for the purpose of encouraging people to go to the trouble of reproducing their kind . . . according to Julian there is nothing wrong with sexual desire; it is natural and innocent . . . it existed before the Fall" (Christopher Kirwan, *Augustine* [London: Routledge, 1989], 194–195).

27. Ibid.

28. Aquinas is by no means the originator of natural law theory, but he is surely the most accomplished systematic refiner of the tradition. More than five centuries prior to the birth of Christ, the earliest recorded Western

thinkers assumed that a natural order was immanent in the universe. They believed that this order was not created by humans but could be discovered by them through reason and careful attention to nature's messages. Moreover, the natural order was thought to be not merely descriptive and scientific, but also normative and action guiding.

Aquinas held that law has three components: it was (1) an ordinance of reason promulgated (2) for the common good (3) by the caretaker of the community. So conceived, law is a foundation for commitment and action, has the animating aspiration of unifying the parts (individual humans) to the whole (the perfect community), and must constitute a public (promulgated) measure of action. For Aquinas the law has two powers: the *coercive power* to command obedience from reasons of prudence—we obey the law because we fear the reprisals of state power; and the *directive power* to impose prescriptive obligations and to allow various propositions to exist as valid law— law embodies a moral dimension which should command our allegiance independent of our fear of state punishment. Law's directive power stems from its ability to facilitate the ends of humans as social beings and members of a community. Law must aim at a common good, which is not merely the aggregation of all individual interests.

Aquinas cites four kinds of law: *Eternal law* exists in the mind of God. It fixes the essence of all things, orders human action to its appropriate ends, and is the origin of natural law. *Divine positive law* is the law of God as revealed through Christ and the Scriptures. Because eternal law resides in the infinite mind of God, it is not directly accessible to finite human minds. Divine law helps to make eternal law explicit and available to humans.

Natural law is founded on human nature, discovered by reason, and is permanent and universal. Humans cannot subtract from it, and compliance with it is necessary if we are to attain our appropriate function. Thus natural law guides humans to their earthly ends and is our "participation" in eternal law. The fundamental principles of natural law, however, do not require the use of elaborate deductive or inductive logical processes. Rather, the basic principles are self-evident, universal, and beyond rational demonstration: God has "instilled [the basic principles of natural law] into man's mind so as to be known by him naturally."

In principle, all humans need and have sufficient knowledge and reasoning power to regulate their actions in accordance with natural law. The use of reason is essential to apply our natural inclinations into concrete, specific commitments and actions. Aquinas tells us that reason unassisted can discover the natural law, which is grounded ultimately in eternal law and the divine reason itself, and translate our inclinations into proper action.

Human positive law is comprised of legal statutes, decisions, and decrees of various governments. It is valid—it can be described accurately as "law"—only if it is in accord with natural law. In fact, the proper role of human law is to make natural law explicit and applicable in particular situations (Thomas Aquinas, *Summa Theologica*). All references from *Fathers of the English Dominican Province*, (trans., 3 vols. (New York: Benziger, 1947), bks. 1–2, question 90, arts. 1–4; question 91, art. 1, 4–5; question 94, arts. 3, 5. See also Lloyd L. Weinreb, *Natural Law and Justice* (Cambridge, Mass.: Harvard University Press, 1987).

29. Ibid., question 98, art. 1.
30. Cole, *Sex in Christianity*, 74.

31. Aquinas, *Summa Theologica*, I, question 99, art. I.

32. "Adam preceded Eve into existence and she was made from him. This . . . gives the first man his proper dignity and authority. Further, man's reason is more fully developed and in greater control of his emotions than woman's, which is additional evidence of his superiority" (Cole, *Sex in Christianity*, 72).

33. "Aquinas regarded seduction of a virgin as less serious than adultery, remarking that it is a 'greater injustice to have intercourse with a woman who is subject to another's authority as regards the act of generation, than as regards her guardianship' " (ibid., 84).

34. Ibid., 85.

35. "If the husband has married because he is consumed with passion, then the wife must 'render the marriage debt' in order to protect him from the sin of adultery, from seeking satisfaction in the arms of another woman. Sex that is motivated by giving the debt or by the desire for children is virtuous and meritorious" (ibid., 87).

36. "The claims of the Church to final truth, to absolute authority, the assertions that the monk and the nun are pleasing in the sight of God, the illusion that celibacy overcomes the power of concupiscence—all these were challenged and condemned by Luther" (ibid., 104).

37. Martin Luther, *Letters of Christian Counsel*, ed. and trans. T. G. Tappert (Philadelphia: Westminster Press, 1960), 275.

38. *Luther's Works*, ed. James Atkinson and Helmut T. Lehman (Philadelphia: Fortress Press, 1966), vol. 44, 369.

39. Some commentators, such as Raymond Lawrence, view Luther as a somewhat salty, happy-go-lucky affirmer of sexuality, with a proclivity for double entendres: "Luther was an energetic and spontaneous character and was obviously very little concerned that everything he said be consistent. He was never very far removed from a joyful, playful, and even mischievous attitude toward his own sexuality" (*Poisoning of Eros*, 179). Others, such as W. G. Cole, however, are less sanguine about Luther as bon vivant: "Despite his own marriage and his view of matrimony as a divine decree, Luther looked upon sex as somehow unclean, and though necessary, an unhappy necessity" (*Sex in Christianity*, 114).

40. Cole, *Sex in Christianity*, 114–117; Lawrence, *Poisoning of Eros*, 177–179.

41. "[There were] two Calvins coexisting uncomfortably within the same historical personage. One was the Renaissance humanist who promoted marriage for the clergy and who celebrated sexuality as a delightful divine gift. The other Calvin was the medieval Catholic, ever anxious to control any sexual impulse lest it get out of hand" (Lawrence, *Poisoning of Eros*, 184–185).
It seems, however, that the "medieval Catholic" dominated the "two Calvins."

42. John Calvin, *Institutes of The Christian Religion*, bk. 2, chap. 8, 44.

43. John Calvin, *Corinthian Commentaries*, 232, 268–269.

44. Many mainstream Protestant churches (for example, Presbyterian, Episcopal, United Methodist) are currently grappling with possible reforms in their official stances on sexual morality: Should gays and lesbians be ordained as ministers? Should a framework for permissible extramarital relationships be developed for certain groups (the elderly, the disabled, adoles-

cents)? Should traditional roles for women be rethought? In part, such reform movements are both responses to declining enrollments and to rapidly changing social attitudes. In the rest of this chapter, I have chosen to concentrate on the official sexual ethic of the Roman Catholic Church because it is the most uncompromising and most influential Christian perspective.

45. The two most important documents emerging from the council were its actual canons and decrees and an official catechism sanctioned by the council and composed after 1563 under papal auspices. The catechism was designed to popularize and to simplify for the public the council's authoritative canons and decrees. Henceforth, differences of opinion within the church about matters of faith would be severely restricted.

46. Cole, *Sex in Christianity*, 98.

47. "The words of St. Jerome were quoted with approval by the Catechism: 'A wise man ought to love his wife with judgment, not with passion; he will govern the impetuosity of his desire, and will not be hurried into indulgence. *There is no greater turpitude than that a husband should love his wife as an adulteress*' " (ibid.).

48. Ibid., 99.

49. Pope Paul VI, *Humanae Vitae*, in *Philosophy & Sex*, ed. Robert Baker and Frederick Elliston (Buffalo, N.Y.: Prometheus Books, 1975), 131, para. 1.

50. Ibid., 135, sec. 2, para. 9.

51. Ibid., 138, sec. 2, para. 14.

52. "Marriage is not . . . the effect of chance or the product of evolution of unconscious natural forces; it is the wise institution of the Creator to realize in mankind His design of love. By means of the reciprocal personal gift of self, proper and exclusive to them, husband and wife tend towards the communion of their beings in view of mutual personal perfection, to collaborate with God in the generation and education of new lives" (ibid., 135, sec. 2, para. 8).

The role of the church is to act as intermediary between humans and God: "[A] teaching founded on the natural law, illuminated and enriched by divine revelation. No believer will wish to deny the teaching authority of the Church is competent to interpret even the natural moral law" (ibid., 133, sec. 1, para. 4). Responsible marriage and parenthood, thus, require that couples "conform their activity to the creative intention of God, expressed in the very nature of marriage and its acts, and manifested by the constant teaching of the Church" (ibid., 136, sec. 2, para. 10).

53. Ibid., 137, sec. 2, para. 11.

54. Ibid., 138, sec. 2, para. 14.

55. Ibid., 139, sec. 2, para. 15.

56. Ibid., 139, sec. 2, para. 16.

57. Ibid., 132, sec. 1, para. 2.

58. Ibid., 138, sec. 2, para. 14.

59. Ibid., 135, sec. 2, para. 9.

60. Ibid.

61. "[The church's teaching on sexual ethics is founded on] the inseparable connection, willed by God and unable to be broken by man on his own initiative [at least not in a morally permissible way], between the two meanings of the conjugal act: the unitive meaning and the procreative meaning. . . . By safeguarding both these essential aspects . . . the conjugal

act preserves in its fullness the sense of true mutual love and its ordination towards man's most high calling to parenthood" (ibid., 137, sec. 2, para. 12).

62. Ibid., 137–138, sec. 2, para. 13.

63. Ibid.

64. "It is an error to think that a conjugal act which is deliberately made infecund and so is intrinsically dishonest could be made honest and right by the ensemble of a fecund conjugal life" (ibid., 138, sec. 2, para. 14).

65. Ibid., 141, sec. 2, para. 18.

66. Ibid., 133, sec. 1, para. 4; 137, sec. 2, para. 12; 138, sec. 1, para. 14.

67. Ibid., 141, sec. 2, para. 18.

68. Ibid., 133, sec. 1, para. 4; 141, sec. 2, para. 18.

69. I will not evaluate here the persuasiveness of this rationale. See, for example, Raymond A. Belliotti, *Justifying Law* (Philadelphia: Temple University Press, 1992), 4–5.

70. "Paul, for instance, wrote first Corinthians with the expectation that the world was about to end. This fact, rather than any ultimate opposition to sexuality, was the reason for his negative remarks on marriage" (Philip S. Keane, S. J., *Sexual Morality* [New York: Paulist Press, 1977], 16).

71. "The Scriptures definitively reject all dehumanizing forms of sexuality such as sexual cruelty, rape, or prostitution. It is quite difficult, however, to push the Scriptures too far on specific questions of sexual morality . . . specific scriptural statements on subjects such as these are likely to be encrusted in cultural contexts that we can never fully recover" (ibid.).

72. Originalism is presumably a nonpoliticized judicial decision making based on strict adherence to the plain meaning of constitutional provisions and legislative enactments ("textualism"), or grounded on the intentions of the framers of those provisions and enactments ("intentionalism"), or derived from the rational or normative order immanent in the law ("formalism").

It should be clear that textualism and intentionalism are in conflict. The alleged literal reading of a provision may be at odds with the intentions of its framers. What we intend is not always reflected clearly in what we say, much less in how others interpret what we intend and say. Thus there may well exist a conflict between the alleged plain meaning of a provision and the animating intent of its framers.

Moreover, all reading requires interpretation that is subject to ideological biases and the currents of history. Presumed literal readings all too often disingenuously mask political preferences. Even the most fervent idolaters of textualism would be hard pressed to respond persuasively when confronted with terms such as due process, freedom of contract, cruel and unusual punishment, and equal protection. These and most other paramount constitutional clauses have no static meaning and are subject to rival, contestable interpretations. Accordingly, textualism is flawed because every significant constitutional provision lacks a preexisting, determinate meaning.

Intentionalism, on the other hand, may pretend to appeal to either (1) the actual intentions of the authors of a provision at the time of framing ("explicit intentionalism"), or (2) the intentions these authors would have expressed had they anticipated the cases and historical events that actually occurred after the framing of the provision ("imputed intentionalism"). Furthermore, proponents must confront an ambiguity between applying (a) what they take to be the true and explicit intentions of the framers and (b) how the framers themselves said and thought their explicit intentions should be interpreted throughout history.

Once intentionalists construct a metatheory to resolve these conflicts and ambiguities, they face additional obstacles: many current social practices did not exist at the time of the framers, and thus the framers developed no explicit intentions about such practices; and it is doubtful that any social practice exists with exactly the same social meaning throughout history. See, for example, Belliotti, *Justifying Law*, 179–182; Mark Kelman, *A Guide to Critical Legal Studies* (Cambridge, Mass.: Harvard University Press, 1987), 215–217.

73. Aquinas, *Summa Theologica*, 1–2, question 94, art. 4.

74. "Sexual intercourse in marriage, [the church holds], must be free and loving. But it cannot be fully so if it is flawed by the fear of a conception the couple cannot afford for reasons of economy and health. Sexual intercourse, [the church holds], should be total; it is love incarnate and supposes that the partners give to one another without reservations. But reservations are precisely what the [indivisibility] premise forces upon them . . . the larger [unitive] aims of the Church, which include the most perfect realization of the ideals of marriage that the circumstances permit, are undermined by the conclusions of [*Humanae Vitae*]" (Carl Cohen, "Sex, Birth Control, and Human Life," in *Philosophy & Sex*, ed. Robert Baker and Frederick Elliston [Buffalo, N.Y.: Prometheus Books, 1975], 155).

75. Sacred Congregation for the Doctrine of the Faith, "Declaration on Certain Questions Concerning Sexual Ethics," in *Social Ethics*, ed. Thomas A. Mappes and Jane S. Zembaty [New York: McGraw-Hill, 1987], 241, para. 1).

76. Ibid., 244, sec. 1, para. 5.

77. Ibid., 245, sec. 2, para. 7.

78. Ibid.; Matt. 19:4–6.

79. See, for example, 1 Cor. 5, 1:6, 9:7,2, 10:8; Eph. 5, 50–7; 1 Tim. 1, 10; Heb. 13,4. There are explicit arguments given in 1 Cor. 6, 12–20.

80. "Questions Concerning Sexual Ethics," 245, sec. 2, para. 7.

81. Keane, *Sexual Morality*, 188.

82. Ibid.

83. Rom. 1:24–27. But, again, we must note "those biblical passages that definitely refer to and point out the evil of homosexual acts are passages that were written in relation to particular problems and situations. Rom. 1:26–28 [the passage quoted above], which is one of the clearest statements against homosexual acts in the Bible, is written in the context of the idolatry of pagan culture and its evaluation of homosexual acts is to be understood in light of this context. The same sort of thing can be said about other passages where homosexual acts are certainly mentioned" (Keane, *Sexual Morality*, 79).

84. "Questions Concerning Sexual Ethics," 247, sec. 2, para. 9.

85. Ibid.

86. This phrase is used by John Mackie in *Ethics: Inventing Right and Wrong* (Harmondsworth: Penguin, 1977), chap. 1.

87. Ibid.

88. See, for example, Ruth Benedict, "Anthropology and the Abnormal," *Journal of General Psychology* 10 (1934): 59.

89. Even fervent believers in Roman Catholicism have questioned the

church's relatively pessimistic view of sexuality: "If we are believers in the Incarnation, we believe *ipso facto* that all things human, save sin, have been radically ennobled by the coming of Christ. Thus for the true Christian . . . there is no choice other than to properly value all the aspects of human sexuality . . . we can confidently assert that our belief in the Incarnation of Jesus Christ supports the goodness and comprehensive character of human sexuality" (Keane, *Sexual Morality*, 98).

CHAPTER 3. THE PRIMACY OF EMOTION

1. Vincent C. Punzo, *Reflective Naturalism* (New York: Macmillan Company, 1969).
2. Ibid., 194.
3. Ibid.
4. Ibid., 193.
5. Ibid., 195.
6. Ibid., 196.
7. Ibid., 195.
8. Ibid.
9. "[In such unions] human sexuality, and consequently the human body, have been fashioned into external things or objects to be handed over totally to someone else, whenever one feels that he can get possession of another's body, which he can use for his own purposes" (ibid.).
10. "The total physical intimacy of sexual intercourse will be an expression of total union with the other self on all levels of their beings. Seen from this perspective, [sexual decorum] is one aspect of man's attempt to gain existential integrity, to accept his body as a dimension of his total personality. . . . A total commitment to another means a commitment to him in his historical existence. Such a commitment is not simply a matter of words or of feelings, however strong. It involves a full existential sharing on the part of two beings of the burdens, opportunities, and challenges of their historical existence" (ibid., 196, 198).
11. He quickly adds, however, that de jure marriage is both important and desirable: "By making their commitment a matter of public record, by solemnly expressing it before the law and in the presence of their respective families and friends and, if they are religious people, in the presence of God and one of his ministers, they sink the roots of their commitment more deeply and extensively in the world in which they live, thus taking steps to provide for the future growth of their commitment to each other" (ibid., 199).
12. Ibid., 198.
13. Russell Vannoy, *Sex Without Love* (Buffalo, N.Y.: Prometheus Books, 1980), 26.
14. I will in fact eventually argue in chapter 7 that sexuality is contingently (but not necessarily) more central and crucial to personal identity than wage labor.
15. Punzo, *Reflective Naturalism*, 192.
16. Ibid., 189.
17. For example, regularly viewing "The Three Stooges" and "The World

Wrestling Federation'' on television probably has some (negative?) consequences for self-making, but doing so is not a moral issue *simpliciter*.

18. Punzo, *Reflective Naturalism*, 189.

19. Ibid., 190.

20. See, for example, ibid., 189.

21. John Hunter, *Thinking About Sex and Love* (New York: Macmillan Company, 1980), 80, 85.

22. Ibid., 105.

23. Ibid., 88.

24. Ibid., 103.

25. Ibid., 90–91.

26. Ibid., 91.

27. Ibid.

28. Ibid.

29. Ibid.

30. Ibid., 108.

31. Rollo May, *Love and Will* (New York: Dell Publishing Company, 1969), 311.

32. See, for example, Vannoy, *Sex Without Love*; and some of the feminist thinkers advanced in chapter 6.

33. See, for example, Roberto Unger, *Passion: An Essay On Personality* (New York: Free Press, 1984), 100.

34. Roger Scruton, *Sexual Desire* (New York: Free Press, 1986), 326.

35. Ibid., 327.

36. Ibid.

37. Ibid., 331.

38. Ibid., 339.

39. Ibid., 307.

40. Ibid., 278.

41. Ibid., 343.

42. Ibid., 339. Scruton also argues that erotic love is a paramount value: "Erotic love involves an element of mutual self-enhancement; it generates a sense of the irreplaceable value, both of the other and of the self, and of the activities which bind them. To receive and to give this love is to achieve something of incomparable value in the process of self-fulfillment. It is to gain the most powerful of all interpersonal *guarantees*; in erotic love the subject becomes conscious of the full reality of his personal existence, not only in his own eyes, but in the eyes of another'' (ibid., 337).

43. Scruton underscores his assertion that the interpersonal attitudes requisite for fulfilling sex are "not merely necessary to our happiness; they are also constitutive of our personal existence. A person who lacks them is . . . 'depersonalized' . . . these attitudes are elements of normal human nature, and to lack them is to be a deviant'' (ibid., 289).

44. Ibid., 319.

45. Ibid., 345.

46. Ibid., 343.

47. Ibid., 310.

48. Ibid., 313.

49. Ibid., 341.

50. Ibid., 320.

51. Ibid., 330.

52. Ibid., 290, 344.

53. Ibid., 320.

54. Scruton tells us, for example, that men and women "develop according to a different rhythm, and seem to possess different intellectual aptitudes" (ibid., 262). Moreover, he says that "distinctions of gender will reflect the separate structures of male and female desire. To the extent that these structures have their roots in natural and biologically determined distinctions, it is both futile and dangerous to tamper with them" (ibid., 281). He also claims that for women "sexual excitement tends to be inseparable from the feeling of dependence," but that "the male impulse towards new encounters may lead to promiscuity on a remarkable scale" (ibid., 307).

Scruton's depiction of homosexuality trades on some crude stereotyping and question begging as well. He talks about the mystery of the other gender and its attendant risks, the greater promiscuity of male homosexuality in relation to heterosexual and lesbian pairings, and the "natural predatoriness of the male" (ibid., 306–311). But mystery and risk may arise between two people regardless of their gender. Two male lovers, for example, may be more mysterious to one another and encounter more significant mutual risks because of their socioeconomic or religious or racial differences than two heterosexual lovers who are relatively similar in such areas. Moreover, society's generally harsh reception of homosexuals may be a major factor in the added difficulties their long-term, committed relationships face and may thus add to the phenomenon of promiscuity. Finally, most of Scruton's invocation of "risk and mystery" rests on the question-begging premise that men and women are inherently strange to one another. Scruton comes close to using "risk and mystery" as tautological (or extensional) equivalents to "different genders."

CHAPTER 4. THE SANCTITY OF CONTRACT
AND THE HORROR OF EXPLOITATION

1. Robert Nozick, *Anarchy, State, and Utopia* (New York: Basic Books, 1974), 333–334.

2. Ibid., 10.

3. Ibid., 58.

4. Ibid., 331.

5. Ibid., 262 (emphasis added).

6. Ibid., 263.

7. Ibid., 152. I must note, however, that in his latest book, *The Examined Life* (New York: Simon & Schuster, 1989), Nozick recants much of his libertarian credo: "The libertarian position I once propounded now seems to me seriously inadequate, in part because it did not fully knit the humane considerations and joint cooperative activities it left room for more closely into its fabric. It neglected the symbolic importance of an official political concern with issues or problems, as a way of marking their importance or urgency, and hence of expressing, intensifying, channeling, encouraging, and validating our private actions and concerns toward them" (286–287).

8. John Rawls, *A Theory of Justice* (Cambridge, Mass.: Harvard University Press, 1971), 11.

9. "Among the essential features of [the original position] is that no one

knows his place in society, his class position or social status, nor does any one know his fortune in the distribution of natural assets and abilities, his intelligence, strength, and the like . . . The principles of justice are chosen behind a veil of ignorance. This ensures that no one is advantaged or disadvantaged in the choice of principles by the outcome of natural chance or the contingency of social circumstances" (ibid., 12).

10. Although Rawls recognizes that such a strategy is generally not recommended for choices made under conditions of uncertainty, he insists that the original position has three features which make a maximin strategy attractive: the choosers have no reasonable idea of the probability of particular distributional schemes, they will thus seek to lock in certainties rather than imagine possibilities, and they will decline serious risk taking (ibid., 152–153).

11. Ibid., 302.

12. Ibid.

13. Ibid., 121.

14. Will Kymlicka expresses the problem nicely: "If each theory of justice has its own account of the contracting situation, then we have to decide *beforehand* which theory of justice we accept, in order to know which description of the original position is suitable. Rawls's opposition to gambling away one life for the benefit of others, or to penalizing those with undeserved natural handicaps, leads him to describe the original position in one way; those who disagree with Rawls on these issues will describe it in another way. This dispute cannot be resolved by appeal to contractual agreement . . . the idea of contracting from an original position cannot *justify* our basic moral judgments, since it presupposes them" ("The Social Contract Tradition," in *A Companion to Ethics*, ed. Peter Singer [Oxford: Basil Blackwell, 1991], 193).

15. A moral agent must be able to universalize her actions: "I am never to act otherwise than so that I could also will that my maxim should become a universal law" (Immanuel Kant, *Fundamental Principles of the Metaphysic of Morals*, in *Kant's Critique of Practical Reason and Other Works on the Theory of Ethics*, trans. Thomas Kingsmill Abbott, 2d ed. [London: Longmans, Green, 1879], sec. 1).

This "categorical imperative" has a rational foundation in logic. Kant gives several examples of the workings of the categorical imperative. One of these illustrations concerns keeping promises. A person may be considering borrowing money, promising to pay the lender back when in fact she knows that she will not be able to do so. If this person wants to evaluate the morality of her proposed action, says Kant, all she need do is ask the following question: "Can I will that everyone act on a maxim, 'When it is expedient for me to do so, I can make a lying promise to ameliorate my difficult circumstances?' " Kant insists that we cannot sanction the proposed action because, if universalized, it would destroy the institution of promise keeping: if the practice were widespread, people could no longer rely on promises, and even false promises would surrender practical currency. On one hand, a false promise requires the institution of promise keeping for its intended effect; on the other hand, the universalization of false promises eviscerates that very institution. Because we are not allowed to make ourselves exceptions to the moral laws, Kant affirms that the act of falsely promising is shown by the categorical imperative to be inherently contradictory.

Another illustration of the categorical imperative focuses on positive duties. Suppose I am confronted by a person in distress whom I can aid with a minimum of inconvenience to myself. I am not inclined to render aid, but, as a sincere Kantian, I ask whether I can act on the following maxim: "While not harming others I will do nothing to help them when they are in need" (ibid., sec. 2).

Although I can conceive of a world in which this maxim could be universalized, says Kant, I cannot will the maxim as a universal law because at some future time I may need and desire the help of others. Again, I cannot make myself an exception to the moral law, so logical consistency demands that I render aid now.

16. Kant contends that one's natural inclinations—love, pursuit of happiness, sentiments of benevolence, self-interest, and so on—are improper motives for moral action. Thus, for Kant, the only unconditional good is a good will: the will to do one's moral duty for its own sake, simply because it is one's duty and because it is required by reason. The goal of moral reasoning, for Kant, is the discovery of truth that silences the voices of irrationality and expediency.

Roger Scruton comments: "Moral reasons close the subject's mind to alternative courses of action . . . *because* the moral being is rational, there are certain courses of action which he cannot consider. If Kant is right, it is man's very rationality that leads him to close his mind to actions for which a thousand prudential reasons might be given" (*Sexual Desire* [New York: Free Press, 1986], 322–323).

17. A classic criticism of Kant's view focuses on the malleability of his categorical imperative. When one strives to discover rationally "maxims that one can will become universal laws," she will find that logic is more flexible than Kant imagined. The way one poses the question of the categorical imperative to oneself will usually permit several rationally acceptable, but mutually inconsistent, answers. The abstract universality to which Kant aspires is purchased at the cost of specificity and concreteness.

For example, suppose in the first illustration I asked: "Can I will that everyone act on the maxim, 'When I am in desperate need of life's necessities, through no fault of my own, I may make a lying promise to extricate myself from the situation if my lie causes minimal harm to others' "? If the situation is described in this way I may find no logical contradiction in affirming the proposed conduct. The conduct would not destroy the institution of promise keeping because it is more carefully circumscribed than the conduct in Kant's formulation. Even if readers disagree with the specific conclusion, it should still be clear that to arrive at her antecedently desired answer to a moral question, an agent requires only a degree of ingenuity in describing her action and in formulating her proposed maxim. The categorical imperative does less substantive moral work than Kant imagines.

Moreover, a paradox dwells deep within Kant's categorical imperative. Although appeals to consequences are presumably irrelevant to his moral analysis, notice how they play an important role in the application of his concept. The key questions in his two illustrations focus on the unacceptable *consequences* of everyone's acting on certain maxims and on the moral agent's preferences about her own future treatment. Logic does not merely weave its impersonal machinations; instead, Kant's prescription requires attention to desired social consequences and first-person inclinations. Finally, even if Kantian universality were achieved, it is not clear how its rational acceptance is sufficient to provide first-person *motivation* for moral action.

Scruton adds: "If there is [a universal standard of moral validity], then, by its very universality, it must avoid all mention of *me*; in which case, how can it have the motivating force required by a genuine first-person reason? Conversely, if it is such a reason—a reason which motivates *me*—its claim to universal validity must be doubted. . . . The conflict stems from the contradictory requirements of abstraction and concreteness—the requirements that I be removed from my circumstances, and that I be identified with them. . . . In abstracting from my values, my everyday aims and preferences, from all that constitutes my contingent condition, I abstract also from the circumstances of my act—and, in particular, from the desires and interests which initially raised for me the question of action" (*Sexual Desire*, 323–324).

18. Scruton eloquently summarizes Kantianism in this way: "For Kant, the sympathy that we feel for the virtuous, and the benevolent emotions that prompt us to do what virtue commands, are not genuine expressions of morality, but merely 'empirical determinations', which intrude into the realm of practical reason only to deflect it from its categorical purposes . . . moral reasoning expresses the view of ourselves which is imposed on us by our existence as persons, and by our interaction with others of our kind. Moral reasoning is the formal recognition of the strictures placed upon us by our interpersonal attitudes, from which our existence as person derives" (ibid., 323–323).

19. Immanuel Kant, *Lectures on Ethics*, trans. Louis Infield (London: Methuen, 1930). Excerpts reprinted in *Sexual Love and Western Morality*, ed. D. P. Verene (New York: Harper and Row, 1972), 155.

20. Ibid.

21. Ibid., 156.

22. Ibid., 158.

23. Ibid., 157–158.

24. Ibid., 159.

25. Ibid.

26. Ibid., 160.

27. Ibid., 162.

28. Ibid., 162–163.

29. Ibid., 163.

30. Raymond A. Belliotti, "A Philosophical Analysis of Sexual Ethics," *Journal of Social Philosophy* 10 (1979):8–11.

CHAPTER 5. THE PROSTITUTION IN CAPITALIST
MARRIAGE

1. Friedrich Engels and Karl Marx, *Communist Manifesto*, ed. Frederick Engels, trans. (Chicago: Charles H. Kerr and Company, 1906). Excerpts reprinted in *Sexual Love and Western Morality*, ed. D. P. Verene (New York: Harper and Row, 1972), 194.

For Marxism generally, see Karl Marx, *Economic and Philosophical Manuscripts* (1844); Karl Marx, "Excerpts from James Mill's Elements of Political Economy" (1844) in *Writings of the Young Marx on Philosophy and Soci-*

ety, ed. L. D. Easton and K. Guddat (Garden City, N.Y.: Doubleday, 1967); Richard Schmitt, *Marx and Engels: A Critical Reconstruction* (Boulder, Colo.: Westview Press, 1987); and Raymond A. Belliotti, *Justifying Law* (Philadelphia: Temple University Press, 1992, 145–161.

2. Engels and Marx, *Communist Manifesto*, in Verene, *Sexual Love*, 204.

3. Ibid., 196–197.

4. Passage quoted in Michele Barrett, *Women's Oppression Today* (London: Verso, 1980), 49.

5. Friedrich Engels, *The Origin of the Family, Private Property and the State* (New York: International Publishers, 1972), 79.

6. Engels and Marx, *Communist Manifesto*, in Verene, *Sexual Love*, 196.

7. Ibid., 201.

8. Engels explicitly used the term "false consciousness" in his letter to Franz Mehring, July 14, 1893, in Marx and Engels, *Selected Works* (Moscow: Progress Publishers, 1968), 690. "Ideology is a process accomplished by the so-called thinker consciously, it is true, but with a false consciousness. The real motive forces impelling him remain unknown to him; otherwise it simply would not be an ideological process. Hence he imagines false or seeming motive forces." Some theorists claim that Marx never explicitly used the term "false consciousness," but they admit that no substantive implications follow if they are correct. See, for example, Martin Seliger, *The Marxist Conception of Ideology* (Cambridge: Cambridge University Press, 1977), 30–31.

The term "false consciousness" suggests an inverted representation of reality that is systematically misleading and socially mystifying, in that it misrepresents what are in fact the interests of the ruling class as the natural, common interests of society. This misrepresentation, which flows from superstructure, justifies, stabilizes, and reinforces the social and political status quo. A person who holds a view resulting from false consciousness is unaware of the underlying motives and causal processes by which she came to accept that view.

The term "false consciousness" is used specifically when oppressed classes adopt the dominant prevailing ideology and perceptual prism. When these dominant ideas do not truly correspond to the experience of the oppressed classes, ideological distortion occurs. See, for example, Jorge Larrain, "Ideology," in *A Dictionary of Marxist Thought*, ed. Thomas Bottomore (Cambridge, Mass.: Harvard University Press, 1983), 218–220; Hugh Collins, *Marxism and Law* (Oxford: Oxford University Press, 1984), 40; R. G. Peffer, "Morality and the Marxist Concept of Ideology," in *Marx and Morality*, ed. K. Nielsen and S. C. Patten (Guelph, Ont.: Canadian Association for Publishing Philosophy, 1981), 67–91.

Such distortions have a functional explanation: They legitimate the ruling class's monopoly on power by depicting current social relations as natural, appropriate, or inevitable. In this fashion, the interests of the ruling class misrepresent themselves as universal human interests.

A belief is ideological only if it would perish upon the revelation of its causal origins. Because the relationship between false consciousness and nonideological perception cannot be interpreted validly as a species of the general relationship between illusion and truth, ideological distortion cannot be overcome solely by intellectual criticism. Ideological distortion is not the opposite of truth, but is, instead, a narrow or one-sided rendering of truth that functions to preserve the practices of the ruling class.

Accordingly, false consciousness dissolves only when the internal contradictions of an economic system—especially evident when relations of production can no longer efficiently make use of developing technology—are *practically* resolved.

Marxism is not committed to the simplistic position that all members of subordinate classes, or all subjects generally, are *necessarily* victims of the mystifying effects of ideological distortion. It should be obvious that at least some (and perhaps all) of the people some of the time will be able to pierce the smokescreen of false consciousness.

Certainly, certain views may be the unconscious, conditioned reflection of economic and social oppression, and subordinate classes often become accomplices in their own torment by internalizing the very dominant ideologies which contributed to their mistreatment. But if applied relentlessly, the notion of false consciousness loses much of its critical bite. If the notion is advanced as a nonrefutable thesis, if all denials of Marxism are taken to be affirmations of the doctrine of false consciousness, then the notion of false consciousness is trivial. Any subjective report that denies any basic Marxist conclusion seems too easily and automatically to stigmatize itself. Marxists dismiss the content of a view because it allegedly can be explained by its determinants. Moreover, such a posture demeans the experiences, not merely the ideologies, of Marxism's philosophical rivals. In fact, subjective reports of one's inner condition or of one's ideological commitments are neither incorrigibly true nor self-refuting. The challenge for a Marxist is to delineate, without begging the question, under what circumstances such reports and commitments do and do not reflect veridical perceptions correlated to wider experience. Thus, Marxism cannot automatically deny the veracity of a perception or experience which does not support the conclusions of Marxism. On the other hand, critics of Marxism cannot automatically accept the veracity of such perceptions and experiences as evidence refuting Marxist conclusions.

9. Engels and Marx, *Communist Manifesto*, in Verene, *Sexual Love*, 201–202.

10. In its most general Kantian-Marxist sense, "exploitation" occurs when someone uses another person merely as an object for her own benefit without regard for the humanity of that person. In its more particular Marxist sense, exploitation occurs when one class, the proletariat, produces a surplus whose use is controlled by another class, the capitalists. See, for example, Karl Marx and Friedrich Engels, *The German Ideology* (1845); Karl Marx, *Capital*, vol. 1 (1867); Peter Singer, *Marx* (Oxford: Oxford University Press, 1980), 25–34.

Moreover, the capitalist economic mode differs from other economic modes in that this kind of exploitation occurs without the use of explicit duress, physical threat, or other noneconomic force. It is through the capitalists' vastly superior economic bargaining power over workers, their ownership of the means of production, and the lack of real alternatives for workers that exploitation flourishes in a capitalist regime. Finally, capitalism, shrouded by its pretensions to neutral, economic processes, is especially pernicious because it can mask the nature and effects of the exploitation of workers (ibid.).

Capitalists exploit workers by siphoning the surplus value produced by their labor. Capitalists purchase workers' labor power at its value, which is equivalent to a subsistence wage, and sell products at their value. Because the value workers create is greater than the value of labor power itself, surplus value results. The exploitive nature of the relationship is reflected in the fact that workers do not receive wages equivalent to the value they produce. (Marx, *Capital*, vol. 1; Schmitt, *Marx and Engels*, 74–85; David Conway, *A Farewell to Marx* [Harmondsworth, Eng.: Penguin, 1987], 98–105; Singer, *Marx*, 23–25, 50–54; and John Elster, *An Introduction to Karl Marx* [Cambridge: Cambridge University Press, 1986], 81–101).

Workers' labor is "forced" in the sense that only limited and equally debilitating alternatives are available for workers seeking to satisfy their subsistence requirements (ibid.).

Despite the considerable dispute over precisely which set of necessary and sufficient conditions captures the meaning of Marxist exploitation, the following elements are relevant: workers benefit capitalists; capitalists economically force, in the relevant Marxist sense of that term, workers to supply that benefit; and capitalists wrongfully fail to supply reciprocal benefits to workers. See, for example, Conway, *Farewell to Marx*, 98–105; Allen Buchanan, *Marx and Justice* (Totowa, N.J.: Rowman and Littlefield, 1982), chap. 5; Allen Wood, "The Marxian Critique of Justice," in *Marx, Justice, and History*, ed. M. Cohen, T. Nagel, and T. Scanlon, (Princeton, N.J.: Princeton University Press, 1980), 3–41.

11. Engels and Marx, *Communist Manifesto*, in Verene, *Sexual Love*, 203.

12. Ibid., 205.

13. Ibid., 203.

14. Although Marx was not a proponent of a fixed, universal human nature, he viewed alienation as estrangement from historically created human possibilities. His minimalist view of species-being included the conviction that human fulfillment is intimately connected with imaginative, unshackled use of productive capacities. Labor is a distinctively human activity and possesses central normative significance. Humans presumably shape their social world and forge their personal identities through interaction with their material world and its dominant productive process. It is only through free and creative activity that a person realizes unalienated being. See, for example, Marx, *Economic and Philosophical Manuscripts* (1844); Conway, *Farewell to Marx*, 34–41.

For Marx, the conditions and reality of alienation are not dependent on workers' subjective reports. Regardless of whether workers self-consciously announce the requisite feelings of estrangement, the objective social condition of the proletariat is permeated with alienation. See, for example, Elster, *Karl Marx*, 81–101.

Conversely, nonalienated labor honors our species-being because it is freely chosen, it is collectively designed by workers without a hierarchy of power, it involves creativity and joy, its product is socially useful and appreciated by consumers, and the process of its production effaces the distinction between work and play. The allocation of the products of nonalienated labor is based on need and all surplus is a community, not individual or capitalistic, resource. It is clear that fully nonalienated labor can occur only within a communist framework which abrogates commodity relations among humans, and that Marx employs a "thin" (nonessentialist) theory of human nature.

15. Alan Soble describes the situation well: "Those who claim to know the details of human nature have a firm idea where people are headed and what human behavior will look like when human beings are free, but they have difficulty showing that this 'knowledge' is not mere ideology, simply reproduces dominant values, or flies off into utopianism. On the other hand, those who do not claim to know the details of human nature do not have to worry about putting an epistemological foot in the mouth. But they have very little to say about what human beings will be like when they are free; furthermore, whatever human desires do turn out to be, the agnostic is committed to accept them just because they are the desires of free people. The latter is Engels's preferred view" (*Pornography* [New Haven, Conn.: Yale University Press, 1986], 43).

16. See notes 10 and 17.

17. One of Marx's most intriguing and baffling pronouncements concerns the relationship between a society's economic substructure ("the base") and its ideological superstructure ("the superstructure"). A society's mode of economic production includes its forces of production (natural resources, instruments and means of production, workers and their skills, raw materials) and its relations of production (the formal and informal organization of relations among people, or among people and commodities, in the productive process). The base consists, strictly speaking, of the relations of production. The superstructure consists of our political and legal institutions, and our forms of social consciousness (what we think, believe, how we understand and experience the world).

For Marx, the development of the forces of production results in changes in the relations of production. Moreover, there will come a time when the existing relations of production no longer effectively and efficiently allow the growth of the productive forces. This internal contradiction divides society and will result in revolution and the fall of the obsolete set of productive relations. See, for example, Schmitt, *Marx and Engels*, 30.

New relations of production will triumph because they have the capacity to facilitate the continued growth of society's productive forces. Thus, Marx provides an economic explanation for political revolution.

18. I have, of course, ignored here the numerous *noneconomic* sources of oppression that must be factored into any refined analysis of the Dominic-Vittoria relationship. Because of this I can talk only of the *possibility* that their relationship is noncoercive.

19. "By [mutuality] we mean a relation in which neither person uses the other, neither sees the other primarily as a means to the satisfaction of his or her own self-interest. The relation is genuinely mutual; it is only achievable together, and consciously . . . [It is] a relation in which neither the interest or self nor the interest of the other are pitted against one another, because for both persons, cooperation simultaneously replaces competition" (Virginia Held, "Marx, Sex, and the Transformation of Society," *Philosophical Forum* 5 [1973]:172–173).

20. "Genuine mutual consideration between [parties] making love is neither the joint pursuit of self-satisfaction nor the joint bestowing of charity, but the mutual pursuit of and awareness of mutual feelings and values" (ibid., 173).

21. "[The] practice, of course, in those countries claiming to base practice on the work of [Marxists] is almost as repressively sexist as in capitalist

countries . . . the record of socialism in even being aware of, much less in adequately addressing itself to, the distinctive problems and concerns of women has made of socialism so far almost as dismal a social movement for women as its predecessors and competitors. And the judgment may be applied to both social democratic and communist movements and governments" (ibid., 170–171.).

22. "The sexual division of labor, rooted in the institution of heterosexuality is at least as responsible for women's oppression as is the institution of private property—a point that Engels failed to address and that led him to valorize the proletariat family . . . over the bourgeois family" (Rosemarie Tong, *Feminist Thought* [Boulder, Colo.: Westview Press, 1989], 51).

23. Ibid., 63.

24. "For a Marxist to drive a wedge between sexual activity and wage-labor would be strange. After all, the critique of labor in capitalism is in part a denunciation of what that labor does to the body, ruining it by stress and exhaustion, polluting it in unhealthy working environments, and desensitizing it. Furthermore, a distinction in virtue of the special nature of sexual activity would in effect repudiate the Marxist theme that what is special about human beings is their labor" (Soble, *Pornography*, 136–137).

25. Ibid., 138.

26. Carole Pateman, "Defending Prostitution: Charges Against Ericsson," *Ethics* 93 (1983):562.

27. Sara Ann Ketchum, "Selling Babies and Selling Bodies: Surrogate Motherhood and the Problem of Commodification," read at American Philosophical Association Eastern Division Meeting (Dec. 1987), 7.

28. Margaret Jane Radin, "Market Inalienability," *Harvard Law Review* 100 (1987):1880–1881.

29. Ibid.

CHAPTER 6. THE POVERTY OF CONTRACT

1. See, for example, Alison M. Jaggar, *Feminist Politics and Human Nature* (Totowa, N.J.: Rowman and Allanheld, 1983); Rosemarie Tong, *Feminist Thought* (Boulder, Colo.: Westview Press, 1989).

2. "Even if one is always a man or a woman, one is never *just* a man or a woman. One is young or old, sick or healthy, married or unmarried, a parent or not a parent, employed or unemployed, middle class or working class, rich or poor, black or white, and so forth. . . . Experience does not come neatly in segments, such that it is always possible to abstract what in one's experience is due to 'being a woman' from that which is due to 'being married', 'being middle class' and so forth" (Jean Grimshaw, *Philosophy and Feminist Thinking* [Minneapolis: University of Minnesota Press, 1986], 84–85).

3. Ibid., 17.

4. Ibid., 102.

5. Ibid., 105.

6. Jaggar, *Feminist Politics*, 38–39.

7. "What [gender-neutrality] fails to notice is that men's differences from women are equal to women's differences from men. There is an *equality* there. Yet the sexes are not socially equally. [This] approach misses the fact that hierarchy of power produces real as well as fantasied differences, differ-

ences that are also inequalities" (Catharine MacKinnon, *Feminism Unmodified* [Cambridge, Mass.: Harvard University Press, 1987], 37).

8. Jaggar, *Feminist Politics*, 43.

9. Tong, *Feminist Thought*, 46.

10. Jaggar, *Feminist Politics*, 110–111.

11. "The great moving power of all historical events [is found] in the dialectic of sex: the division of society into two distinct biological classes for procreative reproduction, and the struggles of these classes with one another; in the changes in the modes of marriage, reproduction and childcare created by these struggles; in the connected development of other physically-differentiated classes (castes); and in the first division of labor based on sex which developed into the (economic-cultural) class system. . . . The sexual-reproductive organization of society always furnishes the real basis, starting from which we can alone work out the ultimate explanation of the whole superstructure of economic, juridical and political institutions as well as of the religious, philosophical and other ideas of a given historical period" (Shulamith Firestone, *The Dialectic of Sex* [New York: Bantam, 1970], 12–13).

12. "That women were, historically, the first group to be systematically dominated; that women's subordination causally maintains other forms of domination; that women's subordination is the form of domination that should be tackled first . . . that the domination of women provides a conceptual model for understanding all other forms of oppression" (Jaggar, *Feminist Politics*, 101).

13. "*The freeing of women from the tyranny of their reproductive biological by every means available, and the diffusion of the childbearing and childrearing role to the society as a whole, men as well as women*" (Firestone, *Dialectic of Sex*, 206; emphasis in original).

14. Carol Gilligan, *In a Different Voice* (Cambridge, Mass.: Harvard University Press, 1982).

15. Ibid., 25, 151–174.

16. Rosemarie Tong describes the differences further: "First, women tend to stress the moral agent's continuing relationships to others, whereas men tend to stress the agent's formal, abstract rights. . . . Second, when making a moral decision, women espouse a somewhat more consequentialist point of view, calculating the effects of the moral agent's action on all who will be touched by it, whereas men espouse a somewhat more nonconsequentialist point of view, according to which principles must be upheld even if some people get hurt in the process. Third, women are usually more willing to accept excuses for a moral agent's behavior. . . . Finally, women usually interpret a moral choice within a context of the historical circumstances that produced it, whereas men usually abstract that choice from its particularities and analyze it as if it represented some universal type of moral choice" (Tong, *Feminist Thought*, 162–163).

17. Ann C. Scales, "The Emergence of Feminist Jurisprudence: An Essay," *Yale Law Journal* 95 (1986):1385.

18. Catharine MacKinnon (with Ellen C. DuBois, Mary C. Dunlap, Carol Gilligan, and Carrie J. Menkel-Meadow), "Feminist Discourse, Moral Values, and the Law—A Conversation," *Buffalo Law Review* 34 (1985): 73–75.

19. Jaggar, *Feminist Politics*, 114.

20. Ibid., 126–127.

21. United Nations Secretary General Kurt Waldheim, "Report to the U.N. Committee on the Status of Women," reported in *Ms.* (April 1981), 18.

22. "While female secretaries earned a median wage of $278 per week in 1985, the median for male secretaries was $365; moreover, in twenty-four other narrowly defined occupations in which females earned *less* than they would have as secretaries, males earned more in every case than a female secretary" (Susan Moller Okin, *Justice, Gender, and the Family* [New York: Basic Books, 1989], 145).

23. "The professional and service occupations that are more than two-thirds female—such as education, humanities, home economics, library science, and health science—are far worse paid than those that are still more than two-thirds male—such as science and engineering" (ibid., 144).

24. Barbara R. Bergmann, *The Economic Emergence of Women* (New York: Basic Books, 1986), 133.

25. "The exclusion of women from a big share of all of the jobs in the economy is what creates two labor markets where there should be only one. The discriminatory assignment of jobs to one sex or the other is what sets the level of demand in each market. . . . [This compels] women to have to sell their labor at a low price" (ibid., 125–126).

26. "[A housewife's] work is unpaid work, whereas more than four-fifths of her husband's total work is paid work. . . . This both affects the predominantly houseworking wife's power and influence within the family and means that her social status depends largely upon her husband's . . . the economic dependence of wives can seriously affect their day-to-day physical security. As Linda Gordon has recently concluded: 'The basis of wife-beating is male dominance—not superior physical strength or violent temperament . . . but social, economic, political, and psychological power' " (Okin, *Justice*, 151–152).

27. Philip Blumstein and Pepper Schwartz, *American Couples* (New York: Morrow, 1983), 53, 52.

28. Lenore J. Weitzman, *The Divorce Revolution* (New York: Free Press, 1985), 323.

29. "By far the most important property acquired in the average marriage is its career assets, or human capital, the vast majority of which is likely to be invested in the husband" (Okin, *Justice*, 163).

30. "Typical, contemporary, gender-structured marriage is an excellent example of socially created vulnerability, partly because the asymmetric dependency of wives on husbands affects their potential for satisfactory exit, and thereby influences the effectiveness of their voice within marriage" (ibid., 167).

31. The resulting argument is summarized from Ti-Grace Atkinson, "Radical Feminism," in *Women and Values*, ed. Marilyn Pearsall (Belmont, Calif.: Wadsworth Publishers, 1986), and Ti-Grace Atkinson, "Lesbianism and Feminism," in *Amazon Expedition*, ed. Phyllis Birkby, Bertha Harris, Jill Johnston, Esther Newton, and Jane O'Wyatt (Washington, N.J.: Times Change Press, 1973).

32. Atkinson, "Radical Feminism," 125.

33. Jaggar, *Feminist Politics*, 255.

34. "Motherhood under patriarchy is forced labor. Men determine whether children are born, under what conditions they are reared and what

counts as successful childrearing. Women have responsibility only for the daily details of a process whose totality is male-controlled" (ibid., 260).

35. Shulamith Firestone, "Dialectic of Sex," in *The Philosophy of (Erotic) Love*, ed. Robert C. Solomon and Kathleen M. Higgins (Lawrence: University Press of Kansas, 1991), 251.

36. Ibid., 256.

37. Elizabeth Rapaport, "On the Future of Love," in *The Philosophy of Erotic Love*, ed. Robert C. Solomon and Kathleen M. Higgins (Lawrence: University Press of Kansas, 1991), 378–379.

38. Catharine MacKinnon, *Toward a Feminist Theory of the State* (Cambridge, Mass.: Harvard University Press, 1989), 146.

39. Ibid., 147.

40. Joan C. Williams calls such admissions "a standard disclaimer." "But the disclaimer does not solve the underlying problem. . . . [Authors of such disclaimers do not] explain why men and women whose behavior does not adhere to gender stereotypes should be denied the dignity of being 'real' men or 'real' women. . . . This insult reflects a gender system that (a) mandates correlation of behavior patterns with genitals and (b) consequently admits of only two, consistently dichotomous, behavior patterns" ("Deconstructing Gender," *Michigan Law Review* 87 (1989):813 n. 61).

41. Catharine MacKinnon, "Feminism, Marxism, Method and the State," *Signs* 8 (1983):636 n. 3.

42. Ibid., 650–651.

43. Ibid., 646.

44. Ibid.

45. Ibid., 649.

46. Ibid.

47. Ibid., 650–651.

48. Ibid., 651.

49. Ibid.

50. "But with rape, because sexuality defines gender, the only difference between assault and (what is socially considered) noninjury is the meaning of the encounter to the woman . . . rape law . . . uniformly presumes a single underlying reality, not a reality split by divergent meanings, such as those inequality produces. . . . To attempt to solve [contested sexual encounters] by adopting the standard of reasonable belief without asking, on a substantive social basis, to whom the belief is reasonable and why—meaning, what conditions make it reasonable—is one-sided: male-sided" (ibid., 652, 654).

51. MacKinnon, *Toward a Feminist Theory*, 140.

52. Ibid., 177.

53. Ibid., 215.

54. Andrea Dworkin, *Intercourse* (New York: Free Press, 1987).

55. Ibid., 16–17 (emphasis added).

56. Ibid., 63.

57. Ibid., 64, 66, 67.

58. Ibid., 142.

59. Ibid., 128.

60. Ibid.

61. Thus, Joan Kelly argues: "The current political goals of the women's movement . . . are neither to participate as equals in a man's world, nor to restore to women's realm and values their dignity and worth. Conceptions

such as these are superseded in the present will to extirpate gender and sex hierarchy altogether, and with them all forms of domination . . . [this] will require a restructuring of all social institutions to change our subjective experience. . . . Schools and all socializing agencies will have to be rid of sex and sexual bias. Work and welfare will have to be placed in the humane context of the basic right to all to live, work, and love in dignity. . . . A feminist politics that aims at abolishing all forms of hierarchy so as to restructure personal relations as well as relations among peers has to reach and transform the social organization of work, property and power" ("The Doubled Vision of Feminist Theory," *Feminist Studies* 5:1 [1979]:223–224).

62. Jaggar, *Feminist Politics*, 184.

63. "More women could afford the housekeeping services that now exist for the very rich alone. . . . These new services would be cheaper in real economic terms because specialists working at what they enjoy are more efficient than amateurs doing chores they may detest" (Caroline Bird with Sara Welles Briller, *Born Female: The High Cost of Keeping Women Down* [New York: Pocket Books, 1969], 186–187).

64. Okin, *Justice*, 185–186.

65. Ibid., 171.

66. Ibid.

67. Ibid.

68. Ibid., 176.

69. Ibid., 177.

70. Ibid., 181.

71. Ibid., 183.

72. Ann Ferguson, "The Che-Lumumba School: Creating a Revolutionary Family-Community," *Quest: A Feminist Quarterly* 5:3 (1980):15–17.

73. Jaggar, *Feminist Politics*, 303–307.

74. Jill Johnston, *Lesbian Nation* (New York: Simon and Schuster, 1974).

75. Charlotte Bunch, "Lesbians in Revolt," in *Women and Values*, ed. Marilyn Pearsall (Belmont, Calif.: Wadsworth Publishers, 1986), 129, 130, 131.

76. Marilyn Frye, "Some Reflections on Separatism and Power," in her *The Politics of Reality* (Trumansburg, N.Y.: Crossing Press, 1983), 96.

77. "Heterosexuality keeps women separated from each other. Heterosexuality ties each woman to a man. Heterosexuality exhausts women because they struggle with their man—to get him to stop oppressing them— leaving them with little energy for anything else . . . the straight norm is not really a sexual norm at all, but a powerful instrument in the perpetuation of the power relationship between the sexes" (Rita Mae Brown, "The Shape of Things to Come," in *Lesbianism and the Women's Movement*, ed. Nancy Myron and Charlotte Bunch [Baltimore: Diana Press, 1975], 71).

78. Atkinson, "Lesbianism and Feminism," 12.

79. "Reproductive freedom is incompatible either with the compulsory heterosexuality and mandatory motherhood that have characterized all male-dominated societies or with the economic inequality that necessarily characterizes capitalism. Because it cannot be achieved within the existing social order, reproductive freedom is in fact a revolutionary demand" (Jaggar, *Feminist Politics*, 319).

80. CARASA (Committee for Abortion Rights and Against Sterilization Abuse), *Women Under Attack* (New York: CARASA, 1979), 11.

81. Dworkin, *Intercourse*, 128.

82. MacKinnon, *Toward a Feminist Theory*, 215.

83. Dworkin, *Intercourse*, 67.

84. Ibid., 10.

85. Anthony Violanti, "Men and the Power of Myth," *The Buffalo News* (November 24, 1991), F1.

86. Christine Swanton, Viviane Robinson, and Jan Crosthwaite, "Treating Women as Sex Objects," *Journal of Social Philosophy* 20:3 (1989):7.

87. Ibid., 8.

CHAPTER 7. TOWARD SYNTHESIS

1. Raymond A. Belliotti, *Justifying Law* (Philadelphia: Temple University Press, 1992), 206–207, 233–238.

2. Richard Bernstein, "Pragmatism, Pluralism, and the Healing of Wounds," *American Philosophical Society Proceedings* 63:3 (1989):10.

3. Ibid., 16.

4. Ibid., 16–17.

5. Ibid., 15. "For there is a danger of *fragmenting* pluralism where . . . we are only able to communicate with the small group that already shares our own biases, and no longer even experience the need to talk with others outside of this circle. There is a *flabby* pluralism where our borrowings from different orientations are little more than glib superficial poaching. There is a *polemical* pluralism where the appeal to pluralism . . . but becomes rather an ideological weapon to advance one's own orientation. There is a *defensive* pluralism, a form of tokenism, where we pay lip service to others 'doing their own thing' but are already convinced that there is nothing important to be learned from them."

6. Ronald Dworkin, *A Matter of Principle* (Cambridge, Mass.: Harvard University Press, 1985), 167.

7. Ibid., 171. "I think that the problem of objectivity . . . is a fake because the distinction that might give it meaning, the distinction between substantive arguments within and skeptical arguments about social practices, is itself a fake" (ibid., 173–174).

8. "A moral vision may contradict, for example, what we know or think it rational to believe on other grounds, be they logical, metaphysical, or empirical. But we cannot any longer hope that these kinds of criticisms will leave just one moral vision intact. Ultimately, there is still a point at which one has to say: 'This is where my spade is turned' " (Hilary Putnam, *The Many Faces of Realism* [LaSalle, Ill.: Open Court Publishing Company, 1987], 86).

9. "We cannot isolate 'the world' from theories of the world, then compare these theories of the world with a theory-free world. We cannot compare theories with anything that is not a product of another theory" (Cornel West, *The American Evasion of Philosophy* [Madison: University of Wisconsin Press, 1989], 197; see also Richard Rorty, "The World Well Lost," *Journal of Philosophy* 69 [October 26, 1972]:665).

10. A normative project is rational "not because it has a *foundation* but because it is a self-correcting enterprise which can put any claim in jeopardy, though not *all* at once" (Wilfred Sellars, "Empiricism and the Philosophy of Mind," in *Minnesota Studies in the Philosophy of Science*, vol. 1, ed.

Herbert Fiegl and Michael Scriven [Minneapolis: University of Minnesota Press, 1956], 289).

11. Putnam, *Many Faces of Realism*, 70.

12. Ibid., 77.

13. Dworkin, *Matter of Principle*, 169.

14. Putnam, *Many Faces of Realism*, 67.

15. "Giving grounds . . . justifying the evidence, comes to an end; but the end is not 'certain propositions' striking us immediately as true, i.e., it is not a kind of *seeing* on our part; it is our *acting*, which lies at the bottom of the language-game" (Ludwig Wittgenstein, *On Certainty*, ed. G. E. M. Anscombe and G. H. von Wright, trans. Denis Paul and G. E. M. Anscombe [Oxford: Basil Blackwell, 1969], sec. 200).

16. See Chapter 5.

17. Thomas A. Mappes, "Sexual Morality and the Concept of Using Another Person," in *Social Ethics*, ed. Thomas A. Mappes and Jane S. Zembaty (New York: McGraw-Hill, 1987), 248–262.

18. Ibid., 249–250.

19. Ibid., 250.

20. Ibid., 262.

21. Robert Nozick, "Coercion," in *Philosophy, Science, and Method*, ed. Sidney Morgenbesser, Patrick Suppes, and Morton White (New York: St. Martin's Press, 1969), 440–472; Michael D. Bayles, "Coercive Offers and Public Benefits," *The Personalist* 55:2 (Spring 1974):139–144.

22. Mappes, "Sexual Morality," 255.

23. Ibid., 256.

24. Ibid.

25. Ibid., 257.

26. Ibid.

27. Ibid.

28. Ibid., 258–259.

29. Ibid., 259.

30. Ibid.

31. Ibid., 255–256.

32. Joel Feinberg, "Civil Disobedience in the Modern World," in *Philosophy of Law*, ed. Joel Feinberg and Hyman Gross (Belmont, Calif.: Wadsworth Publishers, 1986), 134.

33. "Insofar as a given act is an instance of one of the [prima facie moral principles], that is a moral reason in favor of doing it, and if it is not, at the same time, a negative instance of one of the other categories on the list, then it is a decisive reason. If it is a positive instance of one type and a negative instance of another, say a promise that can only be kept by telling a lie, then one's actual duty will be to perform the [prima facie obligation] which is the more stringent in the circumstances. That is all a moralist can say in the abstract with any degree of certainty" (ibid.).

34. The best analysis of "exploitation" that I have read is advanced by Joel Feinberg, *Harmless Wrongdoing* (New York: Oxford University Press, 1988), 176–210.

35. Ibid., 184.

36. Ibid., 200.

37. Ibid., 193.

38. Ibid., 178–179.

39. Virginia Held, "Marx, Sex, and the Transformation of Society," *Philosophical Forum* 5 (1973):175.

40. Feinberg, *Harmless Wrongdoing*, 181.

41. Ibid., 201.

42. Ibid., 202.

43. Joel Feinberg, *Offense to Others* (New York: Oxford University Press, 1985), 25–43.

44. Ibid., 44. It should be obvious that the following factors militate in favor of exonerating the actors from moral culpability: relatively meager offense that was reasonably avoidable by the offended party; assumption of risk by the offended party; usual susceptibility of the offended party; an act that bore social value and special importance to the participating parties; a lack of alternative opportunities to engage in the act; performance of the act in a place where acts of its type are common and expected. The converses of these descriptions would, of course, militate in favor of holding the actors morally culpable.

45. Coletta Reid, "Coming Out in the Women's Movement," in *Lesbianism and the Women's Movement*, ed. Nancy Myron and Charlotte Bunch (Baltimore: Diana Press, 1975), 103.

46. Ibid.

47. "[Nude] centerfolds contribute to an environment in which more direct and familiar types of exploitation of women by men is encouraged, and it does this by spreading the image of women as sexual playthings. The pictures then have a direct causal influence on the way the woman's role is conceptualized in society and that in turn makes certain kinds of exploitation possible" (Feinberg, *Harmless Wrongdoing*, 191).

48. Linda LeMoncheck, *Dehumanizing Women* (Totowa, N.J.: Rowman and Allanheld, 1985), 53.

49. Notice, for example, that a student who completes all of her course work (120 credit hours) with Bs will earn a cumulative grade point average of 3.00. If this student has sex with Hott and receives an A in his course, her cumulative average will rise to 3.025. If she refuses to have sex with Hott and receives a C in his course, her cumulative average will drop to 2.975. Thus, unless there are other special circumstances, the gains and losses seem meager.

50. LeMoncheck, *Dehumanizing Women*, 92–93.

CHAPTER 8. A WALK ON THE WILD SIDE

1. Raymond A Belliotti, "Do Dead Humans Have Rights?" *Personalist* 60 (1979):201–210.

2. Jeremy Bentham, *Introduction to the Principles of Morals and Legislation* (1789), chap. 17.

3. Joel Feinberg, *Harm to Others* (New York: Oxford University Press, 1984), 33–34.

4. Belliotti, "Do Dead Humans Have Rights?" 201.

5. James Rachels pointed this out to me more than seventeen years ago.

6. All the following arguments and their discussion are adapted from Belliotti, "Do Dead Humans Have Rights?" 202–206.

7. Feinberg, *Harm to Others*, 83–95; George Pitcher, "The Misfortunes of the Dead," *American Philosophical Quarterly* 21 (1984):183–188.

8. Feinberg, *Harm to Others*, 83.

9. Ibid., 89–90.

10. Ibid., 91–92.

11. Ibid., 91.

12. Ibid., 79–83. "Death can be a harm to the person who dies in virtue of the interests he had antemortem that are totally and irrevocably defeated by death. The subject of the harm in death is the living person antemortem, whose interests are squelched" (ibid., 93).

13. For example, "It should be clear that one can assert that humans have interests that can only be fulfilled after they are dead and simultaneously agree that the bodily organs of the dead can be justifiably used for the benefit of the living. These two claims are compatible because the former does not entail that the interests being considered are absolutely inviolable, while the latter *may* only mean that the interests of the living have a higher priority than the [antemortem] interests of the dead" (Belliotti, "Do Dead Humans Have Rights?" 207).

14. Jerome Neu, "What is Wrong with Incest?" *Inquiry* 19 (1976):27.

15. "One of the most interesting features about the prohibition of incest is its universality; there are rules prohibiting sexual congress between certain close relatives in every society of which we know" (Mary Noble and J. K. Mason, "Incest," *Journal of Medical Ethics* 4 [1978]:64).

16. Neu, "What is Wrong with Incest?" 35.

17. Ibid., 29–30.

18. Alison Jaggar, "Prostitution," in *Philosophy of Sex*, ed. Alan Soble (Totowa, N.J.: Littlefield, Adams and Company, 1980), 351.

19. Lars Ericsson, "Charges against Prostitution: An Attempt at a Philosophical Assessment," *Ethics* 90 (1980):335–366.

20. Ibid., 337, 343–344.

21. Ibid., 338.

22. Ibid., 355.

23. Ibid., 341–342.

24. Ibid., 346.

25. Ibid., 347.

26. Ibid., 353.

27. Ibid., 354.

28. See, for example, Kate Millett, *Sexual Politics* (1969; reprint New York: Ballantine, 1978), 164, 172, 174.

29. "In the present circumstances of our sexual lives it is not possible to separate power from sex. The expression of sexuality and what it means to be feminine and a woman, or masculine and a man, is developed within, and intricately bound up with, relations of dominance and subordination" (Christine Swanton, Viviane Robinson, and Jan Crosthwaite, "Treating Women as Sex Objects," *Journal of Social Philosophy* 20:3 [1989]:13).

30. Carole Pateman, "Women and Consent," *Political Theory* 8 (1980):150.

31. "Voluntary and informed consent to one's sexual subordination may be justified in isolation, or in a society in which the sexual ideology dictates more equality, but it cannot be justified . . . given the prevailing social reali-

ties" (Linda LeMoncheck, *Dehumanizing Women* [Totowa, N.J.: Rowman and Allanheld, 1985], 154).

32. "How actions are widely perceived and interpreted by others, even if wrongly or seemingly irrationally, is crucial to determining their moral status because, though such interpretations may not hold up against some 'objective reality,' they are part of the 'social reality' in which we live. . . . Although the prostitute may want the meaning of her actions assessed relative to her own idiosyncratic beliefs and values, the political and social meaning of her actions must be assessed in the political and social context in which they occur" (Laurie Shrage, "Should Feminists Oppose Prostitution?" *Ethics* 99 [1989]:351, 358).

33. "A history of sexual activity is a negative mark that is used to differentiate kinds of women . . . a person's sexual practice makes her a particular 'kind' of person" (ibid., 355–356).

34. "Women who provide sexual services for a fee submit to sexual domination by men, and suffer degradation by being treated as sexual commodities" (ibid., 347).

35. Ibid., 352.

36. "Prostitution exists to meet the desire of men to degrade women. Studies made by men reveal that very few even pretend they frequent prostitutes primarily for sexual gratification" (Barbara Mehrhof and Pamela Kearon, "Prostitution," in *Notes from the Third Year,* ed. Anne Koedt and Shulamith Firestone [New York: Notes From the Second Year, 1971], 72).

37. "Like rape, prostitution perpetuates the oppression of women by encouraging the view that women are mere sexual objects, hence reinforcing male dominance and female inferiority" (Jaggar, "Prostitution," 360).

38. "When she sells her sexuality she sells herself" (ibid., 363).

39. Ericsson, "Charges against Prostitution," 355–356.

40. See, for example, Alan Soble, *Pornography* (New Haven, Conn.: Yale University Press, 1986), 140.

41. LeMoncheck, *Dehumanizing Women,* 53.

42. Ibid., 28–29.

43. Ibid., 105.

44. "She treats the man as if he were an object, one more fungible anatomical mechanism to prod to orgasm" (Soble, *Pornography,* 160).

45. The male purchaser of sex typically views the female vendor "as if she were an object, to the extent that she has been hired for a specific purpose and so has the status of any object that is consumed in order to satisfy a buyer's needs" (ibid.).

46. "Treating the other person as an object is equivalent to ignoring a whole slew of properties of that person in favor of a select few" (ibid.).

47. Jaggar, "Prostitution," 356–357.

48. "Just as the capacity to labor becomes a commodity under capitalism, so does sexuality, especially the sexuality of women. Thus, prostitutes, like wage laborers, have an essential human capacity alienated. Like wage laborers, they become dehumanized and their value as persons is measured by their market price. And like wage laborers, they are compelled to work by economic pressure" (ibid., 357).

49. The liberated female prostitute would "have the authority to determine what services the customer could get, under what conditions the cus-

tomer could get them, and what they would cost" (Shrage, "Should Feminists Oppose Prostitution?" 359).

50. Consider, for example, Madonna as a cultural phenomenon. Her dancing, singing, acting, and physical attractiveness are unremarkable. Her goal seems to be to achieve an enduring celebrity despite ordinary theatrical talents. She has largely succeeded in this quest through techniques of sexual explicitness, shock, and exploiting the exotic appeal of various subcultures to the bourgeoisie. It would be a mistake, however, to portray her as an abject victim of patriarchal oppression. One could persuasively argue that she uses sexuality for her own *feminist* agenda. *She* is the one who controls the fashions to which she employs her sexuality: the working conditions and the production process, the products, and their dissemination. Her performances send the messages she desires for the purposes she intends.

CHAPTER 9. MORAL REASONING

1. Richard A. Posner, *Sex and Reason* (Cambridge, Mass.: Harvard University Press, 1992).

2. Ibid., 3–4.

3. Ibid., 85.

4. "Economic analysis, with its useful concepts of substitution and complementarity, search costs and signaling, inferior goods and externalities, and much else besides, not only can explain a great deal of variance in sexual behavior and regulation over time and across cultures with a minimum of assumptions, and can integrate a bewildering variety of scholarly literatures on sex; it can also generate a range of hypotheses that have the scientifically appealing property of being at once intellectually interesting, theoretically important, socially relevant, counterintuitive, and refutable (hence testable)" (ibid., 435).

5. Ibid., 30.

6. Ibid., 89.

7. Ibid.

8. Ibid., 90. "*Optimal* here means, of course from an evolutionary standpoint—the standpoint of spreading one's genes—because a strategy that was not optimal in that sense would tend to be weeded out by natural selection. And *strategy* carries with it no implication of *conscious* strategizing. It is a metaphor for the suiting of means to end; in this it resembles the economist's concept of rationality" (ibid.).

9. Ibid.

10. Ibid., 91.

11. Ibid.

12. Ibid., 93.

13. Ibid., 95.

14. Ibid.

15. Ibid., 436. "While a person's preference among the possible sexual objects (male, female, or whatever), if costs are the same, is given, not chosen, the decision to engage in a particular sex *act*, that is, to act on a preference (whether it involves a more or a less preferred sexual object) in light of all pertinent costs and benefits, is a matter of choice" (ibid., 87).

16. Ibid., 86.

17. Ibid., 173.

18. Ibid.

19. Ibid.

20. Ibid., 175.

21. Ibid., 174.

22. Ibid., 175.

23. Ibid., 296. "Homosexual preference, especially male homosexual preference, appears to be widespread; perhaps to be innate . . . to exist in most, perhaps all, societies, whether they are tolerant of homosexuality or repressive of it; to be almost completely—perhaps completely—resistant to treatment; and to be no more common in tolerant than in repressive societies" (ibid.).

24. Ibid., 298. "But women who dislike men—perhaps because they were sexually abused as children or subjected to sexual harassment as college students or as workers, or because they work in an occupation such as prostitution which shows men at their worst, or because they have signed on (perhaps for some of these same reasons) to the radical feminist critique of heterosexuality—may turn away from sex with men and become practicing lesbians. This is a form of opportunistic rather than 'real' homosexuality, but it differs from male opportunistic homosexuality in not resulting from a scarcity of heterosexual opportunities" (ibid., 299–300).

25. Ibid., 308.

26. Ibid., 303.

27. Ibid., 304.

28. Ibid., 304. "The fact that lesbians, who are the opposite of effeminate, also seem, like male homosexuals, disproportionately creative . . . is evidence against the effeminacy thesis, although an alternative explanation is that, until recently, married women were unlikely to have a career, and lesbians are presumably a disproportionate fraction of all unmarried women" (ibid., 304–305).

29. Ibid., 305.

30. Ibid, 305–306. "Since there is less sexual strain in a lesbian union, the prospects for stable lesbian marriages are better. An additional consideration is that whereas men, whether heterosexual or homosexual, generally find young persons more attractive sexually than older ones, few women have a strong preference for sexual partners younger than themselves" (ibid., 306).

31. Ibid., 3.

32. Ibid., 4.

33. Ibid., 437.

34. Ibid., 223.

35. Ibid., 230. Posner is quick to add, however, that the moral revulsion *simpliciter* of the masses to an act is not grounds for *legal* prohibition. He cites "the principle that government has no business regulating beliefs, preferences, or even conduct, as long as it is private" (ibid., 233). He further argues, on empirical grounds, that restoring traditional Christian morality, the source of much of the strong moral feeling of the masses, is not necessary to make our society more civilized (ibid., 233–237).

36. See, e.g., Stephen Jay Gould, *Ever Since Darwin* (New York: W. W. Norton and Company, 1977), 252–254. James Rachels adds, "While there has been a lot of careful work done on insects and other animals . . . there has been no comparably detailed research on the more complicated case of hu-

man beings, on which comparable conclusions could be based. Sociobiological speculations about human nature have been based on impressions, facile generalizations, and hazy analogies" (*Created from Animals* [Oxford: Oxford University Press, 1990], 75–76).

37. See, e.g., Peter Singer, *The Expanding Circle* (New York: Farrar, Straus and Giroux, 1981), 63–83. James Rachels explains, "Suppose it were true that male dominance is an unavoidable consequence of human nature. It would not follow that the feminist analysis of its evil is false. . . . What would follow, perhaps, is that male dominance is ineradicable. But that would only be like discovering that a dread disease is forever incurable. We might have to live with that knowledge, but we surely would not be forced to think it a good thing. Nor would we have to cease our efforts to ameliorate the suffering of the disease's victims. . . . Nothing in sociobiology could imply otherwise" (*Created from Animals*, 78).

38. Posner, *Sex and Reason*, 110.

39. Ibid.

40. Ibid., 230.

41. "*The sale of a human being in any circumstances and for any reasons is morally repulsive, and if permitted could undermine the taboo against slavery.* A variant of this argument . . . is that . . . baby selling promotes 'commodification' . . . the tendency, characteristic of capitalist societies, to view goods and services as things that can be exchanged in a market. Fair enough, but some of us believe that this and most societies could use more, not less, commodification and a more complete diffusion of the market-oriented ethical values that it promotes" (ibid., 413).

42. See, e.g., John Rawls, *A Theory of Justice* (Cambridge, Mass.: Harvard University Press, 1971); Norman Daniels, "Wide Reflective Equilibrium and Theory Acceptance in Ethics," *Journal of Philosophy* 76 (1979):256; and Raymond A. Belliotti, "Toward a Theory of Judicial Decisionmaking," *The Catholic Lawyer* 28 (1983):215.

43. Daniels, "Wide Reflective Equilibrium," 258.

44. Several coherent and legitimate moral ideologies should survive this process, though they will often seem to be in conflict. To resolve such conflict we might take the following steps: First, discern individual moral decisions where the competing sets of values reach similar conclusions. Second, extract general principles from such cases. Third, develop a common framework of shared commitments and data from the prior stage. Fourth, resolve remaining nonmoral factual disputes. Fifth, those specific judgments still in conflict are adjudicated by drawing out the implications of the *shared* framework; arguing by analogy with and disanalogy from the agreed-upon decisions; and exposing internal inconsistencies, unnoticed consequences, and poorly defined or unclear concepts in the *unshared* frameworks of the competing ideologies. Such a process will produce some convergence of answers based on the given data and reasoning, but many specific moral questions, often those upon which the most paramount consequences hinge, will continue to be up for grabs. Once we accept rational disagreement as part of a robust conception of moral theory, this is not bad news (Belliotti, "Judicial Decisionmaking," 250–251).

45. Careful readers will be surprised to see me favorably invoke Rawls's method of reflective equilibrium here after I criticized his methodology in Chapter 4. Rest easy: there is no contradiction. What I find suspicious in

Rawls's methodology is its explicit claim to value-neutrality and its implicit claim to societal consensus based on the conclusions of allegedly free choosers in the original position. Thus, I dispute the *particular* tool Rawls selected as his phase-1 device for selecting moral principles: his portrayal of free choosers who are stripped of all constitutive attributes—a portrayal that seems to permit, at best, a monolithic glob of reason to discern moral principles rather than a heterogeneous group of real, contentious people—and his claim to have established an ideal vantage point that is value neutral. Such aspirations may be the vestiges of a foundationalist spirit: hoping to secure at least the base of moral theory with a series of allegedly nonmoral starting points.

I would amend the method of wide reflective equilibrium in the following ways: abrogate lingering foundationalist and scientific pretensions; accept as salutary the presence of protracted moral disagreements on complex issues; understand that phase-1 devices for selecting moral principles are suspicious, especially where they aspire to value neutrality and thereby often ignore the voices of historically disadvantaged groups by pretending that ideal observers represent *all* of us; and loosen the distinction between phase-1 and phase-2 assessments.

In regard to the last point: we cannot appeal to an antecedent and disembodied theory of persons as an axiomatic starting point in our quest for moral theory. Instead, a theory of persons partly constitutes particular versions of moral theory, and the acceptability of a moral theory helps determine the acceptability of its component theory of persons. The notion of "acceptability" used here is much looser and contestable—appealing to concrete experiences of human personality more than formal categories. No attempt is made to establish moral conclusions *deductively* from facts about human nature.

46. See, for example, Roberto M. Unger, *Passion: An Essay on Personality* (New York: Free Press, 1984), 7–12, 100.

INDEX